The Dance Bible

The complete resource for aspiring dancers

Camille LeFevre

The Dance Bible

The complete resource for aspiring dancers

Camille LeFevre

A QUINTET BOOK

First edition for the United States and Canada
published in 2012 by Barron's Educational Series, Inc.

Copyright © 2012 Quintet Publishing Limited

All rights reserved. No part of this publication may be
reproduced or distributed in any form or by any means
without the written permission of the copyright owner.

All inquiries should be addressed to:
Barron's Educational Series, Inc.
250 Wireless Boulevard
Hauppauge, NY 11788
www.barronseduc.com

Library of Congress Control Number: 2012937940

ISBN: 978-0-7641-6527-6

QTT.DANB

Conceived, designed, and produced by
Quintet Publishing Limited
The Old Brewery
6 Blundell Street
London N7 9BH
UK

Project Editor: Alison Hissey
Consultant: Lisa Jo Sagolla
Designer: rehabdesign™
Copy Editor: Janice Baiton
Illustrators: Claire Scully and Dawn Painter
at The Quiet Revolution
Art Director: Michael Charles
Editorial Director: Donna Gregory
Publisher: Mark Searle

Printed in China by 1010 Printing International Limited

9 8 7 6 5 4 3 2 1

To all of the dancers and choreographers,
and dance teachers, companies, presenters,
critics and scholars, who've guided and
inspired me through the years: Thank you.
Thanks to the dance companies that
generously provided images for these
pages. And to my friends and family, who
cheered me on through the writing of this
book: love and gratitude.

Camille LeFevre

CONTENTS

INTRODUCTION

Whether an art or entertainment, celebration or ritual, dance can't be explained in words. Dance must be danced to be fully understood. No book on dance is a substitute for actually getting into a studio, taking technique classes, honing the art of movement, and experiencing the thrill of performing in front of an audience. This book, however, is a valuable and comprehensive introduction for anyone studying dance or thinking of embarking on a career as a dancer.

Dance is an integral part of all human societies. Moving to music or rhythm is one of the first things toddlers do. Dance as a means of expression, communication, even worship can be found in cultures around the world. Inexperienced dancers may have the passion to move, but are unsure what style of dance to commit themselves to. This book helps them decide.

Dancers need commitment and creativity, art and passion to succeed.

" There is no other art in which you are your own artistic tool. It is so full. You use your body, you use your mind and you grow your self both in the moment and through time. In modern dance, you get to use your entire range—all your training plus who you are as a person.

Laura Thomasson, dancer and choreographer **"**

The first two chapters provide an overview of dance forms around the world. The book covers Western concert dance forms performed on a stage—such as modern, jazz, ballet, lyrical, and contemporary—as well as site-specific dance, which is performed anywhere but a stage. Dances with European origins, from folk dance to flamenco, are discussed.

Non-Western dance forms from India and Asia are included, as are dances from Africa—some of which have migrated from public and religious spheres to the concert stage, or into such street forms as break dancing, hip-hop, and krumping. The studio dance scene with its competition circuit is covered, as well

Zenon Dance Company performing Daniel Charon's *Storm*, a sweeping, heroic modern-dance work in which the dancers are seen by the audience in silhouette (opposite top) during one section in the work; here they're also seen from the wings mid-leap (above).

Ragamala Dance preserves the ancient traditions of Bharatanatyam while expanding the form to incorporate new global perspectives on art and dance, as in this photo from a performance called *Yathra* ("Journey"). The dancer in the foreground is Aparna Ramaswamy.

as dance in musical theater, film, and television.

The majority of the book is devoted to dance as an everyday practice. Various chapters focus on training and cross-training regimens and the technique fundamentals of various dance forms; how to integrate mind, body, and emotion to hone and develop expression; and care of the dancer's body on and off the stage.

Above all, this book gives readers a glimpse into the dance profession as it exists today. Because dance is also a business, the book addresses the demands the profession makes on dancers, and what's required to enjoy a successful and

fulfilling career. Chapters cover the communication and marketing skills a young dancer needs to succeed, supplementing dance with other paying work, and planning for a lifelong career in dance—whether dancing or working otherwise in the profession.

Dancers need commitment and creativity, art and passion, practicality and business savvy to succeed. As a dancer, you are your own product. This book shows you how to prepare for a life as a professional dancer, the thrills and perils you'll experience, maintaining your well-being in a physically demanding art, and remaining resilient in the face of adversity.

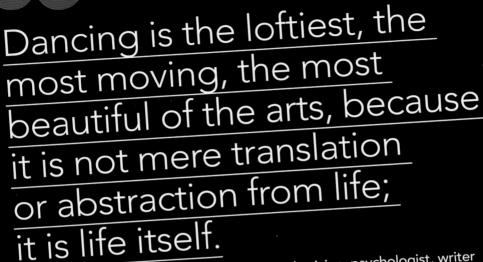

Dancing is the loftiest, the most moving, the most beautiful of the arts, because it is not mere translation or abstraction from life; it is life itself.

Havelock Ellis, physician, psychologist, writer

Being a dancer is about conveying thoughts, emotions, and imagery with an immediacy that fully engages and entertains real people. You are, after all, conveying through your own body powerful truths about the human experience.

Zenon Dance Company's repertory encompasses postmodern work by such choreographers as the award-winning Morgan Thorson, who examines voyeurism and posturing in *Deluxe Edition*.

1
WHAT IS DANCE?

This chapter introduces you to dance, the world's most diverse, beautiful, and physically demanding, yet ephemeral, art. Where does the impulse to move come from? What are the various purposes to which the dancing body can be put in religion, art, and everyday life? Throughout human history, dance has been a means of cultural identity, social interaction, worship, and entertainment—as well as an art form. This brief overview of dance throughout the world highlights some of the people, and peoples, whose commitments to dance have contributed to our knowledge of dance, and dance history, today.

DEFINING DANCE

At its most basic, dance can be defined as the impulse to move. From the first time, as babies, that we're gently rocked or cradled, we experience the power of movement in our own and someone else's body. Watch any toddler hearing music with a lilting melody or strong beat, and they'll kick, bounce, sway, and wiggle with almost instinctual enthusiasm. Even if, as people grow up, some seemingly lose their sense of rhythm, dance is still an integral part of life.

Around the world, since the first human gestured with deliberation or stomped to a percussive sound, the impulse to move has been transformed into dance with a wide array of styles, purposes, and meanings. Depending on where you are, dance might be an expression of cultural identity, of spirituality, or of religious worship. Whereas the dances of royal courts were composed to reinforce political power, courtship dances (whether in a country barn or a downtown club) are a means of social interaction, communication, even seduction.

Ceremonial dances often celebrate community, and competitive dancing pits well-rehearsed contestants against one another. Dance is also an art form. As one of the performing arts (along with music and theater), concert dance is created for the stage, to be watched by a paying audience inside a concert hall. But this dance genre is also extremely varied. Concert dance can range from such classical forms as ballet and kabuki, to modern, postmodern, and jazz dance. Even such forms as Bharatanatyam and Kathak,

Native American powwow styles, and ballroom and break dancing have been reimagined for the concert stage.

Dance is performed the world over, whether in a public space for a community or on the stage for a paying audience.

All of these dance styles share commonalities, however. The material for making dances is the human body. Dance is a nonverbal form of expression. And unlike music (which has a score and can be recorded), or theater (which has a script), or visual art (which is tangible), dance is ephemeral. As the dancing body moves through time and space, its movements can never be repeated exactly the same way again, nor can the kinetic quality of the live dancing body be fully captured electronically or digitally.

The dancing body is as momentary and elusive as dust motes dancing in the sunshine, or leaves dancing across a lawn. In other words, defining dance is like defining life itself.

Definition, from Merriam-Webster Dictionary
[Middle English *dauncen*, from Anglo-French *dancer*.
First known use: fourteenth century]

Noun:
- an act or instance of dancing
- a series of rhythmic and patterned bodily movements usually performed to music
- a social gathering for dancing
- a piece of music by which dancing may be guided
- the art of dancing

Intransitive verb:
- to engage in or perform a dance
- to move or seem to move up and down or about in a quick or lively manner

Transitive verb:
- to perform or take part in as a dancer
- to cause to dance
- to bring into a specified condition by dancing

There is no end to the variety of purposes to which the dancing body can be put.

Gerald Jonas

> # The truest expression of a people is in its dance and in its music. Bodies never lie.
>
> Agnes de Mille

DANCE AS CULTURAL IDENTITY

Around the world, almost every nation, country, region, and tribe has created a singular style of dance that expresses its people's cultural and social identity. Over time, and through colonization and globalization, some of those dance forms have died out—or have been fused with other styles, resulting in new hybrid dances. Still, many people continue to practice the dances of their ancestors, in order to keep alive the spirit of their forerunners and bring their traditions, lifestyles, and ethnicities into the present. Here are some examples of the ways in which dance and cultural identity are linked around the world.

African dance

Throughout Africa, dance has been, and remains, an integral part of claiming and celebrating one's culture. The dance called Adzohu (or Adzogbo) from Ghana, with its fierce gestures of spear throwing and other battle-like movements, originally prepared its practitioners for war. Today, the dance is performed at social and cultural events to reinforce cultural identity.

ISRAELI FOLK DANCE

The folk dances of Israel were created during the country's founding in 1948, to help forge a new cultural identity for a new land. The Hora originated in the Balkans and predates the State of Israel; still, it is often considered Israel's official dance, and is performed all over the world at Jewish events such as weddings, and Bar and Bat Mitzvahs. The Hora is also considered the foundation of modern Israeli folk dance. The Hora's dance formations vary from a circle to a straight line, and may be choreographed for a group or couples.

Native American dance

Native peoples around the world perform their traditional dances to reinforce their identity and cultural traditions. The dances of North America's "First Nation" or "First People" differ in costume, time of year performed, and style. Yet the dances are similar in many ways: Most dances are traditionally performed by men and occur in circles; the music is created through drumming, chanting, and flutes; and the dances celebrate family events and seasonal activities, unite communities, and enact religious ceremonies.
Here are some examples:

Pueblo blue-corn dance: The dancers act out the planting, tending, and harvesting of corn, the tribe's staple crop.

Choctaw social dances: Traditionally performed for the ballgame (a forerunner of lacrosse) ceremonies, the players sing while others participate in fourteen different line, circle, and couple dances.

Plains Indian fancy dance: Performed during powwows, the men's fancy dance features elaborate feather headdresses that bounce and sway as the dancer stomps rhythmically on the ground. In the women's fancy shawl dance, the dancers circle slowly with rhythmic footwork.

Native American traditional dances vary by tribe and are an essential part of cultural identity.

Is dance a part of your cultural identity?
Ask yourself these questions:
- How is dance an integral part of my life?
- How is dance a central part of my parents' lives, even grandparents' lives?
- Where do I dance? Why do I dance?
- Do I dance the same dances as my family members? Or am I creating my own dance tradition?

DANCE AS WORSHIP

Although dance in the West in the twenty-first century tends to be seen primarily as a form of entertainment, in fact, in many countries dance has traditionally been bound up with religious and spiritual beliefs. The intensity of dance, and the physical and emotional sensations it invokes in participants and observers, have led it to be both revered as holy and banned as dangerously profane.

Bharatanatyam

In Hinduism, the gods dance. Nataraja, or the Lord of the Dance, is depicted as Shiva, the Cosmic Dancer, whose raised leg, bent knee, and arcing arms signify the movements of the heavens. In India, the dancing human body is also a vehicle of worship.

The most popular dance form in India is Bharatanatyam—a solo form for highly trained female dancers. It originated as a devotional dance performed in Hindu temples. Many ancient temple sculptures and Bharatanatyam postures are similar, and heavenly dancers depicted in Hindu scriptures represent earthly Bharatanatyam dancers and vice versa. The intricate, complex form includes *abhinaya* (dramatic art of storytelling), *nritta* (pure dance movements—including hundreds of transitional, hand, and feet movements—that depict rhythm), and *nritya* (combining abhinaya and nritta).

The poses created by Bharatanatyam dancers reflect the poses of Hindu temple statues.

BANNED DANCE

In many Judeo-Christian religious traditions, dance has been considered a distraction from concentrating on God. Protestant reformers in sixteenth-century Europe banned dance as a form of worship. Today, many religious groups, including Baptists and Jehovah's Witnesses, ban dance of all kinds (sacred and secular).

Orishas around the world

For the Yoruba of West Africa, the dancing body is where the human realm and the realm of the gods and ancestors meet. The Yoruba believe in more than 400 deities or orishas that manifest as aspects of Olodumare, or God. A priest or priestess evokes his or her deity during communal celebrations with chanting, dancing, and drumming. When the orisha takes possession of the dancing devotee, it successfully enters the community. According to the Yoruba, "Without human beings there would be no gods."

This religion grew around the world and developed into such practices as Candomblé, Lucumí/Santería, and Shango in Trinidad. Its spiritual lineages can also be found in Nigeria, the Republic of Benin, Togo, Brazil, Cuba, Dominican Republic, Guyana, Haiti, Jamaica, Puerto Rico, Suriname, the United States, Uruguay, and Venezuela.

Native American dances

Many Native American tribes, including the Hopi and Plains Indian tribes, believe in the transformative power of dance to integrate body and spirit. For millennia, the Hopi calendar has centered on a cycle of dance ceremonies that invoke the life-giving spirits of nature.

Liturgical dance

In medieval Europe, the Christian church banned many forms of dance, but not liturgical dance. These dances largely took place as processions through a labyrinth. During the *pelota*, a religious leader tossed a ball to the dancers during the procession. Dancing was also permitted during some religious festivals, once the pagan dance rituals marking the seasons were assimilated into the Christian calendar. Today, liturgical dance occurs in many churches as an expression of prayer or worship. The dance may be free-form or choreographed, but is meant to respond to religious ideas or the lyrics of religious music.

> To watch us dance is to hear our hearts speak.
>
> Hopi saying

DANCE AS POWER AND REBELLION

Throughout history, dance has been used to reinforce, or rebel against, power and authority. Dances have also been outlawed in an attempt to control a community. During Europe's colonization of native peoples around the world, much indigenous dance was banned as a means of political and social repression. Enslaved or disenfranchised peoples were denied their dances as a way of separating them further from their cultures, and to keep them from organizing or building community identity. Still, they found ways to dance.

After plantation owners in the southern United States banned slaves from using drums, the slaves originated a dance called the Ring Shout, in which they created rhythm by stomping their feet and clapping their hands.

Elsewhere in the world, political leaders have ordered the death of dancers as a means of eliminating a culture. After capturing Phnom Penh in 1975, the Khmer Rouge imprisoned and killed Cambodia's royal court dancers, who were potent symbols of the country's feudal past.

European court dance

During the Italian Renaissance of the fifteenth century, spectacles of pageantry, dance, costumes, and scenery, called *balli* (the Italian word for "dance"), were performed in the Italian courts. The dancers were courtiers, who participated to publicly display their wealth, influence, and standing. When Louis XIV, who loved to dance, took the French throne, he enshrined himself at the center of elaborate spectacles as the Sun King, and his nobility danced in attendance around him. His ballroom galas opened with the *branle*, in which participants lined up behind the king and queen according to rank. Next the king and queen danced together, then with the highest-ranking nobility, on down the line.

In this way, the king used dance to control his underlings and to ensure they strived for royal favor.

Rebel dances

• In the sixteenth century, Portugal imported African slaves to work in the fields of Brazil. The slaves created Capoeira—which combines dance, martial arts, sports, and music—as a means of expression, identity, physical protection, and rebellion. In the 1800s, the colonial government jailed practitioners of Capoeira; the dance was considered illegal even after slavery ended. As Capoeira developed in urban areas, audiences began creating circles around the dancers to protect them from

several violent confrontations, the United States government discouraged all ceremonial dances until the 1930s. Since many dances were lost in the process, intertribal gatherings or powwows were created to, in part, pass the dances on to younger generations.

Capoeira, a once-banned dance created by slaves in Brazil, is now performed around the world.

detection. Today, Capoeira is practiced around the world and Brazilians take great pride in the dance.

- During the 1880s, the Ghost Dance—a religious movement to restore the Great Plains' ancestors, fertile prairie landscape, and buffalo destroyed by white settlers and the U.S. Army—spread throughout Native American communities. After

- As teenagers in mid-century America embraced rock and roll, some of the couple dances practiced by their parents mutated into more expressive styles like the Jitterbug, the Pony, and the Twist. But many teenagers eventually abandoned couple dances for more free-form styles of movement during the rebellious counterculture era of Vietnam War protests, drugs, and free love. The Punk and New Wave music movements in Britain, and rap in the United States, gave rise to still more innovative dance forms that reflect youthful rebellion and protest in popular culture.

If I can't dance, I don't want your revolution.

Emma Goldman

DANCE AS ART: CLASSICAL DANCE

A classical art is one that's evolved over a long period of time. The classical dance forms ballet, kabuki, Kathakali, and Bharatanatyam, for instance, are more than 400 years old. A classical dance form's technique is structured and specific, codified and stylized. Revered experts, teachers, or gurus teach younger practitioners the unique steps, positions, techniques, and styles of the choreography. The dance has been kept vital, and continues to inspire both its artists and its audiences. Classical dance has withstood the test of time.

Ballet

Ballet (from the Italian *ballare*, meaning "to dance") originated in Italian Renaissance courts of the fifteenth and sixteenth centuries. When Catherine de' Medici married the French heir to the throne, Henry II, she brought ballet to the French courts. In 1581, Balthasar de Beaujoyeulx choreographed the first *ballet de cour*, *Ballet Comique de la Reine*. In the seventeenth century, Louis XIV pushed ballet to become a performing art. Pierre Beauchamp, his dance teacher, codified the five positions of the feet and arms.

In the eighteenth century, ballet technique became more virtuosic. Jean-Georges Noverre helped develop the *ballet d'action*, in which dancers' movements express character and further the narrative. The introduction of the proscenium arch in the seventeenth century established the traditional theater space still used today.

As ballet spread, the Royal Danish Ballet and the Imperial Ballet of the Russian Empire were founded in the 1740s, and the Danes and Russians developed their own ballet techniques. Companies formed in London, Canada, Australia, and throughout the United States, particularly in New York. A Russian dancer and choreographer, George Balanchine, introduced a style to the United States known as neoclassical ballet. More recently, such choreographers as Jiří Kilián, Alonzo King, and William Forsythe have pioneered contemporary and post-structural ballet.

Kabuki

Japan's kabuki dance-theater is a stylized art form predicated on the transformation of a male actor and dancer into a beautiful young woman (the actors are called *onnagata*), through elaborate makeup and costuming, gestures, and movement. The onnagata are intensively trained in their art, and undergo long apprenticeships before they perform on stage. In kabuki, there is no distinction between dance and drama. Spoken words, music, movement, scenery,

> The purpose of art is higher than art. What we are really interested in are masterpieces of humanity.
>
> Alonzo King

A kabuki dancer displays the typical makeup and costume of this Japanese form of dance-theater.

themes and stories from Hindu mythology with elaborate makeup and costuming, and choreography that incorporates articulate gestures and dynamic footwork, in spectacles running from dusk to dawn.

Kathak originated in northern India among temple dancers called *kathaks* or storytellers. In this dance form, dancers illustrate stories from the *Ramayana* and *Mahabharata* with facial expression, broad gestures, and lively footwork.

Kathakali is just one of several classical dance forms that originated in India.

and props are fully integrated into lengthy spectacles that tell dramatic stories of love, war, and revenge.

Kathakali and kathak

Kathakali, which originated in Kerala (in southern India), is one of the oldest and most theatrical dance styles in the world. In its most traditional form, Kathakali animates

DANCE AS ART: MODERN DANCE

In the early twentieth century, dancers and choreographers began to rebel against the formalism of classical dance forms. These dancers drew on classical dance influences, but aimed to make their work more expressive, breaking down traditions and creating new forms of art. Modern dance is popular throughout the world, and has incorporated many different cultural influences.

Modern dance originated in the early twentieth century, in rebellion against the formalism and spectacle of ballet. American dancers Isadora Duncan, Ruth St. Denis and her husband, Ted Shawn, and the German dancers Mary Wigman and Hanya Holm began exploring a freer, more expressive, and more individualized form of concert dance. They innovated their own choreography, danced in bare feet, and wore simple flowing costumes. In the mid-twentieth century, many dancers adopted the skin-tight leotard as rehearsal attire and performance costume, to display the physique of the dancer's body.

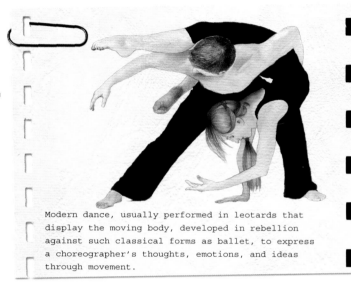

Modern dance, usually performed in leotards that display the moving body, developed in rebellion against such classical forms as ballet, to express a choreographer's thoughts, emotions, and ideas through movement.

Postmodern dance

In the 1970s, choreographer Twyla Tharp was fusing ballroom, ballet, and modern dance in her work. Meanwhile, other choreographers were rebelling against all codified, formalized concert dance by stripping dance down to the essentials of human movement. They claimed any movement could be dance and anyone could be a dancer, and used novel composition methods. The Judson Dance Theater in New York became the hotbed of postmodern dance, with such choreographers as David Gordon, Yvonne Rainer, Trisha Brown, Steve Paxton, Lucinda Childs, and Deborah Hay creating avant-garde works. Some of these choreographers eventually returned to the concert stage with more-formal dances

Choreographer Merce Cunningham and
his longtime partner composer John
Cage devised a chance methodology for
their works. They would throw the
I-Ching or roll dice to determine
what music or movement phrase would
come next in a composition. This
method also dictated that lighting,
costumes, set design, choreography,
and sound/music were created
independently, and came together—for
the first time—during the premiere.
They believed "chance operations"
could not only free the imagination,
but could also reveal serendipitous
connections between the components
of a work. They both redefined dance,
and expanded the collaborative role
of dance with other arts disciplines.

created for their companies.

Today, the legacy of postmodernism lives
on in much contemporary, experimental
dance. So does modern dance in the works
of such choreographers as Mark Morris,
Doug Varone, Bill T. Jones, and Stephen
Petronio.

German dance-theater

In Germany during the 1980s, many
choreographers expanded the modern-
dance form to include postmodern
concepts, and such theatrical elements as
drama, literature, film, and video. Pina
Bausch's company, Tanztheater Wuppertal,

was a standard-bearer of dance-theater
work, performing Bausch's expressive,
multimedia works in showers of petals or
pools of water. Other dance-theater
choreographers included Wim Vandekeybus
and Anna Teresa De Keersmaker.

African-American modern dance

African-American dance artists have often
blended modern dance with African and
Caribbean influences. Such choreographers
as Katherine Dunham, Pearl Primus, and
Alvin Ailey integrated African and
Caribbean movements with ballet and
modern dance to create strong, dramatic
concert dances that reflected the African-
American experience.

Choreographers have blended Western and
African influences to create dramatic new
forms of modern and contemporary dance.

DANCE AS ART: FROM STREET TO STAGE

Although many forms of contemporary dance emerged out of classical dance, the street has also had a huge influence on what is performed today in theaters and concert halls. The nineteenth and twentieth centuries saw many dances that were originally practiced by marginalized or oppressed peoples transformed into works of art.

Flamenco

Flamenco is traditional song and dance that was created by the oppressed Gypsies of Andalusia in southern Spain to express their pain and suffering. The form synthesizes influences from the Arab, Jewish, and Gypsy people persecuted before and during the Spanish Inquisition, who sought refuge in caves or were herded into ghettos. Flamenco became a public performing art in the nineteenth century with the emergence of the *café cantante*. In the 1950s, flamenco festivals introduced new audiences around the world to the art form. Today, flamenco is choreographed and performed on concert stages by such companies as Zorongo Flamenco Dance Theater, Joaquin Cortés Flamenco Ballet, and Virginia Iglesias Flamenco Dance Company.

The passionate dance form flamenco, with its percussive footwork, has moved from the caves of Andalusia to Spanish cafes to concert halls around the world.

Tap dance

The roots of tap dance lie in English clogging, Irish step dancing, and the dances of black slaves, such as the Juba Dance. Tap is characterized by the sound a dancer's shoe makes as it hits the floor. Prominent modern tap dancers have included Brenda Bufalino, Savion Glover, Gregory and Maurice Hines, LaVaughn Robinson, Jason Samuels Smith, Chloe Arnold, and Dianne "Lady Di" Walker.

Breakdance and hip-hop's groundbreaking street-dance techniques can now be found in competitions, during festivals, and on the concert stage.

Jazz dance

During the Jazz Age of the early twentieth century, new music inspired new dance forms—such as the Charleston, Jitterbug, Boogie Woogie, Swing, and Lindy Hop—that arose, in part, from African-American and nightclub cultures. While many of these dances are still practiced as distinct styles, they also influenced the evolution of jazz dance featured in such Broadway productions as *Chicago* and *Cabaret*. Also, concert jazz dance today is an amalgam of jazz, modern, ballroom, and other dance styles, from ballet to hip-hop.

"Breakin' Convention"

For many years, Sadler's Wells Theatre in London has hosted the "Breakin' Convention." The festival explores ways in which the groundbreaking street-dance techniques and styles of hip-hop dance (from popping and locking to krumping and juking) can be merged with the theatrical potential of stage performance. Dancers and companies from Asia, Africa, Europe, the United States, and the United Kingdom present their innovations during the festival, in an effort to push both street and stage forms into new performance modes.

Flamenco does not act out tragedy, it is a tragedy. It makes no poetry, it is poetry. It does not need exuberance to express itself. It is content to cry out.

Anselmo Gonzalez Oliment

> # Dancers are athletes of God.
>
> Albert Einstein

DANCE AS COMPETITION

Carnival

Rio de Janeiro's annual Carnival is a world-famous festival held before Lent every year, and dates back to the 1700s. The carnival parade is filled with people and floats from various Samba schools (which may be an actual school, or a community or group of neighbors). Samba was created when African slaves came into contact with and incorporated other dance genres in Brazil, such as the polka, the maxixe, the lundu, and the xote. The schools compete with specially designed floats, storytelling dances, and vibrant costuming. The competition is one of the highlights of Carnival.

The competitive dance industry

In the United States and Canada, competition dance is an industry run by production companies, which conduct regional and national dance-offs or competitions. Dance students, from about the age of six to eighteen years old, are trained in dance schools to compete in

Rio de Janeiro's world-famous annual carnival includes performers from various Samba schools, who compete wearing colorful, attention-getting costumes.

small and large groups. In front of judges, they perform highly energetic, physically demanding routines that blend such dance styles as ballet, jazz, hip-hop, lyrical, modern, and tap. The dance schools typically arrange for their students and classes to compete, dancing choreography created by the school's teachers.

Ballet competitions

Throughout the world, various ballet competitions for different age groups and levels of proficiency provide young performers with the opportunity to receive coaching and critical assessments of their dancing. Some competitions require participants to perform both classical and contemporary works of ballet, with preliminary elimination rounds. Others are residencies: The repertory is announced once the dancers arrive, and improvements during rehearsals and coaching are factored into one's final score.

Ballroom dancing

Also called "dancesport," competitive ballroom dance occurs around the world under the auspices of the World Dance Council (which regulates professional dancesport at the international level) and the World DanceSport Federation (the international governing body of dancesport, as recognized by the International Olympic

Competitive ballroom dancing is often considered a sport, and is practiced by professional dancers who compete for titles, prestige, and awards. The dancers perform required and free-form choreographies based on such styles as Cha-Cha, Rumba, and Waltz, while wearing elaborate formal wear.

Committee). The term *dancesport* applies only to the International Style of competitive ballroom, which includes waltz, tango, foxtrot, quickstep, and Viennese Waltz, as well as Samba, Cha-Cha, Rumba, Paso Doble, and Jive.

DANCE AS ENTERTAINMENT

Dance is one of the oldest forms of entertainment, whether enjoyed in a community setting, on the screen or theatrical stage, or while out with friends in the street or in a club. Social dance as entertainment runs the gamut, from the cowboy two-step to disco, West Coast swing to salsa, and hip-hop to freaking. Social dance is a means of communication, and often seduction, between people. Just as parents today may frown upon grinding as too sexually explicit for young people dancing in public, so did the pope ban the tango in 1915, and even the Twist raised the ire of critics in the 1960s for being too provocative.

Michael Jackson and the music video

In the 1970s, new audiovisual technologies led to the creation of music videos: clips from live concerts, or creatively edited montages of images and action intended to visually enhance the music-listening experience. Many musicians who were also dancers, from Michael Jackson, Paula Abdul, and Madonna to MC Hammer and Britney Spears, have incorporated new dance moves into their music videos.

Jackson was one performer who maximized the potential of this new medium. His 1983 video *Beat It*, choreographed by Michael Peters, was a dance drama modeled after the Jets and Sharks confrontation choreographed by Jerome Robbins in *West Side Story*. In this groundbreaking work, the dancers' muscular, lightning-fast, highly articulate moves astounded audiences with their virtuosity and the ability to communicate menace and reconciliation.

Reality television

Television shows in the United States like *Solid Gold* and *Dance Party USA* led the way for such competitive-dancing programs as *America's Best Dance Crew*, *So You*

Michael Jackson's innovative dance moves and music videos electrified viewers and spawned many imitations.

All That Jazz
Black Swan
Dirty Dancing
Flashdance
The Red Shoes
Saturday Night
  Fever
Save the Last Dance
Singin' in the Rain
Stomp the Yard
Strictly Ballroom
Top Hat
White Nights

Reality tv
shows that
focus on
competitive
dance have
become
immensely
popular around
the world,
showcasing
dance as
entertainment.

Think You Can Dance, and *Dancing With the Stars* (which pairs professional competition dancers with B-list celebrities). These shows have acquired wide audiences, and have spread to many other countries. Opinions vary, however, on whether these competitions are having a positive or negative impact on dance as an art form. Are they simply slick, flashy entertainment? Or do they introduce people to an array of dance forms, especially upcoming generations of dancers and choreographers who are integrating these influences into their classical dance training?

2
WHAT DO YOU DANCE?

According to legend, the ancestral peoples of the Bantu, in Africa, would welcome guests with the greeting, "What do you dance?" This chapter anticipates that question by providing an overview of various dance styles, as well as their origins, techniques, and aesthetics, that a student passionate about dance might consider as a hobby or a career. Do you see dance as an art form, and want to perform on the concert stage in a dance company? As a competition dancer, you might study ballet, jazz, modern, or lyrical dance, which could lead to a career in musical theater or on Broadway. Or perhaps you're interested in dance forms such as flamenco, or in dance from India or Africa? Hip-hop, break dancing, and krumping—American dance forms with African roots—have migrated throughout the world, inspiring dancers to put their own creative take on dances equally at home in the street, at the club, or on the stage. This chapter also indicates how all of these dance forms have intermingled to produce new styles of dance.

BALLET

Ballet is an excellent foundation for all forms of dance, because of the strength, grace, precision, and poise it brings to the body.

The foundational principles of ballet were created to, over time and through rigorous training, develop a dancer's grace, poise, posture, and strength. These principles include the following:

Turnout: outward rotation of the leg from the hips, for greater leg extension

Pull up: lengthening the spine from the top of the neck to the lumbar region

Alignment: weight distributed evenly between both feet, ankles straight; knees directly over toes; hips turned out and knees straight; shoulders down; torso slightly forward; chest lifted (so ribs do not stick out); neck relaxed and chin up

Pointing the foot: high flexible arch (curve under the foot) accentuates the pointed toes for long leg lines

Flexibility: increases range and suppleness of movements

Port de bras (carriage of the arms): five basic positions, a graceful and expressive accompaniment to the movements of the legs

Styles of ballet

Since classical ballet began developing in the French courts of Louis XIV, the basic ballet steps have been taught around the world and have formed the basis of a variety of distinctive styles with variations in technique. The result is slight differences in the physical profile of the dancer and the ballet aesthetic from region to region, company to company. Although all styles are technically rigorous, here are some variations:

Ballet students wear leotards, tights, and soft ballet slippers.

Paris Opera Ballet School (French)—dramatic and alluring presentation

Bournonville (Danish)—low, quick footwork, melodic arms

Vaganova (Russian)—soft and pliant beneath clear lines

Cecchetti (Italian)—features eight port de bras and forty adages

Royal Ballet School and Royal Academy of Dance (English)—influenced by Cecchetti, pure line free of mannerisms

Alicia Alonso (Cuban)—drama embedded in pure technique

George Balanchine (American or neoclassical)—extreme speed, height, length, and plié; effect of compressed time and space; syncopated musicality

William Forsythe (deconstructionist)— pulls, pushes, twists the line and geometries of ballet

Even professional ballet dancers, who dance almost exclusively in pointe shoes, dress in rehearsal clothes in order to pay close attention to the shapes, lines, and curves their bodies make in space.

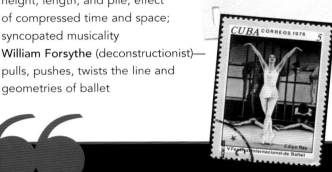

A stamp printed in Cuba, dedicated to the International Ballet Festival, shows a scene from the ballet *Oedipus the King*, circa 1976.

Plié is the first thing you learn and the last thing you master.

Suzanne Farrell

MODERN DANCE: TRADITIONAL

Modern dance originated, largely in the United States, to challenge the conformity and techniques, philosophy, aesthetics, narratives, and production values of classical ballet. It's a dance form of individualization, which arose out of the individual artist's need to express new ideas about life in the twentieth century.

In contrast to ballet, modern dancers are barefoot. Modern dance often works with feet and legs in parallel, with a flexible torso, and uses weight and gravity to create movements and shapes. The choreography uses all levels in space, including the floor, and dancers may be positioned sideways or even with backs turned to the audience. The staging for modern dance is often minimal, and costuming ranges from leotards to street clothes. Choreographers continually innovate new steps, shapes, and phrases, and they may also dance in their own work. A modern-dance piece may be a solo, a small-group work, or a piece for a full company.

Some traditional modern-dance techniques

Rather than performing a strict, prescribed set of steps and techniques, the modern-dance pioneers created their own dance vocabularies to reflect their thoughts, emotions, and experiences. Some of the trailblazers codified their technique, and taught it to dancers in their own companies and schools. Many of these techniques are still taught today and are incorporated into contemporary modern dance.

Doris Humphrey created the technique of "fall and recovery," with the apex of this movement continuum located in suspension. She believed that all movement patterns belong to one of three categories—opposition, succession, and unison—and that all movement characteristics belong to one of three categories—sharp accent, sustained flow, and rest.

Martha Graham's technique of severe contraction and release in the torso generated the sharp, angular movements that distinguish her intensely dramatic dances with mythological themes. She also emphasized weight shifts, oppositional forces in the body, and spirals that twist and curve the torso.

Lester Horton's technique includes "fortification studies" that focus on "descent/ascent" and "laterals," and the development of specific areas of the body such as the tendons or abdominals.

"Dance is the hidden language of the soul."

Martha Graham

Modern dance in Europe

Many seeds of modern dance were planted and germinated in central Europe during the early 1900s.

- **Émile Jaques-Dalcroze** created the Dalcroze Method, which uses eurhythmics, *solfège,* and improvisation to teach musical concepts through movement, and conversely to "tune" the body as a musical instrument.
- **Rudolph Laban** invented the dance notation system "Labanotation," created Laban Movement Analysis to interpret and describe movement using his theories of effort and shape, and developed "movement choirs" (masses of people choreographed in unison).

- **Mary Wigman**, after studying with Rudolf Laban, pioneered a methodology of "absolute dance" through which essential emotions were expressed independently of any narrative or theme.
- **Hanya Holm**, after studying with Wigman in Germany, moved to the United States and developed an expressive choreographic approach focused less on technique and more on how the body moving in space (via direction, plane, and pattern) was a form of creative exploration.

Xiaochuan Xie and Tadej Brdnik from the Martha Graham Dance Company, performing onstage in 2011 in the Canary Islands.

MODERN DANCE: CONTEMPORARY

As the modern-dance pioneers taught subsequent generations of dancers their techniques, those dancers in turn began creating their own choreography and companies, and subsequently taught the next generation of dancers, and so on. Today's modern-dance choreographers blend aspects of the pioneers' modern-dance vocabularies with ballet, jazz, African dance, hip-hop, club dance, everyday movements, and their own choreographic innovations to create work referred to as modern dance, contemporary dance, or contemporary modern dance.

Second- and third-generation modern dance

Merce Cunningham studied tap and ballroom dance as a child, and performed with the Martha Graham Dance Company before founding the Merce Cunningham Dance Company. His influence on modern dance remains profound. With his partner, composer John Cage, Cunningham introduced such radical innovations as creating music and movement independently, and using chance procedures and later computer programs to remove any vestiges of narrative, emotion, meaning, or cause and effect from his choreography.

Paul Taylor was a swimmer and painter who soloed with the Martha Graham Dance Company until founding his troupe and finding his choreographic voice. His lush, loose choreography, often made up of pedestrian movements, gives vibrant resonance to the explorations of life performed by the Paul Taylor Dance Company. Taylor often uses insects and

Seán Curran, an Irish step dancer who became a member of Bill T. Jones/Arnie Zane Dance Company, now choreographs work for Seán Curran Company and other groups. This image shows *Hard Bargain*, which is in the repertory of Zenon Dance Company.

animals as metaphors for the dark and light sides of the human psyche, but his work also addresses such issues as war, spirituality, and mortality.

Mark Morris grew up learning flamenco, folk dance, ballet, and later, modern dance. These influences are embedded in his choreography for the Mark Morris Dance Group. His work is renowned for its musicality (even if some critics disdain his work as mere music visualization), because of Morris' profound talent for translating the tone, structure, melody, and imagery of music into choreography. His dances can be humorous, exultant, emotionally wrenching, or sexually transgressive. "I love the way in which I make up dances," Morris has said. "It's a complicated way and the product is usually clear. Clear and simple. I don't need everybody to know that there are all of these fabulous things going on. If you *can* see it, that's wonderful."

THE BATSHEVA DANCE COMPANY

The Batsheva Dance Company in Israel was founded in 1964 by Martha Graham and Baroness Batsheva De Rothschild. In 1990, Ohad Naharin was appointed artistic director, and began developing a movement technique he calls "Gaga." The technique includes words that signal ways in which parts of the body initiate movement. For instance, when Naharian says "Luna," he's talking about the circular areas (or "moons") at the base of the fingers and toes, and the joints in the hands and feet. He means, focus on those areas, to develop a flow of energy through the joints. "My technique is distinguished by stunningly flexible limbs and spines, deeply grounded movement, explosive bursts, and a vitality that grabs a viewer by the collar," Naharian has said. Naharian has inspired many dancers to become choreographers, such as Andrea Miller, who choreographs for Zenon Dance Company and her own company Gallim Dance.

Amy Behm Thomson, of Zenon Dance Company, in Andrea Miller's 2009 *Picnic, Lightning*.

POSTMODERN DANCE

Postmodern dance was a supernova that burned hot and fast in the 1960s and 1970s. Its first iteration, Judson Dance Theater, grew out of a dance composition class taught by Robert Dunn, a musician who had studied with John Cage. Dancers included Trisha Brown, Lucinda Childs, Judith Dunn, David Gordon, Deborah Hay, Fred Herko, Meredith Monk, Steve Paxton, Yvonne Rainer, and James Waring. Its second iteration was Grand Union. Dancers included Trisha Brown, Barbara Dilley, Douglas Dunn, David Gordon, Nancy Lewis, Steve Paxton, and Yvonne Rainer. The work of these dancers set the stage for such later developments as performance art, dance-theater, and site-specific dance.

Postmodern dance's long-smoldering embers also continue to spark the experiments of dance and movement artists around the world. Organizations such as Movement Research in New York foster processes of experimentation and discovery that result in performance styles now referred to as avant-garde dance, experimental dance, post-postmodern dance, or downtown dance.

"NO TO SPECTACLE NO TO VIRTUOSITY NO TO TRANSFORMATIONS AND MAGIC AND MAKE BELIEVE NO TO GLAMOUR AND TRANSCENDENCY OF THE STAR IMAGE NO TO THE HEROIC NO TO THE ANTI-HEROIC NO TO TRASH IMAGERY NO TO INVOLVEMENT OF PERFORMER OR SPECTATOR NO TO STYLE NO TO CAMP NO TO SEDUCTION OF SPECTATOR BY THE WILES OF THE PERFORMER NO TO ECCENTRICITY NO TO MOVING OR BEING MOVED."

Yvonne Rainer, from her 1965 NO Manifesto

Some features of postmodern dance

- Choreography as an intellectual exercise, more about process than product
- Excising of all references to codified classical dance styles (ballet and modern)
- Performances in alternative spaces or venues
- Lack of expression (on the face and in the body)
- Exploration of everyday movement
- Denial of technical virtuosity
- Other artists (musicians, painters, etc.) as performers
- Incorporation of talking, dialogue, spoken text; film or video; ordinary objects
- Questioning of gender, class, race, capitalism/consumerism

Choreographic methods

- Improvisation
- Chance (throwing dice, coins, I-Ching)
- Repetition
- Stillness

TRISHA BROWN

Trisha Brown emerged from the Judson Dance Theater in the 1960s to create works that took place on rooftops, walls, and water in exploration of gravity and a choreographic methodology of time, space, and movement repetition. In the 1980s, Brown and her company began performing concert dances, which were carefully constructed from repetitive gestures combined into rigorous structures and geometric phrasing, sometimes created through improvisation.

CONTACT IMPROVISATION

According to Steve Paxton, a founder of Contact Improvisation, the process of generating movement through improvisation "is an activity related to familiar duet forms such as the embrace, wrestling, martial arts, and the jitterbug, encompassing the range of movement from stillness to highly athletic." During a contact-improv session, dancers remain in physical contact to support each other as they create movement. Observing the laws of physics, such as gravity and momentum, is an integral part of the process. The dancers, Paxton explains, "do not strive to achieve results, but rather, to meet the constantly changing physical reality with appropriate placement and energy."

A dancer of the Trisha Brown Dance Company performing in one of Brown's original site works, *Roof Piece.*

The ideology of postmodern dance
Dance can be anything, even everyday movement (brushing your hair, walking down the street). Dance can be performed anywhere (on a wall, in a park), not just on a concert stage. Anyone can be a dancer; no formal training is necessary.

SITE-SPECIFIC DANCE

Site-specific dance is dance created for a place other than the concert stage—whether indoor or outdoor, natural or man-made, urban or rural. Choreographers of site-specific dance may draw from such styles as ballet, modern, and jazz dance, ballroom dance, hip-hop, African dance, gymnastics, and aerial work to create a movement vocabulary that reflects the site in which the piece is being performed. They also use the site's history, architecture, and terrain to generate movement for the piece. In this way, site and dance are inextricably connected in a dynamic exchange. Site-specific dance is of one place and no other.

Characteristics of site-specific dance

- It is challenging to create and produce. It requires commitment, trust, and collaboration on the part of the choreographer, presenters/producers, dancers, composer, musicians, visual artists, and the communities in which it occurs, and can require the involvement of city officials, government agencies, insurance representatives, heavy- or industrial-equipment operators, and facility managers.
- It is interdisciplinary. It blends landscape, architecture, technology, history, diverse communities, movement, music, costuming, staging, visual art, and machinery—in any possible combination.
- It requires fearless dancers, who may perform on top of bridges or down the vertical faces of buildings, in polluted rivers, on moving barges, and in abandoned buildings.
- It is community-based and often performed free of charge.

One of Collage Dance Theatre's earliest works was *Laudromatinee*, a spoof on domestic chores and femininity set in a Laundromat.

- It is accessible and reaches a broad spectrum of the public, including culture aficionados, arts advocates, politicians and city workers, knowledge workers and the service sector, community and environmental activists, outdoor enthusiasts, architects and city planners, and intergenerational and multicultural audiences.

Mary Lee Hardenbergh's *Dance of the Waves* on the beach at Acre, Israel on the Mediterranean Sea, May 2010.

- It traverses economic, racial, and religious borders, often while expanding its own context beyond art to involve community, spiritual, and environmental factors.
- It changes viewers' perceptions of the place in which the dance occurred, fosters a sense of community among the people who experienced the dance together, and gives audiences an uplifting sense of how dance is an accessible and integral part of their lives.

"THE MOVEMENT VOCABULARY CHANGES WITH EACH LOCATION, AS DO AUDIENCE VANTAGE POINTS. THIS IS A FANTASTIC CHALLENGE AS A CHOREOGRAPHER. EACH NEW SPACE OPENS NEW WAYS OF LOOKING AT DANCE AND MOVEMENT, AND EACH EXPERIENCE CHANGES MY PRECONCEIVED IDEAS ABOUT SPACE."

Deidre Cavazzi, founder and choreographer, ArchiTexture Dance Company, as quoted in an article in *Dance Magazine*

SOME CURRENT PRACTITIONERS AND THEIR SITES

Joanna Haigood: grain elevators, a clock tower, a can factory, the grounds of Jacob's Pillow

Heidi Duckler: river, gas station, subway station, historic hotel, library, empty swimming pool

Marylee Hardenbergh: river, building windows, cherry picker and Bobcat machinery, farmers' market, museum plaza

Deidre Cavazzi: historic tall ship, four-story atrium, library, hotel, staircases

Stephan Koplowitz: staircases, natural-history museum, water-related sites

Debra Loewen: historic ballroom, lakeside park, building and courtyard under renovation, historical society building

Noémie Lafrance: parking garage, art gallery, empty swimming pool

LYRICAL DANCE

Lyrical dance is a relatively new style that blends ballet, jazz, and modern dance to create fluid, graceful choreography performed to the lyrics of popular music. In other words, the lyrical dancer conveys the emotion of a song's lyrics—such as joy, sadness, anger, and love—through dance. The dancer also uses facial expressions and flowing movements to tell a story that mirrors the lines of the song to which the dance is being performed, as well as the emotionally charged inflections of the vocalist or singer. By adding gesture, pantomime, and other acting elements, the performer can further enhance their interpretation of the music.

Music

Lyrical dances have been performed to pop, rock, hip-hop, and R&B music. Dancers choose powerful songs in order to express strong emotions in their dancing. They may dance to ballads that are slow and melodic, or to dynamic, fast-paced, and aggressive styles of music. The song lyrics may speak of freedom, lost love, betrayal, emotional despair, newfound happiness, or religious faith.

Lyrical dancers often wear long, flowing costumes that capture and enhance the fluid movements of the choreography.

Why lyrical dance is so popular with teenagers and students

"Lyrical is a beautiful and passionate dance form that is attractive to many teens who have deep feelings that they may find difficult to verbalize. Lyrical provides a release of the strong emotions that go along with growing up."

Holly Derville-Teer, teacher, Chehalem Valley Dance Academy, Newberg, U.S.A.

Where to see lyrical dance
- dance competitions
- music videos/MTV
- live concerts by popular singers
- themed stage shows for singers
- Cirque du Soleil

Lyrical dance is performed to a variety of types of music, from pop to hip-hop.

Characteristics of lyrical dance

- The dancer may accentuate a silence or pause in song with a gesture.
- The choreography may blend technically demanding movements with everyday moves to create more drama.
- Connections between movements are critical to creating the fluid aspect of lyrical dance. The dancer holds each move for as long as possible (or as long as is relevant to the lyrics), and transitions seamlessly into the next to integrate movement and emotion.
- Changes in tone, in coordination with the lyrics and music, are essential. Fast low leaps, sharp, short moves, and easy, languid movements convey different emotional states.

"LYRICAL DANCE IS MOVEMENT–FLOW IN TIME AND SPACE WITH THE SPECIFIC INTENT OF EXPRESSING THE EMOTIONAL CONTENT OF A SONG AND ITS VERSE. WITHOUT LYRICS, DANCE EXPRESSING THE MUSIC CAN BE CONSIDERED MUSIC VISUALIZATION. IT'S A POPULAR FORM BECAUSE VERSE AND MELODY CAN EVOKE STRONG EMOTIONS THAT STIMULATE A DESIRE TO MOVE RHYTHMICALLY IN SOME WAY. DANCE IS AND HAS ALWAYS BEEN CONSIDERED POETRY IN MOTION."

Marlene Skog, assistant faculty associate, Dance Program, University of Wisconsin, Madison, WI

MUSICAL THEATER

Musical theater is a stage entertainment combining instrumental music, live singing, spoken dialogue, and dance. Story, emotions, and characters are developed and communicated through the words, music, movement, and technical aspects of the production. The dance technique used in musical theater is a combination of ballet, modern and jazz dance, ballroom dance, and gymnastics.

Broadway, in Manhattan, New York, is one of the most famous centers of musical theater in the world.

From a historical perspective, the role of dance in musical theater evolved from minstrel shows and tap dance, burlesque and vaudeville, the Ziegfeld Follies (a series of Broadway productions staged in New York in the early twentieth century), and the work of many choreographic icons. In the twenty-first century, dance became the focus in a new genre of Broadway shows, with plot and character secondary, called dance musicals.

Great choreographers of musical theater

George Balanchine (*On Your Toes*) introduced extended ballet sequences, which enhanced plot and deepened characterizations as they were deftly woven into the musical's narrative.

Agnes de Mille (*Oklahoma*) introduced the "dream ballet," which integrated dance (performed by professional dancers doubling for the lead actors) into the plot to illuminate the protagonists' emotions.

Jerome Robbins (*West Side Story*) strongly believed in the storytelling power of ballet and broadened its scope and relevance to include the streets and tenements of ethnic New York.

Bob Fosse (*Chicago*) introduced playful sensuality and ribald sexuality in his choreography.

Gower Champion (*42nd Street*) drew from his ballroom-dance background to ensure props, choreography, and performers were seamlessly integrated into plots and songs.

Tommy Tune (*Nine*) brought down the level of razzmatazz while injecting choreography with fresh wit and inventive staging.

Michael Bennett (*A Chorus Line*) deployed dance as storytelling in nearly every scene and song, while retaining its artistic and entertainment value.

Susan Stroman (collaborated with Prince on a *Show Boat* revival) introduced dance montages drawing from African-American dance forms.

The dance musical *Riverdance*, in which traditional Irish step dancing is used to tell the story of Irish immigration to America, had its beginnings as a short number in the 1994 Eurovision Song Contest.

MUST-SEE DANCE MUSICALS

Burn the Floor (Jason Gilkison, director/choreographer)
Come Fly Away, Movin' Out (Twyla Tharp, director/choreographer)
Contact: The Musical (Susan Stroman, director/choreographer)
Fame: The Musical (Bob Fosse, director/choreographer)
Footloose: The Musical (A. C. Ciulla, choreographer)
Riverdance, Lord of the Dance (Michael Flatley, director/choreographer)

I have not wanted to intimidate audiences. I have not wanted my dancing to be an elitist form. That doesn't mean I haven't wanted it to be excellent.

Twyla Tharp

> Jazz is such rich music. I don't use it as atmosphere or background. The music is the subject matter … I learned more about the United States studying the history of jazz dance than I ever did from any history class I ever took.
>
> Danny Buraczeski

JAZZ DANCE

Jazz dance is a broad term referring to a choreographic fusion of European and African dance traditions that is inspired by, and created and performed to, jazz music.

Traditional jazz dance

Until the mid-twentieth century, "jazz dance" referred to such African-American vernacular dance styles as tap dance, Cakewalk, Black Bottom, Charleston, Jitterbug, Boogie Woogie, Swing, and Lindy Hop. Many of these dance styles are still taught, still practiced by enthusiasts who belong to dance clubs, and still performed on the concert stage.

Contemporary jazz dance

After innovations in free-form jazz made some jazz music less danceable, and tap dance diverged down its own evolutionary path, jazz dance developed into today's popular style. The form often includes elements of ballet, modern dance, hip-hop, and acro (a dance style that includes acrobatic elements).

Jack Cole

Considered the father of theatrical jazz dance, Jack Cole developed a unique style in which he integrated jazz, ballet, and such "ethnic" forms as Bharatanatyam to create what he called "urban folk dance." His singular style included isolations (movements confined to specific parts of the body), angled foot positions, lightning-fast changes in direction, and long dramatic slides on the knees. Cole technique is now a part of nearly every jazz dance concert or routine performed in competition, on the concert stage, in musical theater, in nightclubs, and in television commercials. "In the theatre you want to see real people doing real things, expressing valid emotions in an artistic, meaningful way, disclosing bits of insight that will transfix you and make you understand something about life, and about yourself," Cole said in a *Dance Magazine* interview. "I just try to touch the dancer at the center of his emotion. I try to remind him of what he is— a dancer, and actor, a real person."

Other notable jazz-dance choreographers

Bob Fosse: turned-in knees, rounded shoulders, rolling hips, sideways shuffling, finger snaps, strutting; sensual style

Gus Giordano: clean lines, "Giordano *port de bras*," weighted; regal style

Danny Buraczeski: angular, swinging, pulsing, rhythmically complex, coiled, curvy, and flowing; profoundly musical style, called "the thinking man's jazzman"

Contemporary jazz dance is often a blend of ballet, modern dance, hip-hop, and acro styles of dance.

WHERE TO SEE JAZZ DANCE

- On the concert stage (Hubbard Street Dance Company, Giordano Jazz Dance Chicago, Zenon Dance Company)
- In musical theater, on Broadway
- During dance competitions

Danny Buraczeski is renowned for his tremendous musicality in choreographing dances to jazz music. In *Avalon*, for his company JAZZDANCE by Danny Buraczeski, he transformed music by Lionel Hampton into kinetic choreography of power and grace.

INDIAN DANCE

The classical dance forms of India include Bharatanatyam, Kathak, Kathakali, and Odissi. Each of these dance forms, many of which originated in the temples or royal courts of India, has its own distinctive style, technique, and aesthetic. Generally, however, the dancer's hips are open and knees bent. Flat feet beat out intricate, complicated rhythms enhanced by ankle bells. Jumps are usually low and small. The dancer's head may quickly and subtly change direction, while neck isolations emphasize facial expressions. The dancer moves her torso with graceful side-to-side movements or turns on the axis of her spine. The hand and arm movements are elaborately poetic: Indian dancers deploy a vast repertoire of gestures to communicate the events, stories, ideas, and emotions of the music and poetry they're interpreting.

Bollywood

"Bollywood" (Bombay + Hollywood) is a style of Hindi-language cinema. In Bollywood musicals, the films integrate lively song and dance segments into formulaic narratives that may combine romance (embedded within melodramatic love triangles), family drama, danger, villains, and stunts. The choreography may blend classical Indian dance with popular styles of Western dance. Usually, the protagonist leads a chorus of backup dancers in settings that suddenly shift location.

ANANYA DANCE THEATRE

Ananya Dance Theatre is a contemporary company of women artists, primarily of color, who work at the intersection of artistic excellence and social justice. Dr. Ananya Chatterjea, founder and artistic director, created a movement vocabulary for her company that is rooted in the Indian dance form Odissi. She integrates the sculptural sensuality, powerful footwork, and emotional articulation of Odissi with yoga's pure lines and breath release, and with the energy of the Indian martial-arts tradition Chhau.

Ananya Chatterjea (middle) performing in *Tushaanal: Fires of Dry Grass*, a work exploring the experiences of women who live near the gold mines of South Africa.

RAGAMALA DANCE

Ragamala Dance performs Bharatanatyam, a form that dates back more than 2,000 years and originated in the temples of southern India. The Ragamala dancers trained in the style of internationally renowned dancer Alarmél Valli, which emphasizes linear geometry and structure, rhythmic complexity, and expressive subtlety and depth. "In Bharatanatyam, the form is but the foundation on which the creative dancer builds structures, both in time and space, drawing from her individual experience of music, movement, and life. Every song or poem, therefore, is re-created by the dancer, becoming her personal statement," Valli has said. Founder Ranee Ramaswamy, as well as her co-artistic director and daughter Aparna Ramaswamy, integrate elements of music, theater, poetry, sculpture, and literature into their multidimensional dance works. Ragamala's repertoire ranges from solo works to large-scale performances with live orchestra, sets, video projections, and floor paintings. The company's work is part dynamic living tradition and part innovative exploration of the permeable creative boundaries of Bharatanatyam.

Ashwini Ramaswamy, another daughter of Ranee Ramaswamy, in Sacred Earth.

"BHARATANATYAM PROVIDES ENDLESS CHALLENGES AND INSPIRATIONS. EVERY PRACTICE AND PERFORMANCE OFFERS A NEW CHANCE TO INTERPRET THE MUSIC, TO GO BEYOND WHAT YOU THOUGHT POSSIBLE, AND TO CONTINUE IN THE LIFELONG PURSUIT OF UNITING SOUL AND BODY AS ONE. IT'S AS SPIRITUAL, MENTAL AND PHILOSOPHICAL AS IT IS PHYSICAL, WHICH IS WHY THIS CAREER IS A LIFELONG JOURNEY. I WOULDN'T HAVE IT ANY OTHER WAY."

Ashwini Ramaswamy, dancer with Ragamala Dance

AFRICAN DANCE

African dance often refers to the dances of sub-Saharan Africa, which vary widely and were developed as a means of cultural or religious expression, to educate children, to celebrate during festivals, and to reinforce social cohesiveness. Many African-American modern-dance choreographers draw on African dance traditions to infuse their work with social and political meaning, add vitality that resonates with their cultural heritage, and create new forms of concert dance that excite, entertain, and enlighten audiences. The best-known of these companies is the Alvin Ailey American Dance Theater, which still performs *Revelations*, its signature work of African slavery and freedom, around the world.

Contemporary choreographers from Africa create work that blends storytelling, dance, and music to convey the realities of life in countries such as Nigeria, the Congo, or South Africa. Such work often questions and challenges social values through dynamic choreography that's a matrix of African dance, modern dance, hip-hop, and other forms.

Congolese choreographer and dancer Faustin Linyekula performing for dance students at the Walker Art Center.

Faustin Linyekula and Les Studios Kabako

The Congolese choreographer Faustin Linyekula and his company, Les Studios Kabako, create works that conjure stories of the Congo's history of slavery, colonization, and corruption. Movement and music are juxtaposed with props, projected and recorded text, and invitations to the audience in performances of resonant works driven by a desire for truth. Skeins of memory,

SOME AFRICAN OR AFRICAN-INFLUENCED DANCE COMPANIES AROUND THE WORLD

Forces of Nature Dance Theater
TU Dance
KanKouran West African Dance Company
Nora Chipaumire
Voices of Strength
Gregory Maqoma/Vuyani Dance Theatre

propaganda, and imagination unravel during these works, which are kinetic expressions of political realities and hopes for the future.

Hip-hop

A form of artistic and cultural expression, hip-hop originated in African-American communities during the 1970s (particularly in New York City), but has since spread around the world. Hip-hop dance is particularly popular in France and South Korea, where international competitions take place and dance companies perform. But hip-hop also has established practitioners in the Middle East, Africa, Australia, and the Caribbean, where the performers add their own local stylings. In Iraq, for example, dancers mix Western and Arab music with Islamic subject matter to infuse hip-hop with the struggles of Islamic youth.

The primary styles of hip-hop are breaking, locking, and popping, which are usually performed on a mat. In hip-hop, the entire body—from the top of the head to the tips of the toes—is used, along with dramatic isolations of the muscles, joints, and limbs. Hip-hop is also an improvisational form that gets free rein during battles or freestyle dance competitions. Battles usually take place within a cipher—a ring of observers and dancers that surrounds the performers.

Hip-hop is also taught in dance studios. Hip-hop routines choreographed for students to perform at dance competitions are often referred to as new style or jazz funk.

> Dance is for everybody. I believe that the dance came from the people and that it should always be delivered back to the people.
>
> Alvin Ailey

OTHER WORLD DANCES

Flamenco

Flamenco dance is famous around the world for its passionate intensity. To convey *duende*, or the soul of the music, the dancers proudly stand upright, expressively splay their fingers and curve their arms around their heads and torsos, combine lightning-fast footwork with rhythmic stomping, and during duets keep their eyes locked on each other.

In Spain, flamenco is danced informally at weddings and celebrations, in cafés and clubs as entertainment, and by professional groups on concert stages. Originally a solo form, today the dance is also performed by flamenco dance companies throughout the United States and in other countries. Although a dancer must adhere to the music's fifty different *palos* (or forms), the dancer is allowed to improvise, which is often evident in the performer's sudden and vivid emotional expressions.

Susana di Palma, dancer and founder of Zorongo Flamenco Dance Theatre, is internationally renowned for her innovative flamenco/theater works that respond to Spanish literature, art, and politics to shed light on our contemporary world.

European folk dances

Folk dance generally refers to dances that originated in European villages before the twentieth century to note a day of significance or celebrate an aspect of everyday life. Dances might commemorate a marriage, mark the seasons, or reflect the value of work. Young and old alike performed the dances, with little or no professional training; they learned from watching other dancers. Performed at community events or social functions to live music, the dances became part of a village's tradition.

Ethnic Dance Theatre is one of the few companies in the United States dedicated to the artistic performance and preservation of world music, song, and dance. Since its founding in 1974, EDT has performed dances from more than 50 different countries, including Austria, Albania, Bulgaria, China, Costa Rica, Germany, Lebanon, Mexico, Mongolia, Norway, Pakistan, Poland, Saudi Arabia, Spain, Tibet, Turkey, Russia, Uzbekistan, and Ukraine.

Butoh

Butoh appeared in Japan in response to the horrors of World War II, particularly the detonation of the atomic bomb. Its founders, Kazuo Ono and Hijikata, trained in Western dance and in the German Neue Tanze tradition before originating Butoh.

A form of dance-theater, Butoh often features naked performers whose bodies may be painted white or dusted with rice flour. The dancers move through minimal choreography at a glacial pace with extreme control. An internationally prominent butoh company is Sankai Juku. In one of the group's signature motifs, the dancers are suspended upside down, supported by ropes. As they're lowered to the ground, they slowly uncoil their bodies.

BUTOH PRACTITIONERS AND OTHERS INFLUENCED BY BUTOH

Eiko and Koma
Sanna Kekalainen, Arja Raatikainen, Mammu Rankanen
SU-EN Butoh Company
Dai Rakuda Kan
Maureen Fleming
GooSayTen
Minako Seki
Tadashi Endo
Ko Murobushi

3
DANCE
TRAINING

In this chapter, you'll begin to discover the training, discipline, and fortitude required to become a serious student of dance or a professional dancer. No matter what dance style or technique you decide to study, you'll usually spend eight hours or more a day in classes, in rehearsals, and cross training with swimming, yoga, or Pilates, in order to increase your physical strength, stamina, and flexibility. Most dancers begin their formal training—often in a classical technique, such as ballet, or such Asian dance forms as Kathak and Bharatanatyam—between the ages of five and fifteen. Younger children often learn folk dances and other culturally specific dances by watching their parents rehearse and perform in their communities. Here you will find all you need to know about training your body for this complex art form.

WHERE TO STUDY DANCE

Professional Western dance training focuses primarily on three forms: ballet, modern, and musical theater (which includes jazz, modern, and tap). Although African dance, hip-hop, and Asian dance forms are increasingly popular and taught throughout the world, professional dance training usually focuses on ballet, modern dance, or musical theater (which includes jazz, modern, and tap). Students who train with hopes of a career in dance usually immerse themselves in one category while taking classes in the others. Why? Because today many contemporary choreographers are drawing from diverse dance styles in creating their work. They're more likely to select dancers who have strong technique and sound training in at least one form, but are easily adaptable and can incorporate other styles.

Dance studios

For young students who wish to train and perform on the competition circuit, with an eye toward performing on Broadway, cruise ships, in music videos, and with pop singers on the concert stage, for-profit dance studios that offer such styles as lyrical, tap, hip-hop, and jazz—with some grounding in ballet and modern dance—are a good choice. To select a studio:

Mirrors are an essential part of any dance studio, so students can pay close attention to their form, alignment, and the expressive quality of their dancing.

- Consider the style of dance that interests you, and the type of music you listen to.
- Find dance studios close to where you live. Ask for recommendations. Visit their websites to learn about class offerings. Find out the kinds of competitions in which the studio participates and has won awards.
- Tour the dance studio to assess the facilities. Are the studios clean and comfortable, with sprung floors? Are the dressing rooms and bathrooms clean and secure, and do they offer some privacy?
- Learn about the instructors. What are their backgrounds and teaching methods? What do the students say about them?
- Observe or even try out a class. There's no better way to assess a teacher and a class than through real-life participation.

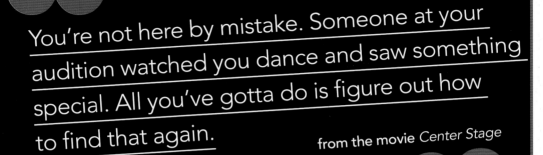

> You're not here by mistake. Someone at your audition watched you dance and saw something special. All you've gotta do is figure out how to find that again.
>
> **from the movie** *Center Stage*

Dance company schools

Across the world, many nonprofit dance companies have their own for-profit dance schools. Members of the dance company may teach in the schools, along with guest instructors. Such schools often audition students before selecting new enrollees. They may teach only the technique of their founders, or they may wish to prepare students for possible careers in their own companies—such as the School of American Ballet, the Rambert School of Ballet and Contemporary Dance, or the Paris Opera Ballet School—or other professional companies.

Repertory companies, such as Zenon Dance Company School in Minneapolis, offer classes in a wide array of dance styles, from modern and ballet to hip-hop and improvisation, for professional dancers and students. Zuzi! Dance Company School in Tucson offers creative movement for toddlers and aerial dance for adults, in addition to ballet and modern dance. Companies specializing in Asian, Middle Eastern, African, and flamenco dance often offer classes as well.

An integral part of dance training is the student performance, whether you're learning ballet or Bharatanatyam.

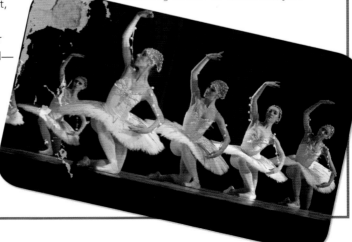

Universities and colleges

Many colleges and universities award bachelor's and/or master's degrees in dance, typically through departments of dance, theater, or fine arts, thus providing preparation for a professional dance career in a liberal arts setting. In the United States, the National Association of Schools of Dance is made up of seventy-four accredited dance programs. Many of these programs concentrate on modern dance, but some also offer courses in jazz, culturally specific dance, ballet, or other techniques. Colleges and universities also offer courses in dance composition, movement analysis, dance history and scholarship, and dance criticism.

Workshops and summer intensives

Spending a summer intensively studying a particular style of dance, with a renowned teacher, is an excellent way of honing your technique or broadening your dance horizons.

- Dance company schools frequently offer special summer intensives with famous visiting or guest instructors, providing students with a once-in-a-lifetime opportunity.
- Universities and colleges with dance departments often provide their students, as well as students from other programs around the world who wish to study on that campus for the summer, opportunities to work with a specific choreographer or study a specific dance technique or style.
- Dance festivals frequently offer classes. Jacob's Pillow Dance Festival in Massachusetts, for example, is open only in the summer, during which the school offers accepted students classes in ballet, musical theater, contemporary, and cultural dance styles, often in coordination with its festival of world dance.

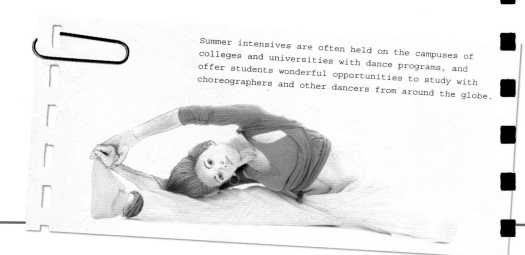

Summer intensives are often held on the campuses of colleges and universities with dance programs, and offer students wonderful opportunities to study with choreographers and other dancers from around the globe.

A variety of skills, from singing and acting to dancing, are essential to training for a career in musical theater.

Considering musical theater?

You'll need to be a triple threat: an accomplished actor, singer, and dancer. Musical-theater programs around the world provide instruction in bringing characterization to songs and choreography; defining characters; vocal techniques and performance; and advancing levels of dance (ballet, jazz, tap, and modern) as a soloist and as part of an ensemble.

Whether you're studying at a renowned school of classical dance, a suburban dance studio, a downtown dance center, or a university, the rules of etiquette are the same:

- Turn off all cell phones.
- Don't chew gum or eat. (Water bottles, placed at the perimeter of the room, are allowed.)
- Be on time. Or rather, come early so you have time to warm up before class begins.
- Position yourself in the room according to your experience. If you're a newcomer, find a place in the back of the room so you can watch and learn from the more experienced students in front.
- Respect your teacher, as well as the other students. Ask questions, but otherwise do not engage in conversation. Give the instructor your full attention at all times.
- Accept corrections from your teacher. Watch the corrections the instructor gives to other students, and apply those corrections to your own dancing.
- Maintain a positive attitude.
- Don't sit between combinations or while other groups are performing. Keep your body warm, flexible, and moving.
- If you are experiencing pain or injury, immediately inform your teacher.
- If you're excused from class because of injury, still participate by closely watching the class. Much can be learned from active observation.

> The body is your instrument in dance, but your art is outside that creature, the body.
>
> Martha Graham

THE ELEMENTS OF DANCE: BODY AND ACTION

Students who study dance in the United Kingdom or United States may encounter the acronyms BASTE or BEST. These shortcuts to describing the elements of dance stand for Body, Action, Space, Time, and Energy; or Body, Energy, Space, and Time. These are the foundational concepts of dance, and are present in the moving body whether running down a sidewalk, dancing at a club, practicing at the barre, moving into a yoga pose, or performing on a concert stage.

A thorough understanding of these concepts is essential to learning movement skills that will evolve into the styles or techniques performed as a dancer.

Posture or alignment is "home base" for every dancer, whether the movement takes them across the floor or into the air.

Body

The body is the material or instrument with which dance is created. Some teachers and choreographers start with the spine, or the breath, or the center of the body (from the sternum to the pelvis) as a point of movement origination. Even in stillness, the dancing body is inherently aware of itself, and its relationship to changes in space, time, motion, and energy around it. Body basics in dance training include the following:

Posture or alignment—"home base" for dancers, this allows the dancer to initiate, hold, and organize movements from a central place of action, with attention to the pull of gravity.

Balance—an inner sense of equilibrium and support throughout the body.

Flexibility—range of motion in muscles, joints, and limbs, and the ability to lengthen or stretch parts of the body.

Strength—not only muscle strength and the ability to lift and hold one's own body or another dancer's, but also endurance and stamina.

Coordination—awareness of how the whole body is moving in space and time.

Action/Motion

There are two basic categories of action/motion:

Locomotor—action that carries the body from one place to another through space, either using the feet (walk, run, leap, jump, hop, gallop, skip, slide, or sashay or chasse), or not using the feet (roll, crawl, knee slides).

Axial—motion organized around the axis of the body, which stays in one place (stretch, sink, pull, bounce, twist/untwist, bend, kick).

Combinations of these actions result in movement sequences or phrases.

Facial expressions, gestures, and changes in posture add layers of movement and meaning to the combination.

"MOVEMENT IS AMBIGUOUS UNTIL YOU PLACE IT AGAINST SOME BACKGROUND.... I USE A GREAT MANY REPETITIONS WITH VARIATIONS TO MAKE THE AMBIGUITIES OF MOVEMENT APPARENT. EXPLORING THE ALTERNATE POSSIBLE MEANINGS OF GESTURE IS ONE OF MY MAJOR CONCERNS."

David Gordon, choreographer, founding member of the Grand Union, theater director

THE ELEMENTS OF DANCE: SPACE AND SHAPE

Space isn't simply air, but the medium through which you move as a dancer. The possibilities for interacting with space are endless—from standing still to traveling from place to place, from moving isolated parts of the body to rapid full-body movement that quickly changes in direction, pattern, level, and quality.

Shapes make meaning

Whether created by an individual dancer, or by several dancers working together, shape is three-dimensional and generates meaning. Shapes with straight lines or angles may convey meanings and qualities such as purposeful and driven, lean and hard, rigid and unyielding, proud and defiant, or clear

Middle-Eastern dancers acquire tremendous flexibility that allows them to extend the parameters of the traditional form into enlarged shapes and gestures.

THE BODY CAN MOVE...

In different directions:
Up, down
Forward, backward
Side to side
Toward, away from
In various patterns:
Straight, zigzag
Curved, twisting
Angular, geometric
Through different levels in space:
High (in the air)
Middle (standing positions)
Low (on the floor)
**With different qualities,
as if space were actually:**
Soft (silk, fur, angora)
Thick (gelatin, mud, milk shake)
Heavy (water, a weight)
Bubbly (soda, champagne)

and clean. Shapes that are more organic or curved may convey meanings and qualities such as soft and yielding, natural and flexible, forgiving and supplicant, cowed or ashamed.

When viewed in silhouette, because of a lighting scheme of contrasts, the choreography's shapes or forms are heightened and placed in bold relief.

The dance company Pilobolus is internationally acclaimed for its ingenious shape-shifting acrobatics, elastic choreography, and tableaux of intertwining, interlocking, and interchanging forms.

Space as place

Venues or places in which dance occurs (or is performed) are sometimes referred to as spaces. A dance space can be a concert stage dedicated to the performing arts, a dance floor at a club or ballroom, a studio for training and rehearsal, an open area outside around which an audience gathers to watch dancers, a designated place within a church or temple, or even a spot in your house or apartment in which you dance.

"I'D BEEN PLAYING JIGS AND REELS FOR A CEILIDH, WATCHING THE SET DANCERS SPINNING AND STAMPING OUT WITH WILD PRECISION THE RHYTHMS OF A DANCE . . . SOME TIME DURING THE COURSE OF THE EVENING THE MUSIC I HAD FOR YEARS ONLY HEARD AND PLAYED BECAME VISIBLE, FILLED WITH SPINNING SWEATY COUPLES, AS THE ABSTRACT SHAPE OF A WHIRLPOOL FILLS WITH WATER, OR AN EQUATION TAKES SHAPE AS A TETRAHEDRON. ONLY AFTER THE DANCERS HAD LEFT THE FLOOR DID I NOTICE THE CIRCULAR PATTERNS OF BLACK SCUFFS AND STREAKS THEIR HEELS HAD MADE ON THE POLISHED WOOD. THIS PATTERN, I RECOGNIZED, WAS AN ENORMOUS ENCODED PAGE OF POETRY, A KIND OF MANUSCRIPT, OR, MORE PROPERLY, A PEDISCRIPT."

Michael Donaghy, from The Shape of the Dance: Interviews, Essays and Digressions

THE ELEMENTS OF DANCE: TIME AND ENERGY

Time

Time encompasses the rhythmic aspects of a dance, as well as the duration (length) and tempo (speed) of movements. Rhythm is a flow or pattern of sound or movement. Underneath rhythm is a pulse or beat (an even or uneven division of time). Patterns of beats create meter, which in dances like the waltz, tango, salsa, and specific African dances are immediately recognizable. In most Western music, the meter or time signature (a form of notation, such as 2/4 , 3/4, or 4/4 time) specifies the number of beats in each measure, the note values (or beat duration), and which note might be accented.

Duration is note value, or the length of time a note or movement lasts. How long or short a movement is also correlates with its tempo. Tempo is the speed of a movement, and how much movement occurs in a specific period of time.

Energy

Although energy refers to the degree or amount of force, tension, or weight a dancer puts into an action or movement, energy is also about the quality or attribute assigned to the motion. Both aspects of energy imbue choreography with psychological and emotional characteristics, which may be either obvious or ambiguous to the viewer. Because of this, energy is one of the most expressive aspects of dance, and one that invites interpretation.

The energy a dancer puts into a movement or phrase might be powerful or limp, strong or weak, tight or loose, heavy or light, struggling or relaxed, jerky or free flowing.

In Pattin' Juba (otherwise known as the Juba dance, hambone, or Juba Jivin'), originally a plantation dance created by African slaves, dancers stomp, slap, and pat their arms, legs, chests, and cheeks. Pattin' Juba dancers also created these rhythms to keep time for other dancers during a walkaround, a competition dance in nineteenth-century blackface minstrel shows.

Other ways dancers "keep time"
- By following the beat or rhythm of the music
- Through breath patterns
- By anticipating and feeling changes in the emotional or rhythmic qualities of choreographic phrases
- By taking cues from other dancers and their movements
- Through changes in the energy or dynamics of choreographic phrases and sections

There are many qualities (or attributes) of energy that can be applied to movement:

- **Sustained:** an even, smooth flow
- **Suspended:** a momentary stillness, with the body actively arrested in space (often after a burst of energy)
- **Swinging/swaying:** a lifted part of the body drops along a curved pathway with a combination of gravity and energy that generates the momentum necessary for the motion to carry the body part back up, on a curve
- **Collapsing:** a sudden or gradual loss of force and release of energy, during which the body crumples, folds, or curls downward with gravity
- **Vibrating:** shuddering, fluttering, or quivering created by tensing a specific part of the body
- **Percussive:** explosive, staccato, or spurts of movement; energy that stops and starts suddenly

Combinations of different energies can occur within a single movement or throughout a phrase of choreography. The choices choreographers and dancers make with energy indicate the emotional tone and intention of the choreography.

The qualities of time and energy manifest differently in dances throughout the world, depending on the cultural values and traditions that inform the dance style. The fast and punctuated moves of hip-hop (above), and its body-revealing clothing, would be out of place in many cultures that value deliberate, thoughtful movements done by dancers in traditional costumes (below).

IN THE STUDIO: THE ESSENTIALS OF DANCE TRAINING

Nearly everyone begins learning a verbal language at a young age, often starting with an alphabet. Similarly, dancers—whether young or already adults—learn the language of dance by starting with basic building blocks or exercises.

Dance students practice these exercises over and over, sometimes every day, to strengthen, loosen, and build the body's ability to move with precision, speed, and grace. Some key areas of training include

- core strength—engaging the abdominals and strengthening the center of the body without tilting the pelvis forward or back;
- hips—flexibility in rotating the legs from the hip sockets, as well as working with legs parallel;
- arms—lifting and moving the arms without letting the rib cage jut out;
- jumps—learning how to leave the floor and land again without jarring knees, feet, and ankles;
- isolations—being able to work one part of the body while relaxing or releasing tension in another.

Floor work

Floor work allows you to stretch and lengthen parts of the body, and to build strength in specific areas, without worrying about the need to balance or bear a lot of weight. Depending on the style of dance being studied, floor work may include spine stretches and curls, torso contractions and twists, foot and ankle exercises, side stretches, arm sequences, and turned-out and parallel leg flexes.

At the barre

The barre is a fixture in most dance studios. It may be a horizontal wood rail attached to the wall or a freestanding structure in the middle of the room. Barre exercises allow the dancer to practice elevating, turning, balancing, and jumping, using the barre for support.

Many exercises done at the barre have their origins in ballet, such as

plié (knee bends);

tendu (leg and foot stretches that brush the floor);

dégagé (same brushing movement as *tendu*, but the working leg leaves the floor slightly when extended);

rond de jambe (the toe of the working leg traces a semicircle on the floor);

frappé (flexed foot darts out to hit the floor);

petit battement (the heel of one foot touches the other ankle, and the lower part of the leg moves quickly out and in);

grand battements (leg kicks brought down in *tendu*);

arabesque (leg stretched behind the body).

Center work

During most dance classes, students will spread out into the room to practice some of the exercises learned at the barre. This portion of the dance class is called center work. Students may practice basic positions (as in ballet, jazz, and codified modern-dance techniques), as well as movement combinations across the floor. A jazz walk followed by a shoulder roll and contraction, or a skip that lands in plié that deepens, rises, and unfurls into arabesque,

The barre is an integral part of every dance studio. The wooden barre supports student dancers as they learn new or practice familiar steps, and is where professional dancers warm up before class or a performance.

or floor roll that lengthens into the prone position are all combinations that use different levels of space, and could be performed differently, depending on the teacher's instructions about the use of energy, time, and shape.

Beneath your feet

Dancers require a sprung floor, whether training, rehearsing, or performing. A sprung floor is constructed to absorb the impact of jumps and leaps, either through wood basket-weave construction, or wood overlying neoprene pads or foam rubber. Often, a layer of marley is laid on top of the wood floor (especially for modern dancers). Marley is a thick but lightweight sheet vinyl that can be taped down for rehearsals and performances, and later removed (good for touring companies and for theaters that don't have a sprung wood floor). Marley's matte, nonskid finish helps prevent dancers from slipping.

What should you wear?

- Ballet: Many classical ballet studios require a strict uniform for students: pink or flesh-colored tights and short- or long-sleeved black leotards for girls/women; thicker ballet tights designed for boys/men, a dance belt, and leotard or tight, tucked-in T-shirt. Women (and men with long hair) wear hair tied back. As girls advance in ballet, they may wear chiffon or wrap skirts. Tight sweaters and shrugs

Dancers rehearse in front of mirrors in order to attend to and correct their form, posture, and steps.

help keep dancers warm during class.
- Jazz: Tights and leotards will allow your teacher to clearly see your shapes and lines. But many jazz dancers like to wear jazz pants, which are usually boot-cut or flared at the bottom. Tops are form-fitting tank tops, T-shirts, or leotards.
- Modern/contemporary: Some teachers will ask students to wear tights and leotards, especially at the beginning and intermediate levels, so they can observe and correct the dancer's line. But clothing

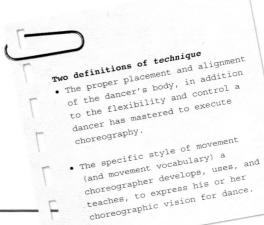

Two definitions of technique
- The proper placement and alignment of the dancer's body, in addition to the flexibility and control a dancer has mastered to execute choreography.

- The specific style of movement (and movement vocabulary) a choreographer develops, uses, and teaches, to express his or her choreographic vision for dance.

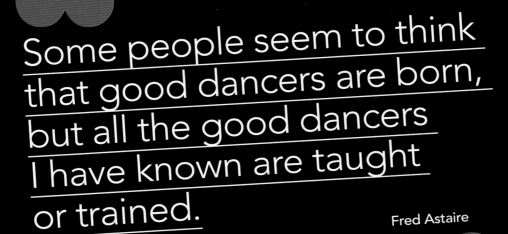

> Some people seem to think that good dancers are born, but all the good dancers I have known are taught or trained.
>
> Fred Astaire

Many dancers never stop taking ballet class. Ballet provides a basis of technique that can be applied to many dance styles.

rules for modern classes are generally less restrictive. Shorts, T-shirts, sweaters, sweatshirts, and sweatpants are usually allowed, as long as they aren't too baggy and don't get in the way of the dancer's movements.

- Hip-hop: Street and athletic clothing is appropriate for hip-hop dance training. For women, a sports bra under a full-length or cropped T-shirt, with leggings or loose sport pants, is the norm. Men wear T-shirts and hoodies, with baggy pants in which they can move freely. Sneakers and athletic shoes are common footwear.

Dance footwear

Proper footwear (unless you're a modern, African, Kathak, or Bharatanatyam dancer) is essential to a dancer's training and success. Shoes are often worn with tights (footless or whole foot) and/or anklets, although some dancers wear their shoes without socks.

- Jazz shoes (booties, sandals, sandal-shoes, sneakers, trainer shoes): Made of leather or canvas, the shoes should have strong arch support, and lots of spring and flexibility. Some jazz shoes have split soles, allowing the shoe to bend freely.
- Ballet slippers: Made of soft leather or canvas (for class), or satin (for performance), the traditional ballet slipper has a flexible, thin sole. Split soles provide greater flexibility to the dancer. The shoes are secured with a single elastic band across the top of the foot, or with two bands crossed in an X at the top of the foot. Traditionally, women wear pink shoes and men wear black shoes.
- Pointe shoes: These shoes are worn by female ballet dancers, and help them dance on the tips of their toes through two structural features—a box with a flat end at the front of the shoe, which encases and supports the dancer's toes, and a shank made of a rigid material that stiffens the sole to support the arch of the

DANCE TRAINING | 70

Sure he was great, but don't forget Ginger Rogers did everything he did backwards . . . and in high heels!

Bob Thaves on Fred Astaire

Ready for pointe?

Ballet dancers are considered ready for pointe work (and pointe shoes) when they can maintain proper turnout while performing center combinations; have strong core strength, pull-up, and alignment; and can securely balance in relevé.

foot while it's *en pointe*. To keep the shoe tightly on the foot, dancers sew satin ribbons to the sides of the shoes and tie the ribbons securely around their ankles. The shoe's exterior fabric can be dyed to match a costume.

- Heeled character shoe: Used in musical theater and sometimes jazz, character shoes are leather, have a 1–3-inch heel, and one or more straps across the instep to secure the shoe to the dancer's foot.
- Jazz shoes: Usually made of leather, jazz shoes typically have a two-part, rubberized sole (sometimes split) for flexibility and traction, and a low (1 inch or shorter) heel. Laces or elastic inserts keep the shoe securely on the foot.
- Ballroom shoes: Women wear 2-inch heels, while men's ballroom shoes are lace-ups with 1-inch heels and leather uppers. In contrast, shoes for Latin dancing are usually more flexible, and have higher heels that shift the dancers' weight more to their toes.

- Tap shoes: Whether lace-up, slip-on, or high-heeled, tap shoes have metal plates (called taps) affixed to the bottoms of the toe and heel, which make percussive sounds when the foot strikes against a hard surface.
- Ghillies: Soft flat shoes of supple leather, with numerous straps that crisscross the instep and wrap around the ankles, for Irish, Scottish country, and highland dancers.
- Foot thongs or dance paws: Often used by lyrical dancers, these elastic, partial, slip-on foot covers help protect the ball of the foot during turns.

Irish, Scottish, and highland dancers often wear a version of ghillies—soft flat shoes of supple leather, with numerous straps that crisscross the instep and wrap around the ankles.

IN THE STUDIO: DANCING WITH OTHERS

Dance training isn't only about the individual dancer honing his or her technique. Dancers also learn how to move with each other as partners, in groups of various sizes, and in large ensembles. When dancing with another person, understanding how the body moves in space and time, and with what quality of energy, becomes even more critical in order to work within an ensemble without injury and with clarity of choreographic intent.

By dancing in a group, students learn to become aware of the space around them and who may be occupying that space.

Canons

A canon is a passage or movement sequence (sometimes called a motif) that is repeated in various ways to generate sections of choreography in a dance work. Canons allow dancers to start performing the same phrase together, but with variations in timing that increase awareness of others moving in space around them.

- Simple canon: Every dancer in the group performs the sequence but with one person at a time stopping while the next dancer performs it. When the dancers start a beat or two before or after another dancer, the overlap slightly alters the rhythm or timing of how other bodies are moving.
- Round canon: The dancers all perform the sequence, but begin at different counts in the phrase. Think of this canon as an intricate visual representation of the children's game, singing in a round.
- Cumulative canon: As one dancer performs the sequence, others join in on various counts. But everyone stops at the same time, regardless of where they are in the phrase.

Spatial awareness

Early on in dance training, students become aware of the space around them. Dancers line up at the barre, or on the floor, where individual exercises help them strengthen the alignment of the body; seeing their image in mirrors helps them to self-correct. As dancers start "traveling" across the floor

- Unison: All dancers do the same steps at exactly the same time and with the same movement energy or quality.

- Duet: two people dancing together (referred to as pas de deux in ballet; used in such concert dance styles as modern, postmodern, jazz, and lyrical)

- Trio, quartet, quintet, etc.: three, four, and five or more people dancing together (used in concert dance styles and folk dance)

- Corps de ballet: in ballet, a group of dancers that performs in unison as a chorus or backdrop for the principal dancers

- Partner dancing: largely refers to ballroom, Latin, and swing dance; featured on such television shows as Dancing With the Stars

during center work, they learn about moving along or off invisible lines in space.

While moving together in groups, dancers learn to keep within their own spacing. Attuning their depth perception, their senses of hearing, sight, and smell, and their understanding of time and energy to those around them helps a dancer maintain a clear personal frame of reference within an ensemble. In short, a dancer must learn to use all of his or her senses, not just the body, when performing with others.

Partner dancing

In most partner dances—such as some folk dances; the tango, salsa, and swing; and ballroom dances like the waltz—the man typically leads; the woman follows. In some dances, their body contact is loose. In other dances, the partners maintain a strict "dance frame" (individual dancers also have their own dance frame), which is critical to successful leading and following.

Practicing with a partner

When dance partners meet to practice, they need to arrive already familiar with their own steps, positions, and spacing. So a good way to begin is for each dancer to mark their parts as the other partner watches (with or without the music). Then, break down the dance into sections and combine both parts, starting slowly and moving through each step with care (without music). Check each other's alignment, spacing, footwork, and timing as you work through each section. As your coordination improves, increase the speed and add to the expressive quality of the movement. Be patient with each other. When you've reached a level of confidence with the sequence, add the music. If you mess up, go back and practice that section, focusing on the moments or steps with which you had difficulty. Later, show the teacher or choreographer what you've accomplished, and ask for corrections and feedback to improve your performance.

THE IMPORTANCE OF PRACTICE

The types of learning a dancer experiences while in class, in rehearsals, and during self-directed practice sessions are quite different. All three learning modes are necessary (along with cross training and mind–body techniques) for a dancer to fully develop their technical skills, movement expression, and artistry.

During private practice, dancers embed the knowledge learned in class and rehearsals more deeply into their bodies through repetition and diligent attention. Problems with alignment, challenges with a particular step or movement phrase, a correction that doesn't yet make sense, a solo, and even a part in a quartet (or other group) are all aspects that dancers study, scrutinize, and improve during practice sessions.

When to practice

- After class or rehearsal. Spend 5–30 minutes in a corner of the studio redoing what you were just taught. Don't forget to cool down afterward.
- Set aside 30–90 minutes a day, several days a week (more before a performance), in a studio or other room with a hardwood floor, to practice steps, combinations, and sections of work. Be sure to warm up and cool down. Balance physical practice with performance visualization (see pages 136–137).
- Before class or rehearsal. After warming up, mark the steps in a difficult passage, or dance through a challenging phrase, to ready your body for dancing full-out.

Mark or full-out?
Mark or marking: Going through the movements of a dance work or routine with correct timing and choreographic accuracy, but at a lower energy level. A way to rehearse choreography before performing; never done during a performance.
Full-out: The opposite of marking; to perform the choreography with all of the expertise, energy, and expression of which you're capable.

Progressive overload

Progressive overload is the practice of gradually increasing the stress placed on muscles during training and practice, to build physical strength. Progressive overload also increases the strength and density of bones; strengthens ligaments, tendons, and cartilage; increases blood flow to the body parts being worked; and develops nerve connections between mind and body; and helps dancers master neuromuscular control when practicing complex choreography.

Gradual increases in intensity, volume, and frequency contribute to progressive overload:

- Intensity: the difficulty of dance steps, exercises, or combinations (speed increases the difficulty).
- Volume: the number of repetitions in correspondence with resistance; the higher the resistance (intensity), the fewer repetitions (volume). For strength, do fewer repetitions with higher resistance; for endurance, do more repetitions with less resistance.
- Frequency: how often you practice and for how long. Allow for rest and recovery between sessions, and vary the sessions to ensure motivation and avoid boredom.

Practice in the studio isn't limited to technique classes. Students and professional dancers may dance full-out before, during, or after class while rehearsing a particular phrase or perfecting a shape.

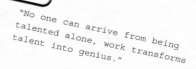

"No one can arrive from being talented alone, work transforms talent into genius."

Anna Pavlova

PRACTICE TIPS

- Warm up and cool down (also see pages 86-87).

- Incorporate variation—to keep motivation high, avoid overworking a body part or area, stimulate concentration, avoid injury.

- Work mind and body—balance muscle strength and endurance, cardio-vascular fitness, flexibility, and dance technique with such mind-body exercises as imaging and visualization (see pages 122-127, 136-137).

- Drink water before, during, and after practice, and eat a sufficient balance of carbohydrates/protein before and after practice.

- Rest, so that the body can adapt to the rigors of class, rehearsal, and practice.

- Be self-aware—set realistic practice goals, because every dancer and every body responds differently to learning, training, and the overload process.

CROSS TRAINING

Professional dancers, and dance students serious about improving their technique, as well as their strength, flexibility, and stamina, incorporate various modes of cross training into their daily and weekly routines. If you're worried about coping with the rigorous schedule of a summer intensive, or just want to have more energy during classes, then swimming, bicycling, running, yoga, and Pilates can give you an extra edge.

- Running: This can help with cardiovascular endurance and build leg strength. Be sure to stretch well before and after a run, as running tends to tighten and shorten up the leg muscles.
- Swimming: This low-impact alternative coordinates the breath and entire body as it moves in a resistant medium.
- Bicycling and Spinning: This is a great way to get off your feet while toning legs and increasing cardiovascular endurance.
- Aerobics: This adds to cardiovascular endurance, muscle strength, and coordination, and can reduce fatigue.
- Strength training: This builds muscle strength and definition.

Yoga

One of the most popular methods of cross training for dancers is yoga, an ancient Hindu spiritual discipline that includes physical postures (*asana*), purification procedures (*shatkriya*), poses (*mudra*), breathing (*pranayama*), and meditation. The body postures increase a dancer's strength, flexibility, and control.
Some of the common yoga styles are:

Swimming is a form of cross training practiced by many dancers, as the exercise is aerobic and low impact.

- *Hatha*: The word is often used as a general term to describe the various types of yoga. A Hatha yoga class will, most likely, have an easy pace and include stretching, simple breathing exercises, and meditation, and provide a good introduction to basic yoga poses.
- *Vinyasa*: The word means "breath-synchronized movement," and classes often begin with a series of Sun Salutations that move through various positions and levels in space in coordination with the breath. Also often called flow yoga, as the poses flow from one to another without interruption.
- *Ashtanga*: The word means "eight limbs," and the style is often referred to as power

Yoga is one of the most popular forms of cross training for its attention to breathing, bodily awareness, and flexibility.

- *Bikram*/hot yoga: A series of twenty-six poses developed by Bikram Choudhury, this style is practiced in a 95–100-degree room, in order to loosen muscles and produce cleansing sweat.
- *Anusara*: Founded in 1997 by John Friend, this style combines attention to physical alignment with philosophy of intrinsic goodness. Traditional Hatha poses are taught in ways that open the heart. Props are often used for support.
- *Kripalu*: Associated with both a Hatha-yoga style and center in Stockbridge, Massachusetts, founded by Amrit Desai. The style emphasizes meditation, physical healing, and spiritual transformation.

yoga because of its fast pace and intensity. This vigorous practice includes long sets and series of poses done in a flowing Vinyasa style.
- *Iyengar*: This style is the most like classical ballet with its focus on alignment, codified postures with precise attention to placement, and strict teachers who rigidly uphold the teachings. The practice also uses props—blankets, blocks and straps, ropes attached to the walls—to support and bring the body into alignment.
- *Kundalini*: This practice, more than any other, explores the effects of breath on the postures. Also called the yoga of awareness, this style works to expand sensory awareness and intuition.

Pilates

Pilates is a body-conditioning system that builds flexibility, strength, endurance, and coordination in the legs, abdominals, arms, and back. Developed by Joseph Pilates, the technique focuses on developing a strong and stable core (the deep muscles of the abdomen and back), as well as the muscles of the trunk and spine. The exercises are practiced on a thick mat or a "reformer," a piece of resistance equipment that precisely works alignment, core strength, and flexibility. The six primary principles of Pilates, around which the exercises are focused, are centering, concentration, control, precision, breath, and flow.

4

THE DANCER'S BODY: ANATOMY AND AWARENESS

The dancer's body is his or her instrument, the means of aesthetic, physical, and emotional expression. Thus it's imperative that every dancer understand the basics of anatomy, or how and why the body moves; the nutritional requirements for fueling an active and healthy body; and the ways in which injuries can be avoided or treated. This chapter introduces these essential topics on the science of the dancing body, and expands into the realm of greater body awareness and functionality. Through such time-tested and world-renowned modalities as Laban and Bartenieff Movement Analysis, dancers learn, on a more profound level, how the body and its ability to move are integrally connected, how those connections can be strengthened, and how the body can move with more stability in space.

BASIC ANATOMY

In general, anatomy begins with organ systems, defined as two or more organs working together for a common purpose or function in the body. The purpose or function under study here is movement. So the two systems we associate most closely with movement—muscular and skeletal—receive closer attention (with a look at the neuromuscular system). The other organ systems are: circulatory, nervous, respiratory, digestive, excretory, endocrine, reproductive, and lymphatic/immune.

Skeletal system

The skeletal system comprises bones; related cartilage, tendons, and ligaments; and the joints connecting those parts together to create movement. In combination, these components provide the structural framework that supports the human body, and gives the body stability and form. This intricate system also protects the internal organs, and is the structure on which muscles and organs are attached. The skeleton's joints permit the body to move in ways that make up, in part, the movement vocabularies of dance.

Types of bone
- Long: Shaped like tubes, and longer than they are wide, these bones are in the arms (humerus) and legs (femur), and function as levers in dance movements.

  - Short: Square in shape (as wide as they are long) and found in the upper part of the hands (metacarpals) and feet (metatarsals), these bones help dancers perform intricate, complex movements.
  - Flat: Thin but sometimes slightly curved, these bones (upper part of pelvis, ribs, sternum, skull) protect soft organs (heart, lungs, brain) and are attachment sites for muscles.
  - Irregular: shaped for specific purposes (vertebrae, lower pelvis), including to protect organs,

support the body, provide anchor points for muscles, and facilitate movement.

- Sesamoid: short or irregular and embedded in a tendon, to protect the tendon from excessive wear while rubbing against underlying bone (the "kneecap" or patella).

Knowledge of the neuromuscular and skeletal systems is essential to dancers, in order to understand why and how their bodies are moving.

Muscular system

The approximately 700 muscles in the body fall into three distinct types: skeletal muscles (about 340 of them), cardiac or heart muscles, and involuntary or smooth muscles (found in blood vessels and arteries, gastrointestinal tract, bladder, etc.). Muscles provide the energy, tension, or force with which we move our skeletal system, particularly our joints. Muscles are made up of contractile fibers, which change size (contract and expand) as required to most efficiently produce movement.

Muscles are also integral to the body's strength, balance, and alignment.

Neuromuscular system

This term refers to the interplay of the muscular and nervous systems, which controls movement. The nervous system has two main parts: central (brain and spinal cord) and peripheral (nerves in the torso and limbs that carry information to and from the brain). The nervous system enables the dancer to respond (consciously and unconsciously) to constant changes in their environment (inside and outside of the body), and to integrate those responses with the body's movements (which the muscles initiated). .

The nervous system accomplishes this through two functional components:

- Somatic: peripheral nerve fibers that send sensory information to the central nervous system, including touch, position in space, and temperature; enables reflexive movements to occur as skeletal muscles contract
- Autonomic: fibers that control and connect smooth and cardiac muscle and glands in two ways—sympathetic (deals with stress, "fight or flight response") and parasympathetic (balances the body and its processes)

Joints

A joint occurs in the skeleton when two or more bones meet and are attached to each other by ligaments or cartilage, to allow varying degrees of movement. Essentially, joint movement is made possible by skeletal muscles, bones acting as levers, friction-reducing cartilage, and ligaments that help prevent dislocation.

Understanding how the joints function as points of articulation in the body increases the dancer's awareness of why the body moves, and how to prevent injury.

Three types of joints

- Fibrous (immoveable): joints held together by a thin layer of strong connective tissue that prevents movement (pelvis and skull bones, teeth in their sockets)
- Cartilaginous (partially moveable): joints

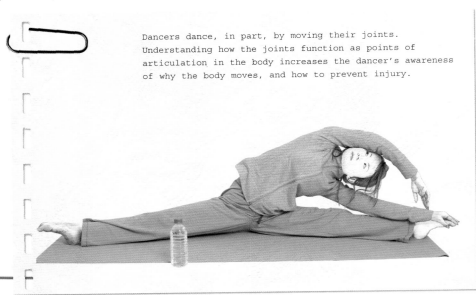

Dancers dance, in part, by moving their joints. Understanding how the joints function as points of articulation in the body increases the dancer's awareness of why the body moves, and how to prevent injury.

connected by fibrocartilaginous discs and ligaments (between vertebrae in the spine)

- Synovial (freely moveable): six joint structures in which a synovial capsule (collagenous structure) surrounds the joint, while a synovial membrane (the capsule's inner layer) secretes synovial (lubricating) fluid, and hyaline cartilage covers and pads the ends of the bones

The six synovial joints and their movements

- Ball-and-socket: One end of the bone is round to fit into the cup-shaped end of the other bone (hip, shoulder); flexion, extension, adduction, abduction, internal and external rotation.
- Gliding (plane): Both ends of the bone are flat (ribs, midcarpals and midtarsals in the hands); gliding motion.
- Hinge: A bone with a concave end meets a bone with a convex end (knee, elbow); flexion and extension.
- Pivot (rotary): one bone moves around another on an axis (radius and ulna in the forearm); rotation.
- Ellipsoid or condyloid: similar to ball-and-socket, but with less motion (MCP and MTP wrist joints); flexion, extension, adduction, abduction, circumduction
- Saddle: back-and-forth and up-and-down movements (CMC joint in the thumb); flexion, extension, adduction, abduction, circumduction

An understanding of anatomy allows the dancer to maintain correct posture when moving.

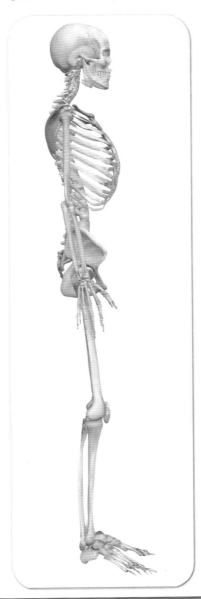

Choreography becomes more dynamic when the dancer's body moves through space on a specific plane but with the added dimension of extension.

Movement planes

The dancing body moves through three planes that correspond to the three dimensions in space. The three planes of movement, as well as positional and directional terminology for movement, start from the standard anatomical or anatomically neutral position (a pose similar to Tadasana in yoga): facing forward with legs in parallel and feet hip distance apart, with proper spinal alignment, and with arms and palms rotated slightly forward. From this position, the planes are easy to understand.

- Frontal: divides the body into front and back; movements are sideways, or abduction and adduction
- Sagittal: passes through the body, halving it into right and left; movements are up and down, or flexion and extension
- Transverse: halves the body into upper and lower; movements are rotational

Terminology related to planes and axes of movement

Dance instructors and choreographers use positional and directional terminology to describe a body part's position. Positional terminology includes the standard

Joint movements

Flexion: bending, folding
Extension: straightening
Abduction: moving away from the center of the body
Adduction: moving toward the center of the body
External rotation: rotating outward
Internal rotation: rotating inward
Plantar flexion: pointing the foot
Dorsiflexion: flexing the foot
Circumduction: moving in a circle (a combination of flexion, extension, abduction, adduction)

anatomical or anatomically neutral position described above, supine (lying on the back), and prone (lying facedown). Directional terminology includes the following:

- Superior (toward or above the head); inferior (toward or below the feet); anterior (toward or in front of the body); posterior (toward or at the back of the body)
- Medial (toward or at the midline/center of the body, inner side); lateral (away from the center, outer side); proximal (closer to the center of a limb or center body); distal (farther from the center of a body part or center body)
- Superficial (closer to or the surface of the body); deep (farther from the body's surface)
- Palmar (front of the hand); dorsal (back of the hand or top of the foot); plantar (bottom of the foot)

Neutral spine: the starting position for movement

Although your spine can bend forward and back, side to side, and move in flexion and extension, proper alignment in dance begins with the neutral spine. This position ensures the spine's stability and strength while retaining its natural curves. To create neutral spine, imagine a straight line extending from the middle of your ear through the center of the shoulder, down through your hip and knee, and to the ankle.

That line is referred to as a plumb line (after the plumb bob used in construction; a cord with a weight attached to its bottom end to measure exact vertical lines). In dance, the plumb line displays the relationships between the joints of the body to the floor, to help maintain accurate alignment and awareness of the body in space. Body parts or joints that deviate from the plumb line can be corrected through stretching and strengthening.

A clear plumb line, or proper alignment, as parts of the body extend from the axis into space helps the dancer maintain control and clarity in form.

WARM UP AND COOL DOWN

Before starting any class, rehearsal or performance, a dancer needs to slowly and carefully warm up the muscles and joints, to prepare the body for intense and sustained physical activity. Cold muscles and joints are less flexible. Joints and muscles that have been warmed up become increasingly flexible and are better prepared for bending, stretching, extending, and leaping. A good selection of warm-up exercises helps the body segue from a normal or restful state to one ready for activity. Similarly, after the dancer is finished for the day, the body needs to cool down in order to return comfortably to a less-active, more normal state. Regardless of the temperature in the room, the dancer needs to properly warm up and cool down the body in order to prevent muscle soreness and injury.

Benefits of the warm-up

- Stretches muscles and increases joint flexibility by increasing blood flow to these parts of the body
- Deepens and quickens breathing, which brings more oxygen into the body while exhaling more carbon dioxide
- Increases heart rate, to deliver more oxygen and glucose (fuel) to the muscles
- Increases internal body temperature, which in turn warms muscles
- Distributes blood to working muscles and joints
- Coordinates muscle–nerve–mind communication
- Gives the dancer time to prepare for class, rehearsal, or performance by turning attention to the body
- Prevents delayed onset muscle soreness (DOMS), which can occur 24–48 hours after vigorous activity

Basic dance warm-up

- Set aside 10–15 minutes for the warm-up.
- Move slowly. The goal isn't to sweat, but to warm the body, engage the lungs, and slightly raise your heart rate.
- Start with extra layers of clothing, to help retain body heat.
- Don't overstretch.
- Begin the warm-up with little hops, short, easy runs, or small prances. These aerobic activities gently engage and warm muscles, increase your respiration (breathing), and raise your heart rate.
- Lubricate the tissues in your joints. Roll your shoulders, wrists, ankles, and hips in comfortable loose circles. Bend and straighten the knees and elbows. Flex and point the feet.
- Get comfortable moving in various directions. Gently swing arms and legs to the back, front, and across the body (or you may want to hold on to the barre).

- Get comfortable moving with rhythm. Swing arms, bend knees, sway from side to side, and rotate the torso in a simple pattern with a gentle rhythm to engage the whole body.
- Gently stretch the large-muscle groups, such as quads, hamstrings, thigh, and calf muscles while sitting on the floor. Hold each stretch for 10–15 seconds.
- Engage your balance by standing on one leg, then bending and straightening the supporting leg and rising to demi-pointe.
- Practice simple movements in your dance style. Ballet: pliés. Tap: gentle shuffles. Modern: drop and release. Jazz, modern, and hip-hop: lunges. Salsa: basic quick-quick-slow step.

Basic dance cooldown

- Set aside at least 10 minutes for the cooldown.
- Gradually decrease heart rate, respiration, and blood flow by walking or slowing down rhythmic movement patterns.
- Gently swing arms and legs from side to side, front to back, and across the body until breathing becomes normal again.
- Stretch leg muscles by doing slow lunges, elevating one leg at a time

The yoga position "downward dog" is a good way to warm up and stretch the body as it engages the hips and shoulders, and lengthens the back and legs.

on the barre, bending the knee back and clasping the ankle, and sitting on the floor in a V-shape and bending forward and side to side.
- Lengthen the torso by bending sideways into a gentle C-shape with the arm arcing over the head.
- Relax the upper back with the "downward dog" pose from yoga; relax the lower back with the "child's pose."
- Put sweatshirts and sweatpants, sweaters and leg warmers back on to keep the body from cooling off too quickly.

Voice and movement warm-up

The *Je Je Kule* is a West African call-and-response game that warms up the voice, the body, and coordination between the two. A designated leader makes up a simple movement for each phrase. After calling out the phrase while doing the movement, everyone in the class follows.

INJURIES: PREVENTION AND RECOVERY

Whether ballet or break dancing, the intense repetition required to learn, practice, and perfect movements means that all dancers are susceptible to injuries from overuse in specific parts of the body, much more so than from sudden trauma. In fact, some statistics have shown that 80 percent of dancers sustain at least one injury a year, compared with 20 percent of rugby or football players.

Injuries of the foot, ankle, lower leg, low back, and hip are among the most common in dancers. The risk of injury increases with age, so new and young dancers need to carefully build strength, endurance, and flexibility to prevent injury.

Common dance injuries

Sprains: Joint sprains happen when a ligament is overstretched, or the joint bends in the wrong direction. Muscle sprains occur after a sudden contraction of a muscle, especially when the dancer isn't warmed up or hasn't enough flexibility. Lifting, arching, and improper technique can strain the lower back. The result is tenderness and swelling in the sprain area.

Stress fractures: an incomplete break in a bone often caused by repeated landings from jumps. Fractures result in pain and swelling. Shin splints can result from stress fractures.

Shin splints: pain in the front of the lower leg as a result of repetitive weight-bearing movements, such as jumping and landing

Bursitis: The small sacs (bursa) cushioning the hip bones become inflamed or irritated, usually because of repetitive friction from a tight muscle or a poorly executed

movement. Results in sharp, intense pain.

Tendonitis: painful inflammation of a tendon caused by overuse, dancing on a hard floor, too much weight or pressure on tight muscle, or an unbalanced range of motion

Knee injuries: Patellofemoral pain (or runner's knee) occurs in the kneecap (patella) and femur, usually after tight

To prevent injury, remember to
- take sufficient time to warm up and cool down after class,
- wear clothes and shoes that fit and don't hamper movement,
- stay hydrated by drinking fluids without caffeine and alcohol,
- build and maintain core strength and proper alignment,
- correctly perform technique,
- increase flexibility through stretching,
- stop if experiencing pain,
- maintain good nutrition, and
- stay well rested.

Wrapping an injured joint is the C or "compression" aspect of R (rest), I (ice), C, E (elevation) treatment for many injuries.

hamstrings and calf muscles, weak quadriceps and repetitive forceful movements cause cartilage to lose its ability to absorb shocks from repetitive jumping and landing.

Torn meniscus: tear(s) in the cartilage that cushions the knee because of twisting, using feet instead of hips to turn out, or loss of control during jumps and landings

Snapping hip syndrome: a snapping sensation (sometimes with a popping noise), along with pain or discomfort, felt when the hip is flexed and extended

Treatment

The most common and immediate treatment for injuries that occur while dancing is often referred to as RICE:

R= Rest: Stop and rest.

I= Ice: Apply ice (or ice packs) immediately to the affected area for 15–20 minutes, several times a day, for the first 48 hours.

C= Compression: Wrap the injured area tightly (but not enough to cut off circulation) with an elastic or compression bandage between icings.

E= Elevation: Raise the injured area on a chair or pillow to decrease blood supply.

(This protocol is also sometimes referred to as HI-RICE, with the addition of H=hydration and I= Ibuprofen.)

Depending on the type of injury, a variety of other treatments after RICE may be necessary, with surgery as a last resort.

For sprains: analgesic and anti-inflammatory medication, immobilization of the area, chirurgical repair in the worst cases

For shin splints: anti-inflammatory medication, rest, stretching

For stress fractures: immobilization of the area, X-rays to determine type and extent of fracture, anti-inflammatory medication

For bursitis: analgesic and anti-inflammatory medication, steroid injections with local anesthetic, therapeutic ultrasound

For tendonitis: analgesic and anti-inflammatory medication, alternating heat and cold along with stretching and strengthening, steroid anti-inflammatory medication

For knee injuries: immobilization of the area with a brace, X-rays or MRI to determine type and extent of injury, heat before strengthening and ice after, anti-inflammatory medication, corticosteroid shot, PRP (protein-rich plasma) injection or surgical scraping

For snapping hip syndrome: anti-inflammatory medication, MRI or ultrasound to determine extent of injury, corticosteroid injections

DANCER NUTRITION

Good nutrition is critical to a dancer's success, as continual training, rehearsing, and performing puts serious strain on muscles, joints, and bones. The earlier a dancer learns how to eat for maximum replenishment, energy, endurance, and concentration, the better. Proper nutrition can help with growing lean muscle, absorbing essential nutrients, repairing injuries, and preventing fatigue. Today, restricting calories to maintain an overly thin body is frowned upon. Doctors and nutritionists advocate eating well-balanced foods that supply the dancer with nourishment and stamina, but without adding excess calories. According to the International Association for Dance Medicine & Science, a dancer's diet should be balanced with 55–60 percent carbohydrate, 12–15 percent protein, and 20–30 percent fat.

Carbohydrate

Carbs are essential to the dancer's diet. During digestion, carbs break down into glucose that's stored in the muscles as glycogen, which fuels energy and keeps muscles working. During strenuous periods of rehearsal and competition or performance, dancers should increase carbs to 65 percent of their diet, according the International Association for Dance Medicine & Science.

Good complex carbohydrates worth incorporating into meals include whole-grain breads (bagels, crackers, toast), fruit (bananas), whole-grain pasta, grains (cereal, brown rice, quinoa, oats, barley), and starchy vegetables (potatoes). Whole grains take longer to break down than white or refined carbs, providing the dancer with more energy for longer periods of time. Eating carbs before and after exercising, class, rehearsals, and

performances—and during long rehearsals—is also necessary to replenish glycogen. Good glycogen boosters are energy bars, sports drinks (with glucose), and bagels.

Although plenty of vegetables are essential to good health, a dancer's diet must also include 55-60 percent carbohydrate, 12-15 percent protein, and 20-30 percent fat to maintain energy levels.

Proper hydration is essential to the performing body, and water is the easiest and safest way to keep fluid levels high.

Calories required

According to the International Association for Dance Medicine & Science, the number of calories a dancer requires per day during heavy training is 45-50 calories per kilogram of body weight for girls/women, and 50-55 calories per kilogram of body weight for boys/men.

To break that down during the day, this example from the Centre for Dance Nutrition is based on a 120-pound professional female dancer who takes a 1½-hour ballet class in the morning and rehearses for four to six hours before an evening performance.

Estimated energy needs: 2,100-2,500 calories, depending on the strenuousness of the rehearsals and performance.
Breakfast: 350-400 calories
Snack after morning class: 200-275 calories
Lunch: 550-650 calories
Post-rehearsal re-fuel: 200-285 calories
Dinner before performance: 550-650 calories
Post-performance re-fuel: 200-350 calories

Protein

Carbs are the body's primary fuel source, but protein stabilizes that fuel (glucose or blood sugar) so dancers can enjoy a continuous supply of energy from morning to evening. Protein also helps repair muscle fiber that's stressed by constant use, and it synthesizes enzymes required for proper metabolism. In addition to chicken, turkey, fish, and red meat (the latter in lesser amounts than poultry and fish), good protein sources include eggs, tofu, seitan (wheat gluten), hummus (tahini and chickpeas), beans and rice, nuts, quinoa, nut butters, and cheese. Meals of protein and carbohydrates (four parts carb to one part protein is recommended) should also include healthful fats for optimal nutrition.

Fat

Dancers should limit their intake of "bad," saturated or trans fats (as in red meat). But other fats are stored in muscles as triglycerides, which break down into fatty acids that the body metabolizes to create muscle energy. Essential fatty acids, which the body doesn't naturally produce but are essential to maintaining healthy joints and muscles, are available by eating salmon, flaxseed, avocado, and nuts.

Micronutrients

Vitamins and minerals are the micronutrients necessary in balanced nutrition. To ensure they're ingesting enough micronutrients, dancers should consume five servings of a variety of fresh fruit and vegetables a day along with whole grains, dairy products, and lean red meat. A multivitamin/mineral supplement can help ensure dancers receive their required micronutrients.

Of these vitamin micronutrients, B vitamins provide energy. Vitamins A, C, and E, the antioxidants, help repair overworked muscles. Vitamin D builds strong bones. Of the macrominerals, calcium is essential for bone strength. Of the microminerals (trace minerals), iron carries oxygen in the blood used to produce energy in muscles, and zinc is necessary to several enzymes that produce energy.

Hydration

Dancers sweat as they generate heat during training, rehearsing, and performing, which is how the body cools itself. But this loss of fluid can lead to dehydration, resulting in dizziness, a lack of energy, an inability to concentrate, sore muscles, and lackluster performance. If you feel thirsty, then you're already dehydrated, as the body takes a while to register its need for water. Dancers should drink a cup of noncaffeinated liquid during breaks in class or rehearsal, and increase that amount afterwards. In exceptionally hot or dry weather, the body needs even more liquid to stay hydrated along with sufficient salt and electrolytes (sodium, potassium, chloride, and bicarbonate), which help the body to retain water.

Eating disorders

Anorexia nervosa: self-starvation. Bulimia: binge eating followed by self-induced vomiting. Disordered eating: ritualistic and compulsive problems with food. Eating disorders such as these plague the dance world, particularly ballet.

According to Dr. Michelle Warren, professor of obstetrics and gynecology at Columbia Presbyterian Medical Center in New York City, "the average incidence of eating disorders in the white middle-class population is 1 in 100. In classical ballet, it is one in five."

Long days filled with classes, cross training, and rehearsing quickly deplete the body of its calories, and dancers get hungry. When

"ANOREXIC DANCERS HAVE BEHAVIOR THAT'S DIFFERENT, A GLASSINESS IN THE EYE, A DIFFERENT CONCENTRATION LEVEL. DANCERS WHO ARE ANOREXIC ARE WITHDRAWN, THEY DON'T CONNECT WITH YOU, DON'T RESPOND IN THE SAME WAY. IF SOMETHING DOESN'T GO WELL, THEIR FRUSTRATION LEVEL IS MUCH HIGHER. THEY ARE VERY COMPULSIVE. IT'S FRIGHTENING."

Eleanor D'Antuono, a former principal with American Ballet Theatre, teacher at the Joffrey Ballet School, quoted in an article in *Dance Magazine*

- Lethargy, lack of stamina
- Loss of muscle strength
- Lack of concentration, difficulty memorizing choreography
- Scalp hair thins, soft hair appears on face and arms
- Orange tint to the skin
- Withdrawn, self-imposed isolation
- Skipped menstrual periods
- Stress fractures/onset of osteoporosis

dancers feel pressured to maintain an ideal (thin) body type, however, and attempt to "control" their hunger through self-starvation, binging and purging, or other food-related compulsions, they can develop an eating disorder.

Dancers who find their life overtaken by an eating disorder are at serious risk of losing their ability to dance, their health, even their life. The long-term complications of eating disorders include osteoporosis (bone loss), which can result in more frequent and serious fractures and breaks; and heart complications leading to loss of consciousness or death.

Causes of eating disorders in dance

George Balanchine, the legendary ballet dancer, teacher, and choreographer, is credited with demanding a particular body type in his ballerinas—long limbs, short torso, skeletal frame, minimal hips and breasts—which has become the accepted aesthetic in Western ballet. In her autobiography *Dancing on My Grave*, ballerina Gelsey Kirkland recalls Balanchine telling her to "eat nothing" and demanding to "see the bones" during her time at New York City Ballet in the 1960s.

Because dance is an intensively competitive, high-pressure, and physically demanding profession, dancers (particularly young dancers who lack confidence and feel the need to please) internalize the Balanchine body type. To reach this idea of perfection while coping with the physical demands of dancing, they reduce their caloric intact and/or excessively exercise. In addition, in the Western world, the thin and anorexic body is idealized and propagated through fashion, advertising, television, and film.

Among dancers, eating disorders can lead to increased bone fractures and breaks, muscle fatigue, deteriorating health, and even death. In dance, the pressure to be thin can be intense. If you feel you have an eating problem, seek professional help immediately.

THE DANCER AND BODY IMAGE

Body image is the physical portrait of ourselves we generate in our minds. Our body image reflects how we perceive our weight, judge our attractiveness, view our body parts, and cope with our physical "flaws."

Nearly everyone is susceptible to finding fault with oneself. But many dancers suffer from an inaccurate or even skewed body image. They may see themselves as grossly overweight (even while anorexic, see pages 92–93) or obsessed about "fixing" another perceived physical defect.

When these preoccupations start taking over the dancer's life, causing significant distress and/or withdrawal, the dancer may have body dysmorphic disorder (BDD). BDD is a psychological illness that often accompanies eating disorders. Regardless of body size, shape, or weight, few dancers escape from some degree of BDD, especially ballet and modern dancers.

BDD behaviors

- Compulsively checking body and image in mirrors, windows, and other reflective surfaces; or covering, removing, and/or refusing to look into reflective surfaces
- Covering the perceived defect with baggy clothing or makeup
- Excessive grooming
- Compulsively touching the area of the imagined flaw
- Constantly seeking reassurance that the body part isn't as flawed as believed
- Excessive dieting and/or exercising outside of class
- Comparing appearance with others

Overcoming BDD

Because the dancer's instrument is their body, finding ways to appreciate oneself and cultivate a realistic body image can require constant diligence. Adjust body image so self-perceptions are more realistic by

- realizing that gifted dancers come in all shapes, sizes, and colors;
- understanding that an excessive or debilitating focus on appearance can take time away from artistic development;
- talking to older dancers about how they coped with BDD;
- researching BDD on the Internet to discover stories, books, and therapies that can help transform negative perceptions into positive ones;
- meeting with a therapist who can help you regain a more balanced perspective on body image.

Body dysmorphic disorder is common among dancers, especially ballerinas, who fear they aren't thin enough to win a coveted role. Dancers can overcome body dysmorphic disorder by accentuating the positive aspects of their bodies, and focusing on improving their technique, expressiveness, and ability to work well with other dancers.

> "I have boobs, I have a huge butt and I have a lot of muscle. I like having curves. I'm proud of them!"
>
> Lacey Schwimmer (above)

THE AGONY OF THE FEET

Isn't it ironic: As beautiful as dance is, the physically strenuous art form creates havoc with feet. Dancers use their feet to achieve extreme positions and unnatural shapes. Whether dancing en pointe or demi-pointe, running or skipping, leaping or landing, lifting or sliding, a dancer's feet bear the brunt of weight, pressure, turning, and overuse.

According to several studies, dancers' feet (and ankles) represent 34–62 percent of all injuries reported. Female ballet dancers sustain more injuries than male ballet dancers or modern dancers (in part because they dance en pointe). Studies have also shown that foot and ankle injuries comprise 23–45 percent of all injuries among dancers in musical theater. Although the United States has a large network of foot specialists for dancers, in other countries podiatrists who specialize in dancer's feet are few and far between.

Of course, the only way to really heal foot problems—from blisters to sesamoiditis—is to rest, which usually isn't an option. Dancers routinely push through pain as long as possible; they don't want to appear uncomfortable, weak or expendable, lose favor with a director or choreographer, or miss out on a coveted role.

As such, a minor ailment can turn into a prolonged agony. Compensating for foot pain can cause unbalances and place stress elsewhere, resulting in another injury. Still, dancers become used to pain; it's simply a part of the dancer's life.

Common foot problems

Blisters

Cause: shoes rubbing against feet because of insufficient padding

Quick fix: Cover with moleskin or burn pad, later disinfect, allow to air and dry out, dab with Orajel or other numbing cream; keep layers of dead skin that build up for padding.

Bruised/broken nails

Cause: nails too long; shoes too wide, square, or soft (causing the foot to slip and nails to pound the floor through the shoe)

Quick fix: Wrap toenails for extra padding; make sure shoes fit correctly; wear comfortable shoes with large or square toe box outside of class.

Bunions

Cause: too-tight/too-narrow shoes (big toe leans toward or crosses second toe; pinky toe crosses to fourth toe); can be genetic

Quick fix: Soften shoe where bunion comes into contact; ice toes; use gel toe spacer between affected toes.

Dancers' feet take a beating, especially feet encased in pointe shoes. Dancers' feet and ankles represent 34–62 percent of all injuries reported.

Corns
Cause: pressure and rubbing from shoes (causing localized thickening of the skin or plug that results in pain and swelling)
Quick fix: metatarsal pads; silicone sleeves for toes; soaking feet; over-the-counter salicylic acid treatment

Hallux limitus or hallux rigidus
Cause: overuse of metatarsal phalangeal joint (big toe) at 90-degree angle resulting in inflammation and limited use
Quick fix: ice; rest; flexibility exercise by stretching the foot into a demi-point position while sitting; toe spacer

Hammer toes
Cause: bent middle digits caused by genetics or too-tight toe box in shoes
Quick fix: Anchor bent toe to straight toe by taping them together; stretch toe box of shoes; use toe splint.

Metatarsalgia
Cause: joint instability caused by overuse, sprain, overstretched ligaments (resulting in pain and tenderness along the ball of the foot)
Quick fix: stretching and strengthening exercises (scrunching towel with toes); padding under ball of the foot; wider toe box in shoes; rest; ice; ibuprofen

Neuromas
Cause: overuse (thickening nerve fibers between toes and metatarsals resulting in burning sensation, cramping, numbness)
Quick fix: padding under the ball of the foot; orthotics; stretching; ice; ibuprofen; steroid injection; nerve freezing

Plantar fasciitis
Cause: overuse, weight-bearing, high demi-pointe, collapsing arches (pain and swelling underneath the foot)
Quick fix: ice; rest; arch supports; stiff shoe sole

Sesamoiditis
Cause: dancing on hard surfaces, improper balance/alignment (inflammation of tendons connected to the big toe caused by overuse of small bones in tendons)
Quick fix: ice; rest

BODY AWARENESS: LABAN MOVEMENT ANALYSIS

Rudolph Laban was a European dancer and dance theorist interested in the relationship between the human body and the space in which it moves. He distilled movement into four basic yet interrelated components.

With those components, he devised a method for interpreting and visualizing movement called Laban Movement Analysis (LMA):

- Body: different parts of the body (alone or in coordination), and how they initiate and follow through with movement, move in patterns or sequences, connect with another.
- Effort (or dynamics): the intention and energy with which a movement is performed; divided into four subcategories or qualities with opposing poles:
  a) Space: indirect/direct (quality of attention or focus paid to movement)
  b) Weight: light/strong (related to gravity)
  c) Time: sustained/sudden (how long a movement takes)
  d) Flow: free/bound (continuity of movement)
    These qualities can be combined in groups of two ("States"), three ("Drives"), or four ("Effort"), to become part of a "Movement Signature."
  - Shape: form of the body, and how and why the shape changes; practitioners describe the modes with which the body interacts and relates to its environment differently, but these modes may include "shape flow" (shivering, shrugging, twisting, breathing), "directional" (movement that bridges the body with object or space, as in punching, swinging,

Laban Movement Analysis allows the dancer to conceive and describe the shapes and movements of the body.

poking), "carving" or "shaping" (interactions with an object or volume of space, as in hugging), and "shape qualities" (actively growing larger or smaller, rising or shrinking).

- Space: the relationship between the moving body, the "kinesphere" (space immediately surrounding the body), and overall spatial geometries, patterns, directions, and points in space the dancer is using.

Labanotation

Laban created a system of movement notation using symbols (some shown below) on a music-like staff, to represent parts of the body and how it moves in time and space. Different symbols, symbol shapes, and shadings notate the level and the direction of a movement, part of the body moving, and length of time the movement takes. Dancers and choreographers use Labanotation to record dances, but it's also used by actors, athletes, and physical and occupational therapists to analyze movement.

forward

left forward diagonal | right forward diagonal

left side | right side

left backward diagonal | right backward diagonal

backward

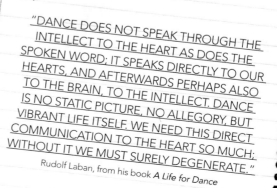

"DANCE DOES NOT SPEAK THROUGH THE INTELLECT TO THE HEART AS DOES THE SPOKEN WORD; IT SPEAKS DIRECTLY TO OUR HEARTS, AND AFTERWARDS PERHAPS ALSO TO THE BRAIN, TO THE INTELLECT. DANCE IS NO STATIC PICTURE, NO ALLEGORY, BUT VIBRANT LIFE ITSELF. WE NEED THIS DIRECT COMMUNICATION TO THE HEART SO MUCH; WITHOUT IT WE MUST SURELY DEGENERATE."

Rudolf Laban, from his book *A Life for Dance*

BODY AWARENESS: BARTENIEFF FUNDAMENTALS

Pioneering physical therapist Irmgard Bartenieff, one of Laban's students, significantly expanded on his work. Today the system is known as Laban/Bartenieff Movement Analysis or Laban Movement Studies, and has four components: Laban Movement Analysis; Anatomy and Kinesiology; Bartenieff Fundamentals; and Labanotation. Bartenieff Fundamentals (BF) is a series of body practices that applies Laban's movement theory to the physical/kinesthetic functioning of the human body. The exercises are based in the belief that the body's movement is closely linked with thoughts, emotions, and everyday interactions in the world.

BF has six basic movement actions: thigh lift, pelvic forward and pelvic lateral shifts, body half, diagonal knee reach, and the arm circle with diagonal sit up. BF gets complicated when these six actions are combined with such concepts as dynamic alignment, breath support, core support,

Bartenieff Fundamentals pioneer Irmgard Bartenieff dancing.

"THE PRINCIPAL OBJECTIVE OF THIS BOOK IS TO SUGGEST ADDITIONAL MODES OF PERCEIVING ONESELF, OTHER PEOPLE, AND RELATIONSHIPS TO THE WORLD AROUND ONE, USING THE LIVE BODY TOTALLY—BODY-MIND-FEELING—AS A KEY TO COPING WITH THE ENVIRONMENT. IN THE PROCESS OF EXTENDING THE QUALITY AND RANGE OF ONE'S BODY MOVEMENT OPTIONS, THE EXPERIENCE CAN EXTEND THE QUALITY OF FUNCTIONAL AND EMOTIONAL LIFE AS WELL. THE POSSIBILITY OF MOVING IN NEW WAYS WITH LESS RISK STRENGTHENS COURAGE TO TOLERATE CONTINUOUS MOVEMENT AND CHANGE WITH STABILITY AND DELIGHT."

Irmgard Bartenieff, from her book
Body Movement: Coping with the Environment

rotation, initiation and sequencing, and spatial intent.

A subtle practice that requires discipline and concentration, BF refines your understanding of how your body connects with your movements, and helps you better adapt to the often stressful and varied situations of daily life.

What is LIMS?

When talking with people about Laban and Bartenieff, you'll probably hear them mention LIMS. The acronym stands for the Laban/ Bartenieff Institute of Movement Studies, a non-profit educational organization in New

Irmgard Bartenieff (1900-1981) studied biology, art, and dance in Germany before meeting Rudolf Laban in 1925. She moved to the United States in 1936, earned a degree in physical therapy from New York University, and become a proponent of Laban's work. She began the professional training program at Laban Movement Studies (now LIMS) in 1978. She applied Laban's theories to her work with polio patients and dancers, then created her own practice called Bartenieff Fundamentals^{SM}. She's well known as a movement researcher, dancer, notation expert, and pioneer in the field of dance therapy.

One of Six: the thigh lift

Dancers, yogis, runners, and sports enthusiasts of all kinds lift their thighs to move through space. A free-moving thighbone in the hip socket, combined with leg strength and toned torso muscles, allows us to move. By practicing the BF thigh lift, you'll learn the proper flow between the upper leg, torso, and lower leg, strengthening this simple movement in the process.

York City. The institute trains movement professionals from around the world to become Certified Movement Analysts (CMAs). CMAs come from all walks of life—not only dance—and apply this movement knowledge to sports, education, and communications.

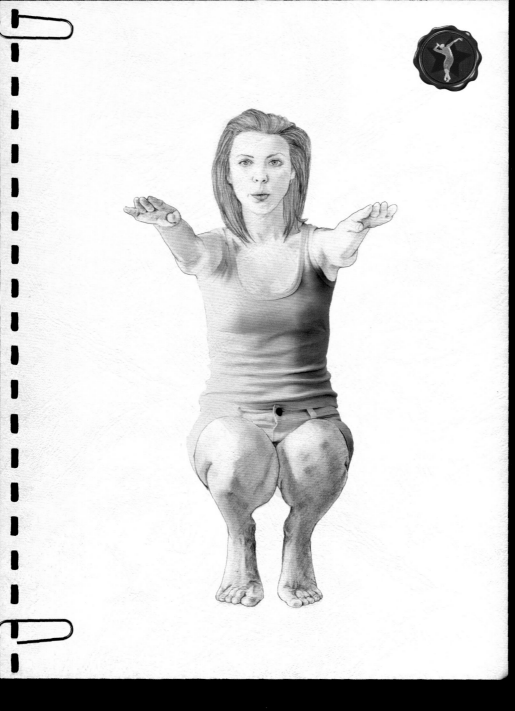

5
REST AND REJUVENATION

According to a study conducted by Dr. Yiannis Koutedakis and Dr. Athanasios Jamurtas, titled "The Dancer as a Performing Athlete: Physiological Considerations," no differences exist between professional dancers, Olympic bobsledders, and Olympic rowers "on the strength and muscle contractile characteristics" of their activities. The researchers also found that lactic acid blood levels are the same in a professional dancer performing a solo and professional football, squash, and hockey players during a game. Dancers are art's athletes, to paraphrase Albert Einstein. And let's face it: Even after a week or season of shows, a tour with a performance in a different venue every evening, a fierce competition, or a day of back-to-back classes and rehearsals, dancers rarely rest. They often return to class, the studio, or the stage the next day. Yet without rest and recovery, dancers become prone to fatigue and injury. This chapter discusses the need for rest, and how to incorporate moments of recovery into a daily routine.

POST-PERFORMANCE BASICS

Immediately after a performance, a dancer's body is running at a high metabolic level and is dehydrated from sweating, with adrenaline, cortisol, and lactic acid coursing through the neuromuscular system. In other words, the body requires rest and replenishment.

After final bows and retiring to the dressing rooms, dancers need to do the following:

- Bring the heart rate to the resting level. A five-minute, gradually slowing walk keeps your body gently moving as you restore your heart rate.
- Cool down. In addition to walking, a 10–15-minute series of simple stretches that extend and loosen the muscles will keep the body from tightening up. (Also see pages 86–87.)
- Rehydrate. Drink plenty of water and/or an electrolyte sports drink.
- Eat. After a performance, dancers need to eat within two hours to restore muscles and glycogen levels and reduce protein breakdown. Don't rely on the cake and champagne reception: First, eat a snack that balances carbohydrates and protein, such as a peanut butter and jelly sandwich, a banana with a protein bar, or a hard-cooked egg and crackers. Then, eat a well-balanced dinner after the reception.
- Clean up. A hot shower may sound wonderful, but if you're injured, the hot water and steam will encourage swelling. Shower with medium-hot water and direct

After a rehearsal or performance, dancers need to replenish their fluids by drinking water, and their energy by eating fruit or carbohydrates.

cold blasts to any particularly achy or injured areas.

Back at home/ the hotel room

After dinner and returning to your room, don't immediately go to bed. Most dancers, after a night of performing, greeting patrons, and then dining, require at least two hours to relax before going to sleep. Instead of climbing into bed, continue restorative techniques such as these:

- Stretching. Gently flex, extend, or lengthen any muscle areas that feel as if they're contracting or tightening.
- Self-massage. Use your hands, a foam roller, and/or tennis balls to carefully massage tight and overworked muscles.
- Limb elevation. Lie on the floor with your legs up the wall (see page 111), or on a chair or on pillows to relax legs, feet, and back, and to decrease knee, ankle, and foot swelling. Elevate your arms on pillows for relaxation.
- Ice. The Radio City Rockettes are known for bathing in ice water after shows, to reduce pain and inflammation. For most other dancers, ice packs (20 minutes on, 20 minutes off, repeat) placed on sore joints and muscles are sufficient.

Sleep

The benefits of sleep are enormous: Organs cleanse, muscles repair, the brain rests, and the entire body is replenished. Six to eight hours of sleep a night are recommended. But what if your mind is still racing, reviewing your performance, considering the choreographer's notes, visualizing a difficult combination, replaying a discussion with another dancer? When experiencing difficulty getting to sleep, try these:

- Get out of bed and do something else for a while. Sew ribbons on your toe shoes, read a book or magazine that you find uninteresting, take a hot bath (if you aren't injured or swelling) with lavender (a relaxing herb), or write down your thoughts in a journal to transfer them out of your mind.
- Make sure the room is dark (with no interfering lights on electronic devices or through windows).
- Drink hot herbal tea, with such relaxing herbs as chamomile or valerian.
- Soak your feet. If your feet aren't swollen but achy, soak them in warm water with Epsom salts.
- Breathe deeply. Concentrate on and listen to your breathing instead of to your thoughts.

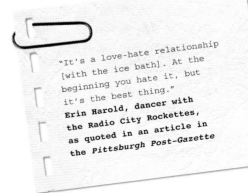

"It's a love-hate relationship [with the ice bath]. At the beginning you hate it, but it's the best thing."
Erin Harold, dancer with the Radio City Rockettes, as quoted in an article in the Pittsburgh Post-Gazette

RECOVERING FROM FATIGUE

One of the most-used "swear words" in dance is *rest*. Yet whether the new dancer has completed a difficult combination in class, the student dancer has learned a complex section of choreography in rehearsal, or the professional dancer has mastered a new work in live performance, fatigue has undoubtedly set in. Rest is what the dancer most needs (along with lots of water and a good meal).

The rigors, excitement, and stress of learning, rehearsing, and performing contribute to high levels of fatigue in dancers—an overall sense of physical exhaustion, as well as tiredness in specific muscles or overused parts of the body. If the dancer doesn't rest, injuries can occur. Fatigue impairs sense of balance and decreases stability in the joints. Fatigue is also cumulative; if the dancer doesn't rest, fatigue builds over time and can lead to burnout (see pages 228–229).

Rest can be as simple as temporarily stopping the level of intensity, or changing up your routine with cross training, somatic practices, or restorative practices. How long dancers need to rest depends on the source of their fatigue, and whether they're recovering from a tough day in the studio or a series of back-to-back performances.

Two types of fatigue

Dancers experience two types of fatigue, which may appear separately or in combination, depending on the individual's situation:

• Peripheral: specific or local, and occurs when a muscle has been contracted or used so often (as in after repeated jumps, leg lifts, or arm patterns) that it runs out of energy and can no longer function.

• Central: mental exhaustion that develops after prolonged repetitive activity; can impair the central nervous system and lead to lethargy, irritability, depression.

Rest is essential for dancers in order to avoid serious injury.

Tips for recovering from fatigue

- 12–24 hours of little or no physical activity after a series of performances
- Incorporate short naps into the daily schedule whenever possible.
- Use periodization: hard workouts alternated with easier routines incorporating rest.
- Get eight hours of sleep every night.
- Eat nutritionally balanced meals
- Treat, don't ignore, injuries.
- Adopt the constructive rest position during breaks (see pages 108–109).
- Minimize stress in other areas of your life.
- Take B vitamin supplements (which promote healing and increase energy).
- Take a break from dance and do cross training instead (swimming, yoga, Pilates, etc.).

Not all fatigue is bad

All dancers experience muscle fatigue. It's inherent to the principle of progressive overload, through which dancers gradually increase the stress put on muscles during class and rehearsals to increase physical strength. (Also see pages 74–75). Fatigue, then, is an essential part of advancing the body's stamina and power, and improving technique. The dancer works until fatigued, rests, then works harder to produce better results, becomes fatigued, rests, and the cycle repeats.

Research findings

Dr. Marijeanne Liederbach, a physical therapist at the Harkness Center for Dance Injuries in New York City, has analyzed 500 injury reports from dancers in a professional ballet company, a university conservatory, and a hospital-based orthopedic clinic. Her data showed that fatigue was the most common variable associated with injury in all three groups. In addition, 79 percent of injuries happened at the end of the day, after five or more hours of work.

Dancers need plenty of rest, fluids, and protein and carbohydrate meals to recover from fatigue.

CONSTRUCTIVE REST

As a dancer, you're always working to change your body's bad habits, improper alignment, and faulty technique. The constructive rest position assists with these endeavors. Constructive rest also lengthens the spine, releases muscle tension, brings a fast heart rate back to normal, and improves physiological conditions throughout the body.

The position also helps you experience breath and weight to realize a more economical use of the body; heightened neuromuscular coordination to improve technique and performances; and a relaxed position in which to work on visualization and imaging techniques (also see Chapter 6).

In her 1937 book, *The Thinking Body*, Mabel Todd (the founder of Ideokinesis, see pages 142–143) talked about the concept of "constructive rest" for dancers, calling it "hook lying." Kinesiologist Lulu Sweigard further developed the position and its applications. Constructive rest has since been incorporated into many fields of bodywork and somatic practice, including the Alexander Technique, yoga, and Pilates.

Todd found that dancers (particularly ballet dancers) overuse their hip flexors, and often move and jump in asymmetrical positions. These repetitive motions can torque the pelvis and back, resulting in misalignment, aches, and pain. Taking time after class, rehearsal, and a performance for constructive rest is an excellent way to hit the body's re-set button.

Constructive rest doesn't require any muscular action or effort. Gravity does most of the work, as it pulls the body toward the ground and thus alleviates strain and balances muscles throughout the body. However, you do need to focus and concentrate in order to gain the physical and mental benefits of constructive rest.

During constructive rest, lie on your back with the head supported (a pillow beneath the neck is suggested) and the knees drawn up with feet on the floor. The pose creates a relaxed position. Then focus on areas of tension in the body, and using breath and imagery encourage your body to relax. The pose is usually held for 20–30 minutes, which allows the body to relax and rejuvenate.

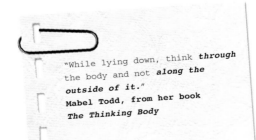

"While lying down, think *through the body* and not *along the outside of it.*"
Mabel Todd, from her book *The Thinking Body*

Getting into position

Lie down on a carpet or mat in a quiet area. Once on your back, bend your knees at a 90-degree angle, allowing your lumbar spine to rest easily on the floor. For many dancers, this position causes the legs to fall to either side. If this happens to you, gently fasten a belt or tie a scarf around your thighs to keep the legs together. Or, you can lean your legs together with your knees lightly resting against each other.

A variation of the basic position is to elevate your legs on a chair, knee rest, bolster, or cushion. Place a small pillow under your head to support the neck in proper alignment.

Using imagery

Start by paying attention to your breathing. Breathe normally, in and out, but pay attention to your breath to help focus your mind.

What areas of your body need to relax? Find a precise location in your body. If your lower back is in pain, for example, imagine your back is a pat of butter slowly melting. Keep the image in the present moment, and visualize it as vividly as possible.

When visualizing the image, engage all of your senses. Feel the warmth, and the sensation of the cool hard butter slowly and easily turning into a warm liquid.

Focus on the process of melting, not the result (a pool of melted butter).

If your mind wanders, bring your thoughts quietly back to the image.

When you're ready, refresh the process with a new image that focuses on another part of the body. Be aware that different images work differently on different days.

Gravity does most of the work during constructive rest, but using the mind to create imagery that relaxes the body maximizes the benefits of the position.

RESTORATIVE YOGA

Sometimes described as "active relaxation," restorative yoga is a slow-paced Hatha yoga in which props support the body during open poses and long stretches. The point of restorative yoga, and its use of props, is to eliminate unnecessary strain, allow the body to stay in position longer, and encourage the release of tension.

The postures are generally adapted from traditional seated or supine yoga asanas. They were designed to calm the nervous system, induce restfulness, and encourage a sense of well-being. Relaxing into the supported poses for a length of time also releases physical and emotional strain.

Restorative yoga is also believed to stimulate the parasympathetic nervous system (PNS), which is responsible for balancing the body and equalizing its response system. Stimulating the PNS lowers heart rate and blood pressure, stimulates the immune system, and maintains endocrine-system health.

Key concepts or conditions
- The body is physically comfortable.
- The body is physically warm (blankets may be used to cover the body).
- Muscle tension and strain are released.
- Poses are inverted or done lying on the floor.
- The room is dark and quiet.
- Eye bags or a pillow provide a slight pressure on the bones around the eyes.
- Poses are held for an optimal length of time.

Props in restorative yoga
- Cotton blankets (can be rolled into various configurations for support)
- Bolsters (placed under knees, spine, neck for support)
- Blocks (support body parts)
- Straps (for binding legs or feet in opening poses)
- Sandbags (further relaxation by weighing down parts of the body)
- Eye bag/eye pillow (calms the eyes and face by blocking out light, puts slight pressure on bones around eyes to further relaxation)

Benefits of restorative yoga for dancers
- Better alignment and posture
- Relief from back pain, mental fatigue, physical exhaustion
- Improves resistance to injury
- Extended range of motion and flexibility
- Releases lactic acid and other toxins
- Improves blood flow and circulation
- Promotes a greater sense of calm, concentration, focus

Three restorative poses

1. Supported child's pose (alleviates fatigue, headaches, neck, and shoulder tension) On a yoga mat or rug, sit down with your legs underneath you and knees spread apart.

Put a rolled-up blanket or bolster lengthwise between your knees, and pull it toward you.

Lie down on the bolster and place your arms to either side. Adjust the bolster (pull it farther forward or back) to find the most comfortable position. Your back should be straight and free of tension.

Turn your head and put one cheek onto the bolster (be sure to turn to the other cheek midway through).

Breathe slowly and deeply for 2–5 minutes.

2. Legs up the wall (relieves lower back tension, drains blood from swollen legs and feet, brings blood to head and heart) Get a bolster or fold two blankets into a similar support; put the props near the wall.

Sit on the floor with one hip next to the wall, lie back and swing your legs straight up onto the wall, so you're at a 90-degree angle. Fit your butt as snugly to the wall as possible.

Put the bolster/blankets underneath your back and hips; they support you from your tailbone to the midback. Shoulder blades rest on the floor.

Place an eye bag over your eyes.

Allow arms to relax on the floor or over your head.

Breathe deeply for 5–20 minutes.

3. Supported back bend (opens and releases the chest and shoulders, stretches lower and middle back) Fold a blanket in half (or thirds) and place it on your mat (change number of folds to increase openness/reduce back strain).

Sit in front of the blankets, then lie back slowly to lower torso onto the blankets. Shoulders touch the floor.

Place a small pillow or the rolled edge of a blanket under your neck for added support.

Place an eye bag over your eyes.

Let arms extend out from the body at the sides.

(Increase the openness of the pose by putting a bolster on top of the blanket and draping torso over the bolster.)

Breathe deeply for about 30 seconds; then adjust pose if necessary. Resume deep breathing.

"Legs up the wall" is a terrific inverted posture for dancers, as it can release tension in the lower back and relax the legs.

CHIROPRACTIC CARE

For most dancers, chiropractic care—in conjunction with yoga, somatic practices, and massage—is a key part of keeping the body in peak physical condition and restoring the body after performance. Because dancers repeatedly perform moves that require extreme flexibility, articulation, and strength, areas of the musculoskeletal system can easily become misaligned, causing discomfort and pain.

These misalignments, from the feet up through the spine and to the neck, inhibit proper joint motion and can cause tight muscles and injury. Joints out of alignment can also affect the dancer's line and technique, leading to unwanted dance habits. Chiropractors alleviate such misalignments through readjustment and other treatments. They may also counsel dancers on nutrition, exercises to build strength, and movement modifications to prevent pain or reinjury.

Many large dance companies have chiropractors on staff or on call, who may also tour with the company. Other companies have favored chiropractors, sensitized to the injuries and requirements of dancers, whom they visit at the chiropractor's practice. A chiropractor may be brought into a studio before performances to treat and prepare dancers for a show. Dancers also seek out chiropractic treatment after performances to release tension and alleviate pain.

Tiny misalignments in the spine can lead to serious injury, so many dancers find a chiropractor essential.

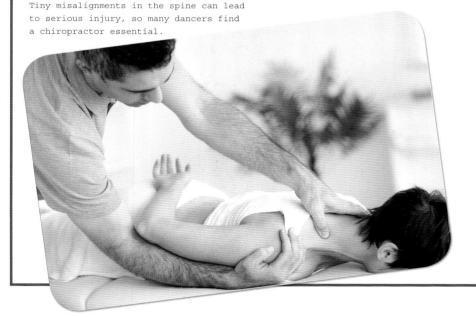

Risk factors leading to misalignments

- Innate: unbalanced musculoskeletal system, improper biomechanical functioning, past injury
- External: improper technique, performance mishap, overuse, fatigue, stress, floor, footwear

Chiropractic therapies

- Hands-on manipulation of the spine and other joints
- Hands-on soft-tissue therapy through various release techniques
- Kinesio taping to extend manipulation and soft-tissue therapies, and reduce inflammation
- Mechanical muscle stimulation through such equipment as laser and ultrasound
- Advice on diet and nutritional supplements to speed healing
- Advice on extending treatments through specific exercises
- Ice pack/cryotherapy recommendations

Adjustment techniques

Chiropractors usually practice a mix of adjustment techniques, which may include the following:

- Diversified: a compendium of hands-on spinal manipulation strategies
- Activator: uses a handheld spring-loaded device that delivers a small, precise pulse that moves vertebrae
- Thompson: the body is positioned on a drop table so its weight exerts gentle force; uses Leg Length System to correct misalignments in spine and pelvis
- Gonstead: considers and treats the sponge-like material between the vertebrae as the source of nerve pressure
- Cox/flexion-distraction: combines gentle adjustments with osteopathic principles
- Sacro-occipital: defines three categories or protocols of distortion in the body, and uses blocks and hands-on manipulation for clearing those blocks
- Nimmo receptor tonus: neuromuscular therapy that uses trigger points to release knotted or banded muscle tissue

"We have daily experience of the connectedness of our physical and emotional body. Why is it still a surprise when knee pain is traced back to an origin in the pelvis/hip? Yes, we are a connected whole! But we head for the eternal manifestation of the pain for treatment (should I brace my knee?), ignoring the patterns that might be the cause (perhaps a pelvic adjustment from the chiropractor?)."
Dancer and choreographer Stephen Petronio, artistic director of Stephen Petronio Company, from an article he wrote for *Dance Magazine*

MASSAGE

The word *massage* is derived from the Latin *massa* meaning "mass, dough," and the Arabic *massa* meaning "to touch, feel or handle." Just as bakers knead bread dough, in other words, masseurs use their hands (as well as elbows and forearms) to knead layers of muscle and connective tissue in the body.

Massage from a certified practitioner can address or help prevent muscle spasms, aches, and injuries.

For dancers, the overuse of muscles during performance (as well as during training and rehearsal), with little time for rest until after the final curtain call, results in muscle stress and fatigue. That is why massage is an integral part of the post-performance recovery process for most dancers.

The body instinctively begins repairing muscles and tissue damage when activity stops. Rest and proper nutrition enhance this recovery process. So does massage, by speeding blood flow, improving circulation, and eliminating toxins (such as lactic acid).

Do not receive massage when you
• feel sick and/or have a temperature above 100°F;
• are injured, bruised, or have a muscle sprain or tear;
• have a skin infection, rash, or open wound.

Research findings

A study conducted by the Touch Research Institute, and reported in the *Journal of Dance Medicine & Science*, found that massage decreased anxiety, improved mood, and enhanced range of motion in dance students. In the study, thirty female dance students received 30-minute massage sessions twice a week for five weeks.

Before and after the study, the dance students completed a questionnaire assessing their mood, levels of pain and anxiety, and range of motion in the neck and shoulders. The dancers also submitted saliva samples (for measuring cortisol levels). Results showed that in addition to better mood and enhanced motion, massage lowered the students' levels of cortisol (a stress hormone) and eased pain in the neck, shoulders, and back.

Self-massage

When a masseuse isn't immediately available, or a dancer's budget can't accommodate a session, some dancers practice self-massage to release muscle tension. Before doing self-massage, dancers need a thorough understanding of anatomy, awareness of the challenging areas within their own bodies, and techniques learned from a professional massage therapist. But even such basic motions as squeezing and stroking a tense muscle can improve blood flow, warm up the area, alleviate tension or pain, and enhance range of motion.

Many dancers include self-massage in their daily routine to address strain or pain in feet, ankles, and legs.

"MASSAGE ALLOWS THE DANCERS TO MOVE BETTER AND HAVE A LARGER RANGE OF MOTION. THEIR MUSCLES CAN FIRE WITH MORE POWER IF THEY'VE HAD THE TRIGGER POINTS WORKED OUT, AND I THINK IT'S ALSO A GOOD MENTAL AND EMOTIONAL BREAK FOR THE DANCERS TO JUST CLOSE THEIR EYES AND HAVE THEIR BODIES WORKED ON."

Paul Papoutsakis, athletic therapist for the National Ballet of Canada

ACUPUNCTURE AND ACUPRESSURE

Some dancers turn to such Eastern therapies as acupuncture and acupressure to alleviate muscle fatigue and help speed post-performance recovery. A dancer may also incorporate these modalities into their overall plan for wellness in conjunction with massage, chiropractic, or various somatic practices. These modalities are also deployed for treating injuries, and are referred to as "alternative" or "complementary" medicine when used in combination with, or as opposed to, Western medical therapies.

Acupuncture

The ancient Chinese medical practice uses very thin, flexible needles to readjust, balance, or regulate the dancer's life-energy or *qi* (pronounced chee). The needles are inserted into more than 400 possible spots in the body along twenty meridians—the pathways through which qi flows. The meridians relate to internal organs and bodily systems, and extend outward to the body's extremities.

The needles stimulate designated acupoints on the body, which are connected by the meridians, to release the qi. Acupuncturists believe that pain indicates the qi is blocked. Acupuncture unblocks the qi and stimulates blood flow through muscles to instigate healing.

Acupuncture needles are usually manufactured of stainless-steel wire; some are made of silver, gold, or copper to use those elements' healing properties. Needle thickness can vary, depending on the dancer and their needs. In most countries, acupuncture needles are sterilized and

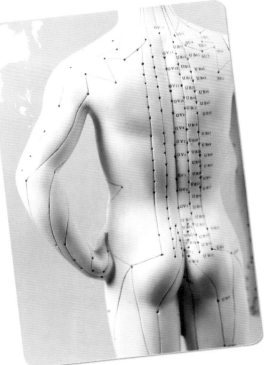

Releasing or redirecting the body's qi, by inserting thin needles along the body's meridians, is one of the goals of acupuncture.

sealed until use, after which they're disposed of. If a practitioner doesn't use disposable needles, make sure needles are thoroughly sterilized between patient use.

Needles are usually left in for approximately 20 minutes. Although some skilled practitioners can insert the needles without causing discomfort, many patients find the procedure painful. If a dancer is seeking out acupuncture for an injury, Western medical doctors suggest the dancer first receive a diagnosis, often through the use of an MRI, to pinpoint the type and location of the injury.

"ACUPUNCTURE AND BODYWORK ARE ABSOLUTELY WHAT KEPT ME FUNCTIONING AT PROFESSIONAL PERFORMANCE LEVEL. WHEN I WAS JUST TWENTY-FOUR I HAD A KNEE INJURY THAT WAS CRIPPLING. I COULDN'T PLIÉ AND WAS SIDELINED… IN TWO SESSIONS I WAS BACK IN REHEARSAL AND CANCELING SURGERY! FROM THERE WE REBUILT A CHRONICALLY DISLOCATING SHOULDER. NEXT WE TOOK ON MY IMMUNE SYSTEM, TAUGHT ME TO EAT PROPERLY, AND HELPED ME GAIN ROBUST HEALTH FOR THE FIRST TIME IN MY LIFE. ALONG THE WAY I LEARNED TO HANDLE INJURIES WHILE ON THE ROAD, HOW TO DANCE SMARTER, RECOVER FASTER."

Elizabeth Carpenter, choreographer and former dancer with Joe Goode Performance Group and Trisha Brown Company, and founder of Oriens Healing Sanctuary

Acupressure

Just as in shiatsu, in acupressure the practitioner uses their fingers (and sometimes fingernails and elbows) to gently and firmly press on the body's acupoints along the meridians. As in acupuncture, the pressure releases the qi, and stimulates healing and recovery. Acupressure is also referred to as compressive massage.

Acupressure can be done anytime to relieve muscle tension and pain, even before and during performances. It can be applied through clothing, and can have an effect after a mere second of pressure. For greater benefits, practitioners will maintain a constant pressure for up to 3 minutes.

When acupressure is applied, the sensation varies from a feeling of tension, to soreness, to penetrating pain. In general, the key to successful acupressure is to rely on the feeling of "hurts so good," meaning the sensation incorporates a firm and releasing pressure without excruciating pain. With some knowledge of anatomy and acupoints, dancers often practice acupressure on themselves and other dancers to immediately release painful or tense muscles.

QIGONG AND TAI CHI

Rest and recovery for dancers doesn't necessarily mean you need to stop moving. Practicing one of the meditative, ancient Chinese movement disciplines—such as Qigong or tai chi—can promote relaxation while you're exercising breath control and movement coordination. Because these practices also loosen muscles and joints, encourage conscious breathing, and induce a sense of calm, they're also helpful before performances and after rehearsals.

Qigong

Qi is the Chinese word for energy or life force (also see page 116), and Qigong (also spelled QiGong, Qi Gong, chi kung) has been a component of Chinese medicine for millennia in conjunction with acupuncture, massage, and the use of herbs. Qigong is a practice that balances qi through rhythmic breathing in coordination with slow flowing movements, balance, and counterbalance over the center of gravity; and a calm, aware, and focused state of mind. Some Qigong styles are more static than others, or may focus on strengthening particular bodily organs or systems.

- Encourages deep, conscious breathing, which relaxes mind and body
- Builds endurance
- Cultivates internal sources of energy
- Sparks the imagination and creativity
- Integrates mind and body to enhance performance
- Maintains inner calm

Benefits of Qigong for dancers

- Reconnection with the body's natural movements and relationship to gravity
- Releases tight muscles and joint tension

"THIS PRACTICE IS ABOUT RECOGNIZING MOVEMENT INITIATION AND TRANSFORMATION IN ONE SELF AND EACH OTHER. LISTENING TO THE FEELING SHIFTS. WE WATCH AND EXPERIENCE HOW ENGAGED, REPEATED UNISON MOVEMENTS FOLLOW THEIR INHERENT RHYTHM AND GUIDE THE DANCING MIND IN A MEDITATIVE WAY. I USE EXERCISES BASED ON PRINCIPLES OF QI GONG AS PART OF THE PRACTICE AND TO GIVE REFERENCE POINTS DURING DANCING."

Choreographer and dancer Melanie Maar, describing her class Rhythmic Unison Transformation for Classclassclass and Movement Research

Tai chi

T'ai chi ch'uan or tai chi is a Chinese martial art also known as "shadow boxing." Like Qigong, tai chi is a low-impact practice that balances qi, and incorporates flowing and controlled movement performed slowly, a low center of gravity, and conscious breathing coordinated with movements. Some styles, however, have a faster pace and include weapons training. The partner exercises are known as "pushing hands."

By practicing ancient Asian movement and martial arts disciplines, dancers can gain greater control of their bodies, acquire a sense of calm, and loosen up muscles and joints.

Benefits of tai chi for dancers

- Improves whole body coordination and control
- Reduces stress
- Increases speed and endurance
- Calms and focuses the mind
- Improves balance
- Restores energy

> **Qigong allows dancers to trust their bodies to go beyond pure technique and tap into their inner power and beauty.**
>
> Christine McQuade

6
THE MIND–BODY CONNECTION

As the dancer's instrument and the choreographer's medium, the body is the means through which the interior realms of ideas and emotions reach the exterior realm of artistic intention, expression, and communication. In other words, dance is inherently a function of mind and body working together. This chapter explores the various ways in which the dancer's mind–body connection is generated through the creation or use of imagery. Dance instructors and choreographers use images to help students improve their alignment and technique, and perform a movement sequence with a particular quality. Imagery and imaging is also an intrinsic aspect of many somatic practices, through which students and practitioners turn inward and use images to heighten awareness of, and correct, neuromuscular habits and patterns that are hampering technique or performance. Dancers and choreographers also explore nature and such arts as painting, sculpture, architecture, music, and literature to find images and ideas for choreographic inspiration.

IMAGING: THE BODY–MIND CONNECTION

Imaging and *imagination*: These words come from the Latin *imago*, and describe the process by which a person forms mental pictures or images. Research has shown that images created in the mind can actually change the body's physiology and its neuromuscular behavior.

In dance, this body–mind connection has various applications.

- To improve dance technique. Imaging helps a dancer—from inside the body—connect a position, movement, or phrase to a particular quality or sensation, which results in the body's movement reflecting that quality or sensation. These types of images are known as "direct" and "indirect."

"PERFORMERS IN MOTION, ACCOMPANIED BY SOUNDS AND DESIGNS, CREATE IMAGES WHICH BECOME THE STUFF OF A DANCE WORK. WHATEVER 'MEANING' THERE IS IN A DANCE IS EMBODIED IMPLICITLY IN THESE IMAGES. A DANCE WORK PRESENTS AN OVERALL IMAGE; AT THE SAME TIME, HOWEVER, WITHIN THAT WORK ARE MANY MINOR IMAGES. THESE CAN BE AS BRIEF AS A SINGLE PHRASE, OR THEY CAN RUN TO A SCENE OF ANY LENGTH."

Joan Cass, from her book *The Dance: A Handbook for the Appreciation of Choreographic Experience*

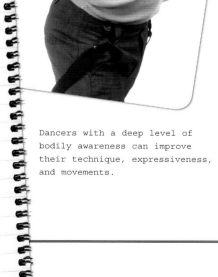

Dancers with a deep level of bodily awareness can improve their technique, expressiveness, and movements.

SOMATIC PRACTICES

The body-mind connection has also given rise to a number of somatic practices or therapies. *Somatic* comes from the Greek word for "living, aware, bodily person," which means experiencing and controlling the body from within—often at the deepest levels (cells, tissues, muscles, nerves, bones)—by using the mind and mental imagery. In other words, in somatic practices the mind and body are connected to achieve a specific outcome. This integration is often referred to as "conscious embodiment." Through these practices, dancers can achieve a deep level of bodily awareness that can inform, improve, and even transform their technique, expressiveness, and movements.

Direct: For example, visualize a plumb line from the ear to the ankle to help you achieve proper alignment.

Indirect: For example, imagine an ice skater gliding across a frozen pond, then travel across the floor using the same quality of motion.

- To improve kinesthetic awareness. We have five senses, plus a "sixth"—the kinesthetic sense, through which we receive information about the position, balance, temperature, speed, and direction of the body. This information is relayed to the mind through proprioceptors or tiny sense organs throughout the body. A kinesthetic image is a sensation or feeling associated with movement, and again can be direct or indirect.

> ❝ The body is the instrument through which the mind is expressed…
>
> Bonnie Bainbridge Cohen from her book *Sensing, Feeling, and Action: The Experiential Anatomy of Body-Mind Centering* ❞

Direct: For example, pull your arms toward you as if they're heavy. Indirect: For example, pull your arms toward you as if you're rowing through choppy water.

- To inspire choreography. Imagery is often used during improvisation to help dancers realize a range of movement possibilities and forms of expression. Imaging is also used to generate dance material that can be combined and refined into choreography.

- To express emotions, thoughts, and ideas. Dance instructors and choreographers use imagery to communicate with an audience. The choreographic imagery may be symbolic (gestures, movements, and characters that convey particular emotions or meanings), representational (recognizable or realistic movements as pantomime), or abstract (either pure physical movement performed for its rhythm, design, or quality; or an emotion or experience distilled to its essence in movement).

Dance imagery in class

During dance class, the instructor may ask you to roll on the floor in a ball, or hold your arms as if you have small air-

In many Indian dance styles, the body is an instrument for articulating images generated through music, mythology, and poetry.

filled balloons under each armpit, or walk as if the floor is covered with deep mud, or contract your torso as if you've been punched in the stomach. These instructions all use imaging to help the dancer

Bodily gestures are physical images that nonverbally communicate messages quickly and effectively, which is why they are sometimes incorporated into choreography. Researchers in kinesics (the study of nonverbal communication) have identified five types of gestural movements:

- Emblems: gestures with immediate meaning, such as the OK sign or the heart hand. (Beware: Gestures are culturally specific, meaning a friendly gesture in one culture might convey an obscenity in another culture.)
- Affect displays: facial expressions (smiling, frowning) and body changes (tensing the shoulder, making a fist) that respond to an emotion, whether done consciously or unconsciously
- Regulators: behaviors that respond to another person (nodding in agreement, looking elsewhere when you're bored)
- Illustrators: used to emphasize or illustrate speech (snapping your fingers, creating a flat plane with your palm)
- Adaptors: gestures of response to self (scratching an itch, rubbing your nose), directed at another (smoothing someone's hair, picking lint from their jacket), or done to an object (folding a scrap of paper over and over, doodling)

visualize—by creating an image in the mind—how to better physicalize and perform a movement.

This process is called dance imagery. A mental visualization of a past experience or memory applied to physical movement, dance imagery helps dancers enhance their technical and performance capabilities. An image can help correct alignment, refine a position or aspect of technique, or add a specific quality to a choreographic sequence.

Types of dance imagery

Eric Franklin, a Zurich-based dance educator and the author of *Dynamic Alignment Through Imagery*, puts dance imagery into the following (and often overlapping) categories:

- Sensory:
  Visual (e.g., rotate your leg in the hip socket like a swizzle stick)
  Kinesthetic (e.g., feel your body tangled up in a large web)
  Tactile (e.g., imagine strong fingers releasing your neck tension)
  Auditory (e.g., smack down your foot as if whacking a bug)
  Olfactory (e.g., walk as if you're in a field of lavender)
  Taste (e.g., work the movement as if you're chewing fresh bread)

In dance styles from flamenco (above) to lyrical, dancers create a strong connection in the body between emotion and movement to ensure an expressive performance.

Using self-generated imagery

Enhance the images given to you in class, and create your own images to strengthen your body–mind connection and deepen understanding of your body and its abilities.

Start during your warm-up. While stretching and loosening, conjure up images (joints softening like melting cheese, muscles releasing like taut ropes gone limp) that engage mind and body. Concentrate on how your limbs are moving in space (swinging like a pendulum, reaching for the sun). Focus on improving your coordination as you practice a simple phrase (limbs and torso moving together like clockwork or like the gears of a well-oiled machine).

- Direct (or literal) and indirect (or metaphorical):
  Direct/literal is a simple imagistic directive (e.g., swing your arm in a circle).
  Indirect/metaphorical creates a picture by adding an event or object to the directive (e.g., circle your arm like a wheel)

- Internal and external:
  Internal are images for inside the body (e.g., imagine your arms filled with sand; feel your stomach sloshing with water).
  External are images for outside the body (e.g., picture yourself on a beach with the sun warming your body)

"HIJIKATA WAS SEEKING TO INCITE AN UNCONSCIOUS MOVEMENT EXPRESSION BY PROBING DEEP INTO THE SUBCONSCIOUS MEMORY. TO INSPIRE THE STUDENTS, HE WOULD RECITE IMAGE AFTER IMAGE, BEAT RHYTHMICALLY ON A DRUM, PLAY MUSIC FROM ROCK AND ROLL TO CLASSICAL JAPANESE, AND INSIST ON KEEPING THE BODY 'IN A CRISIS STATE,' ON THE EDGE, NEVER COMFORTABLE."

About Tatsumi Hijikata, Butoh practitioner and teacher, from an article in *Dance Magazine*

If your dance instructor asks you to image yourself dancing on a beach at sunset, thinking about the sensations of sand beneath your feet and the light at dusk can give your movements more authenticity.

If the teacher instructs you to run as if meeting a long-lost loved one, picture that person and add their smell and their touch to the image to broaden or deepen the expressive dimensions of your movements. If the instruction is to pull back suddenly as if someone has spilled hot coffee down your shirt, add the smell and heat of the coffee to your movement.

Imaging may immediately improve an aspect of your technique or your movement quality in class. Or an image may require a week or more to have an effect.

Establishing and reinforcing a strong mind–body connection requires practice. For example, if you're challenged with moving a part of the body more quickly, sharply, or fluidly, create a specific and localized image (fingers fluttering like butterfly wings, legs scything through space, arms undulating with the softness of rippling silk) to apply to your movement as you rehearse.

Explore how imagery can enhance alignment. Your teacher may tell you to let your tail drop to the floor or lift your head as if it's a helium balloon. Such imagery may resonate, and you immediately visualize, internalize, and apply the image to your body. If an image doesn't make sense, think of a similar image that's more applicable to you.

Make images more alive and kinesthetic by applying two or more senses to them.

Using imagery during warmups can help stretch muscles and loosen joints. For example, imagine your joints warming and softening like melted cheese.

SOURCES OF IMAGERY: NATURE AND MYTHOLOGY

The natural world, as well as mythology based on the earth's creation, and the gods and goddesses embodying natural elements, have long inspired dance. From Polynesian dances based on mythological imagery and nature themes, to dances of the Ewe people on West Africa's coast that incorporate movement that mimics ocean waves, to Kathak dances that express and depict aspects of nature, mythology and nature are imaging sources for dance around the world.

In dance classes, instructors use nature imagery to establish mind–body awareness that can improve alignment or technique. In his book *Dynamic Alignment Through Imagery*, Eric Franklin suggests such visualizations as imaging your metatarsals as logs floating in a river (to spread weight evenly and lightly across the foot), and imaging the sacrum as the body of an eagle with its outspread wings as your ilia (to produce more lifted and graceful movement from the pelvis).

Dance instructors also use nature imagery to strengthen the motor–mind

Dance works based on nature

- Momix's *Opus Cactus*: Inspired by the saguaro cactus and desert of the American Southwest, the work had dancers morphing through shapes resembling a lizard, birds, and tumbleweeds.
- Jennifer Monson's *Birdbrain*: a multiyear project that investigated and used the migratory patterns and habits of birds to create the choreography and structure for the work.
- Dana Reitz's *Sea Walk*: based on the forms, colors, and open spaces and enclosures of shells.
- Sydney Dance Company's *LANDforms*: explored wind, rain, snow, and clouds through choreography.

Nature has inspired much choreography, whether in the site-specific work of Mary Lee Hardenbergh, the dance-deck experiments of Anna Halprin, or modern dances performed on the concert stage.

Eiko and Koma

The duo's Butoh-inspired dance works nearly always concern natural cycles and processes. Rather than literally mimicking birds, animals, or natural elements, the dancers move at a glacial pace—often while in water, on a bed of rice, while emerging from a mound of dirt, or while lying on leaves and twigs—through sculptural shapes and states of being to emphasize the inexorable forces of nature and time.

ANNA HALPRIN

A pioneer of postmodern dance, movement as a healing art, and concert dance in the outdoors, California choreographer Anna Halprin lives on a steep hillside where her late husband (renowned landscape architect Lawrence Halprin) built an outdoor deck that became the platform for her innovations. While practicing and rehearsing outdoors, Halprin recognized ways in which nature flows through and influences the body. She began integrating nature into her choreography and teaching. She developed a holistic view of movement and nature that included choreographing concerts and dance rituals on her deck, and developed this into the Halprin Process. Halprin has taught her movement and healing process around the world and at the Tamalpa Institute, which she founded in the 1970s and is currently directed by her daughter, Daria Halprin.

connection and to inspire creativity and expression during improvisational exercises. Such images can range from a natural object or creature with a distinctive tactile quality, shape, or texture (pinecone, flamingo, sand) to picturing a natural scene (forest, cliff face, meadow).

Choreographers of outdoor site-specific dances often study the site's topography, environmental history, and natural characteristics as inspiration for their movement vocabulary. Companies like Momix and Pilobolus use bodies to re-create nature and biological systems through shape design. Martha Graham is the American choreographer most famous for reviving and recasting mythology and mythological heroines in her modern dances. Her *Cave of the Heart* was based on the Greek tale of Medea, and Graham explored the mythology of American frontier life in *Appalachian Spring*.

MUSIC, MOVIES, THEATER, AND ART

For many dancers and choreographers, dance and music are intertwined. Dancers move to music; choreographers make movement to music; music inspires both. Most ballet classes are accompanied by a pianist who plays music specifically composed for barre and center practice. Choreographers and composers worked together on many iconic ballets; *Swan Lake* or *The Nutcracker* without Tchaikovsky's character-evoking and emotionally picturesque scores is unimaginable.

Song selection for a dance competition is almost as important as the choreography. Such dance styles as flamenco, African and Native American dance, and Bharatanatyam wouldn't exist without the distinctive percussive rhythms and evocative singing that are the basis of the forms.

Choreographers from George Balanchine (neoclassical ballet) to Mark Morris (modern dance) to Danny Buraczeski (jazz dance) are renowned for their "musicality." Their dances illustrate and illuminate the rhythms, themes, melodies, structures, tones, forms, dynamics, and tempos of the music they've selected, which is sometimes called "music visualization" (dance as the movement equivalent of the music).

On the other hand, most postmodern and experimental choreographers don't use music in the traditional sense. They may dance without any sound at all. Or they may create sound collages with snippets of songs or scores juxtaposed with everyday noises, spoken text, electronic sound, and silence that have little, or everything, to do with what's happening on stage.

Composer John Cage pioneered this approach in conjunction with choreographer Merce Cunningham. He created scores with such "instruments" as household objects and pieces of metal; "found sounds" recorded on the street (traffic, voices, sirens); computer-generated sounds; and pianos "prepared" by putting objects on the strings. He and Cunningham decided that score and choreography (as well as sets, costumes, and lighting design) should come together for the first time on stage during the premiere of the work, which allowed for chance meanings, coincidences, and opportunities to occur.

Music as imagery and inspiration

Instructors of creative movement for children, and dance for students and adults,

> "Musicality is when the dancers' movements appear to create the music—and not the other way around."
>
> Kristy Nilsson, dancer, choreographer, and teacher

Many choreographers listen to a piece of music numerous times before finding the inspiration they need—whether in the music's lyrics, rhythm, instrumentation, or composition—to begin making a new work.

often use music during improvisation to inspire imagery that leads to individual creativity and expression. Music is also used while practicing combinations or movement sequences to help guide and stir dancers to manifest emotions in their dancing. Aspects of music that help create imagery, pattern, and feeling include the following:

Melody: a series or succession of tones, rhythm, and pitch that forms a single phrase or motif (the tune you hum or whistle, or that gets stuck in your mind)

Rhythm: the pattern of beats, pulse, and timing

Dynamics: the volume (such as crescendo or increasing in volume, or decrescendo or decreasing in volume) and energy (staccato or sharp and fast, legato or smooth, long, and slow)

Tempo: speed

Canon: form or pattern in which the melody is imitated at regular intervals (can be played at different measures, pitches, and speeds or be reversed)

"ALTHOUGH MUSIC IS ABSTRACT, IT DOES BRING IMAGES TO MIND. WHETHER THESE IMAGES ARE LITERAL OR ABSTRACT, YOU CAN USE SUCH IMAGES TO CREATE MOVEMENT FOR A DANCE. TRANSLATING VISUAL IMAGES INTO MOVEMENT MEANS USING SPACE, TIME, ENERGY, AND BODY SHAPE IN A WAY THAT COMMUNICATES THE MEANING CONNECTED TO A PARTICULAR IMAGE. A PIECE OF MUSIC CAN ALSO CAUSE YOU TO THINK OF A SERIES OF IMAGES THAT TELL A STORY, AND YOU CAN TRANSLATE THESE IMAGES INTO A MOVEMENT STORY, OR NARRATIVE, AS WELL."

Excerpt from *Dance Mind and Body* by Sandra Cerny Minton

The imagery of movies and theater

The dramatic arts, in which narrative, acting, and spoken text are intertwined, can inspire specific images that help a dancer define the emotion behind a movement or the quality of a movement sequence; refine the body language of the character a dancer's creating; and add an element of theatricality (tone, pitch, volume, rhythm) to choreography.

Actor and dancer Penélope Cruz, for example, thought about the cartoon movie character the Pink Panther when performing her dance number in the film *Nine*. "The musical number had to be sexy," she told *Interview*. "And thinking about the Pink Panther would help get me in the mood.... When I was climbing the ropes to the ceiling, all I could think about was the Pink Panther."

Dances are sometimes described as "cinematic" when the choreographer has created vivid or arresting stage pictures with lighting, costume, props, scenery, and movement. Dance-theater artists often integrate spoken text with choreography and the elements of theater (narrative, action, character, costuming, staging, sound/

music, lighting) to create dramatic spectacles, as in the work of Pina Bausch (below). Also, choreography is an integral part of staging a play, whether that play is *Brigadoon* or one without specific dance

Postmodern, experimental, and dance-theater artists often incorporate striking props, costumes, or images in their work, creating arresting stage pictures.

sections. And when choreography drives the narrative or dramatic action of a movie—whether *The Matrix*, *Strictly Ballroom*, or *West Side Story*—those movements may, in turn, inspire a dance maker to include similar steps or moves into their choreography for the stage.

Visual art and literature

Looking to other art forms, such as the visual arts, architecture, and literature, can provide dancers and choreographers with a treasure trove of imagery, shapes, patterns, and textures that inspire movement. Through improvisation or movement exploration, aspects of another art form can be internalized, reimaged, and translated into uniquely choreographic expressions. Dance students often start simply by focusing on just one aspect of the artwork, reinterpreting it through movement. Choreographers may, often in collaboration with their dancers, build on their exploration or excavation of the artwork to create full-length dance works.

- Visual art (e.g., sculpture, painting, mixed-media, photography, ceramics)
  Lines (curved, squiggly, straight; direction; action, as in gathering together, pushing apart, separating)
  Shapes (geometric; amorphous; an abstraction of something recognizable;

quality, as in melting (Salvador Dali's clocks), folding, reaching, absorbing)
Colors (vibrant, dull, primary, nuanced, contrasts between shadow and light, hot or cool)
Textures (both via the material or media used and/or the texture conveyed through the material or media—nubby, greasy, mucky, smooth, metallic, soft, hard, sharp, rough)
Groupings or combinations of people, objects, and forms (number of; spaces between; action; emotional quality)
Symbols (shape, color, and form; archetypal, pop culture, or artistic meaning; placement or action)
Also consider how the artwork was created: Jackson Pollock dripped and poured paint onto his canvases; Vincent Van Gogh painted great swirls of color into vibrant imagery. When re-creating a scene in a painting or photograph, imagine yourself inside the picture to feel its tactile qualities such as texture; smell the odors of flowers, animals, food; interact with the people and objects; experience the air and the textures underfoot.

- Architecture
  Building or structure type (library, parking garage, subway station, museum or art gallery, corporate office, gazebo, hotel)
  Shapes, form, planes, lines (flat, curved,

bulbous, wide, narrow, vertical, horizontal, oval, square, sculptural, angles)

Patterns or rhythms (generated by combinations or integration of shapes, forms, planes, lines)

Materials (stone, metal, brick, concrete, glass, steel)

Textures (smooth, glassy, rough, jagged) slippery)

Rooflines (flat, hipped, peaked)

Style (Romantic, Gothic, Modern, Colonial)

Details (windows, trim and molding; deck, railing, staircase, balcony, turret)

Space (open, closed, circular, square, spiraling up or down; atrium, office, stairwell, exhibition space)

Consider all aspects of an art form—the method of creation may be as inspirational as the finished product.

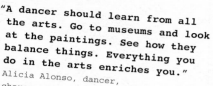

- Literature (e.g., play, novel, short story, graphic novel, poem, spoken word, nonfiction)

  Individual words and word patterns (what they sound like when spoken out loud and with what qualities, such as soft, percussive, color, tone; literal meaning; interpreted meaning)

  Sentences (literal and interpreted meaning, rhythmic pattern, emotion, description or dialogue)

  Characters (role, physique, psychology; quality of actions or gestures as in abrupt, aggressive, noncommittal, gentle; relationship with other characters)

  Genre (love story, mystery, cyberpunk, romance, history, adventure, true crime, biography/autobiography, mythology)

  Narrative/storyline/plot (dramatic, imagistic, linear or nonlinear, flashbacks/

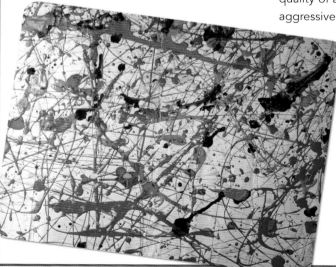

DANCE WORKS INSPIRED BY OTHER ARTS

- *Lines Squared* by Jessica Lang Dance for Richmond Ballet: the paintings of Piet Mondrian
- *colorography, n. The Dances of Jacob Lawrence* by Donald Byrd, Rennie Harris, Reggie Wilson, and Kevin Ward for Dayton Contemporary Dance Company: the life and work of painter Jacob Lawrence
- *Triadic Ballet* by painter and sculptor Oskar Schlemmer: one of the Bauhaus Dances choreographed by Schlemmer with props and forms exploring the human body as a geometric abstraction
- *Rhythmic High* by Room to Move Dance: five dances based on art found in the permanent collection of the High Museum of Art, Atlanta
- *1001 Afternoons in Chicago* by Erin Carlisle Norton and the Moving Architects: based on six short stories written in the 1920s by Chicago journalist Ben Hecht
- *Submerged Ascension* by Deidre Cavazzi and ArchiTexture Dance Company: inspired by and performed in the four-story atrium of the Calit2 building on the University of California—Irvine campus
- *Rapture Series* by Noémie Lafrance: dances inspired by and performed on buildings designed by architect Frank Gehry around the world
- *Vessel: An Opera Epic* by Meredith Monk: Based on the story of Joan of Arc, the piece took place in Monk's loft, a performance space, and a parking garage.
- *St Georges* by Régine Chopinot and Ballet Atlantique: inspired by the windows, spaces, friezes and sculptures of Romantic medieval church architecture

flashforwards, multiple or single narrator(s), multiple or single point(s) of view)
Imagery (symbolic, descriptive, sensory)

Site-specific choreographer Noémie Lafrance has created a series of aerial dance works that take place on the exteriors of architect Frank Gehry's buildings. Shown right is Gehry's Cleveland Clinic Lou Ruvo Center for Brain Health in Las Vegas.

VISUALIZING PERFORMANCE

Many dancers and other athletes incorporate visualization techniques into their training to strengthen the body–mind connection, build kinetic or movement memory, and improve performance. Also called guided imagery or mental rehearsal, visualization is a process of creating and holding, in your mind, an image of or intention for what you wish to accomplish.

Research indicates that an area in front of the brain called the premotor cortex, which is key to motor function and performance, is activated when a person imagines their body moving. When dancers rehearse a step or sequence in their minds, they create neural pathways in the brain for those actions—just as if they were physically moving.

During visualization, you're not actually doing the chaine turn, straddle jump, jazz square, competition routine, or ten-minute solo. But as you mentally map out and rehearse the steps and movement sequences, you're still training. When you return to class or rehearsal, and work to match the physicality of your body movements with the mental blueprint of the performance you wish to achieve, you're more likely to achieve your goals.

Repeated mental rehearsals strengthen your neural pathways, build self-confidence, and refine movement skills. Through visualization, the mind and body are simultaneously trained to physically perform as you've imagined. With visualization, rehearsal can happen almost anywhere.

Mental rehearsal: where and how

- Set aside 10–20 minutes a day for visualization.
- Practice in a quiet space, on the subway or bus, or while lying in bed.
- Start by visualizing a dance step: set a goal for the step (see Setting Goals box).

SETTING GOALS FOR VIZUALIZATIONS

- Be specific: Start with simple and precise goals (e.g., to land softly; to hold arabesque for five seconds without shaking).
- Be realistic: If your goal is ten pirouettes en pointe, start with three. Gradually build up after accomplishing the first three in class.
- Set target dates: Give yourself several weeks to achieve your first goal. Adjust the timetable for your goals as you become better at mental rehearsal and/or your goals become more complex.
- Write it down: Note what you did to achieve your goal and when you achieved it.

Picture your body doing the step. Feel the challenges you're having with the step. Visualize achieving your goal for the step. Mentally perform the step with confidence and accomplishment.

- Gradually add more steps to work your way up to full sequences and/or performances executed with flawless consistency.
- Add the appropriate feelings, motives, facial expressions, and movement qualities to your mental performance.
- Finish by visualizing self-approval, a sense of accomplishment, and audience applause.

Benefits of visualization

- Practice and fine-tune technique, routines, and overall performance
- Reinforce alignment, core stability and strength, and flexibility
- Correct flaws and overcome challenges
- Increase efficiency of movements
- Build self-confidence
- Enhance focus and concentration
- Increase self-discipline
- Overcome fear and intimidation
- Overcome physical, emotional, and psychological obstacles to performance
- Erase negative habits and promote positive attitude
- Release tension and reduce nervousness
- Increase relaxation
- Promote healing of injuries

The [goal] has to be specific. You can't just say to yourself, 'I'll do my best.' You have to have a mental blueprint of that role in your mind.

Linda Hamilton, "Advice for Dancers" in Dance Magazine

SOMATIC PRACTICE:
THE ALEXANDER TECHNIQUE

Australian actor Frederick Matthias Alexander developed the Alexander Technique in the early 1890s to alleviate his hoarseness and breathing troubles after doctors couldn't help him. Alexander began studying his movements in a mirror, and became aware that excess tension in his neck and body were causing his problems. As he investigated ways to speak and move with greater ease, he discovered that by identifying and changing the underlying physical habits producing such problems, he could eliminate these impediments to his performance.

Over time, Alexander expanded the technique to address how posture, movement, balance, and coordination in everyday life could be improved through thoughtful self-observation and attention to ingrained physical habits. Through mindfully engaging in simple exercises, a person could strip away or change unconscious habits, and restore the body's poise and ease of movement.

Today actors, musicians, and dancers around the world use the Alexander Technique to release tension, apply appropriate effort to a given activity, improve coordination, and alleviate pain.

How it works

The Alexander Technique is about self-education. Depending on your situation, an Alexander specialist or teacher may direct you in a variety of simple movements such as sitting or walking. Or they may have you demonstrate the movement pattern that's creating your reoccurring strain, pain, or other difficulties. These difficulties might range from neck kinks to movement limitations to fatigue.

The teacher identifies and analyzes your movements, then guides you verbally, and with light and gentle touch, on how to move more efficiently, more freely, and with better coordination. The goal is greater awareness of the movements you're doing automatically or unconsciously, so you can retrain your thoughts and body to move correctly.

"I HAD PROVED IN MY OWN CASE AND IN THAT OF OTHERS THAT INSTINCTIVE CONTROL AND DIRECTION OF USE HAD BECOME SO UNSATISFACTORY, AND THE ASSOCIATED FEELING SO UNTRUSTWORTHY AS A GUIDE, THAT IT COULD LEAD US TO DO THE VERY OPPOSITE OF WHAT WE WISHED TO DO OR THOUGHT WE WERE DOING."

F.M. Alexander, from his book *The Use of the Self*

The Alexander Technique is often referred to as "the technique under all techniques," because it cleanses the mind and body of habitual thoughts, sensations, and movements.

Key concepts

- Use: the habitual, unconscious ways in which a person moves or uses the body, and the holistic effects (physical, emotional, and psychological)
- Primary control: the relationship between the neck, head, and spine, which is the "master reflex" or organizer of the body
- Inhibition: the process of learning how to stop or correct a learned, habitual movement or "mis-use"
- Directions: the mental directives or instructions given (by ourselves or teacher) to correct mis-use of the body; also the actual directions in which the body moves in space
- Faulty sensory perception: kinesthesia or proprioception is the position–motion sensation or perception through which you detect your body's movements. Faulty sensory appreciation or "debauched kinesthesia" occurs when we don't receive accurate sensory feedback about how we're using our bodies.
- End-gaining: the habit of continually performing a movement in the same ineffectual way, even when it results in discomfort, poor coordination, or injury
- Means-whereby: the conscious thoughts and actions (means) through which (whereby) a student learns to inhibit the end-gaining and mis-use that interfere with the ability to efficiently and painlessly perform a movement

The teacher identifies and analyzes your movements, then guides you verbally, and with light and gentle touch, on how to move more efficiently, more freely, and with better coordination.

BODY-MIND CENTERING

Body-Mind Centering or BMC is a somatic practice created by Bonnie Bainbridge Cohen in the 1970s that develops a deeper awareness of how the mind and body are integrated. Body-Mind Centering calls this awareness "mindful embodiment." The practice uses imagery, breathing, touch, and movement to deepen one's understanding of the body on a "cellular" level (from cells and tissues to anatomical systems)—in other words, from the inside out.

For dancers, the practice can identify and activate a deep sense of support from a better sense of balance and health among bones, nerves, and muscles. The results are greater ease of movement, increased strength, and better flow from movement to movement, as well as a sense of harmonious integration of mind and body.

The basic principles of BMC are
- learning how the mind is central to a well-functioning body, and vice versa;
- learning how to align awareness and movement internally, externally, and through space.

Aspects of BMC
- Bodily systems (such as skin, skeletal, nerve, muscle, and endocrine): Through mindful embodiment, the dancer studies aspects of a bodily system through text and pictures; activates the tissue or organ of the system with imagery that engages the kinesthetic experience; then uses somatization or mindful movement to examine the status of the system's health and well-being.
- Developmental movement: The dancer learns the three "Rs" of movement—reflexes, righting reactions, and equilibrium responses—in order to identify identify inherent and learned movement patterns, whether they're correct or "mis-patterns." Movement and neurological patterns are interconnected, and can affect the balance of thought, physicality, and emotions. Mis-patterns cause imbalances.
- Movement re-education (or re-patterning): The dancer learns learns to integrate movement and perception, and about "vibration and resonance" in the cell,

Benefits for dancers
- More integrated warm-ups through better body-system awareness
- Improved alignment, flexibility, and strength
- Method of retraining by utilizing movement, hands-on, and perceptual awareness to reduce or treat injuries
- Integrated body-mind imagery for use in improvisation, choreography, creating movement vocabularies

tissue, or system under study, which through embodiment, movement, and touch can be retuned, re-educated, or re-patterned to a better state of balance.

• Movement expression: the transformation of mis-pattern and imbalance by allowing activated cells, tissues, and systems to move with more healthy and balanced expression through improved body–mind consciousness.

How BMC works

Body-Mind Centering is an exploratory and experiential process of re-education, through which the dancer learns how movement is supported by the body's anatomical systems. During a typical session, the therapist or instructor uses imagery, voice direction, movement, and touch to help the dancer mindfully visualize and connect with the body on a deep, cellular level. Depending on the dancer's need, the session may focus on improving posture, alleviating pain or discomfort in a specific part of the body, or re-patterning an exercise or movement to increase flow, balance, and efficiency.

Bonnie Bainbridge Cohen dancing at the Body-Mind Centering Association's annual conference in 2011.

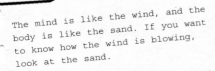

The mind is like the wind, and the body is like the sand. If you want to know how the wind is blowing, look at the sand.

Bonnie Bainbridge Cohen

IMAGE-BASED MODALITIES: IDEOKINESIS

Ideokinesis (*Ideo*=idea, *kinesis*=movement) is a modality for improving neuromuscular coordination (posture and movement) through the application of mental imagery. Originally conceived by Mabel Todd, and named Ideokinesis by Lulu Sweigard, the method uses imagery to communicate with muscles, and the involuntary and voluntary aspects of the nervous system, in order to re-coordinate or improve particular movements.

The purpose of Ideokinesis is to balance the body's neuromuscular structure on an unconscious level. Through visualization, the dancer accesses their sub-cortical system—which coordinates tiny interconnected movements too complex to be voluntarily controlled—to conjoin mind and body in working toward the same goal. Ideokinesis does not use intentional movement; it trusts the body's ability to correct itself at the unconscious level. In this way, Ideokinesis advances change with minimal effort.

To facilitate her work with mental imagery, Todd often practiced lying down in a restorative position she called "hook lying," which stabilizes the spine. Sweigard later adapted this pose and renamed it the constructive rest position (also see pages 108–109).

"THE IDEA OF IDEOKINESIS IS THAT BY IMAGINING YOUR BODY AS, FOR EXAMPLE, A BICYCLE CHAIN, YOUR SKELETAL AND MUSCULAR ALIGNMENT WILL IMPROVE AND YOUR MUSCLES AND BONES WILL WORK TOGETHER WITH GREATER EFFICIENCY. YOU WILL USE LESS EFFORT TO MOVE, AND MANY OF YOUR UNNECESSARY 'HOLDING PATTERNS,' OR PLACES OF TENSION, WILL BE GREATLY REDUCED OR EVEN ELIMINATED. THE IMAGES USED IN IDEOKINESIS CAN BE JUST ABOUT ANYTHING, AS LONG AS THEY REFLECT SCIENTIFIC KNOWLEDGE OF THE MECHANICAL WORKINGS OF THE BODY. EACH PERSON MUST FIND THOSE SPECIFIC IMAGES THAT WORK BEST FOR HIM OR HER."

Julie Grinfield from her article "The Idea of Ideokinesis: Lulu Sweigard's Concept of Imagined Movement"

The nine lines of movement

Sweigard's lines crisscross the body from the feet to the head, and bring muscles, bones, and alignment into balance around the body's central axis.

1. Front spine upward: key to proper alignment
2. Back spine downward: releases lower-back muscle tension
3. Between midfront pelvis and lower thoracic vertebra: shortens the distance between the two, lifts pelvis, releases erector spinae (back) muscles, balances torso and head
4. Top of sternum to top of spine: balances head on top of spine, lengthens spine, releases shoulder and neck muscle tension
5. Across rib cage: narrows and reduces muscle tension for improved flexibility and breathing
6. Across back of pelvis: widens to release buttock muscles, increase hip flexibility, balance pelvis on top of femurs
7. Across front of pelvis (companion to above): narrows to activate inner-thigh muscles, also balance pelvis on top of femurs
8. Center of knee to center of hip joint: release muscle tension in outer hip, balances muscles around femurs, aligns leg, gives greater control of the leg close to pelvis
9. Big toe to heel: centers body weight at the ankle joint, reduces collapse onto the foot's inner arch

André Bernard, master teacher of Ideokinesiology, practicing the technique on a student.

IMAGE-BASED MODALITIES: SKINNER RELEASING TECHNIQUE

Skinner Releasing Technique (SRT) is an approach to dance training that uses image-based floor work to stimulate unstructured improvisations that release tension and create effortless movement. SRT is based on the premise that letting go of ingrained neuromuscular patterns liberates movement to become more expressive and powerful. As with many dance techniques, SRT also focuses on increasing a dancer's alignment and flexibility, strength and speed, technical clarity and movement efficiency. The technique is taught, practiced, and influences contemporary dance artists around the world.

What to expect

In SRT classes, students are encouraged to release stress, nervousness and tension, preconceptions, habitual ways of thinking, and feelings of fear and awkwardness. This occurs through the use of guided imagery, sometimes with music, which stills the mind, ushers in a deep state of mind–body awareness, and activates the imagination. Students find inner balance by moving in various directions, rather than staying in one place. The process is gentle, experiential, and intuitive.

Part of the class is like meditation; moving in this state often produces unexpected and inventive results. The class may also include working with a partner (called a "partner graphic"), where one person works with another body to increase the receiver's awareness of alignment, patterning, release, and movement potential.

During the class, students and practitioners integrate the technical aspects of dance and movement. The intent is to increase energy, recover natural alignment, improve strength and flexibility, and inspire creativity and spontaneity.

"SKINNER RELEASING IS A DANCE TECHNIQUE THAT HAS THE SAME OBJECTIVES AS OTHER CONCERT DANCE TECHNIQUES: ALIGNMENT, FLEXIBILITY, STRENGTH, SPEED, DYNAMIC RANGE, MUSICALITY, AND CONTROL OF NUANCE. THIS TECHNIQUE, HOWEVER, IS A SYSTEM OF KINESTHETIC TRAINING THAT REFINES THE PERCEPTION AND PERFORMANCE OF MOVEMENT. IMAGES ARE GIVEN WHICH ARE METAPHORS OF KINESTHETIC EXPERIENCE OF TECHNICAL PRINCIPLES. THE POETIC IMAGERY KINDLES THE IMAGINATION, THEREBY INTEGRATING TECHNIQUE WITH CREATIVE PROCESS."

Joan Skinner

About Joan Skinner

In the 1950s, while dancing with Merce Cunningham's and Martha Graham's dance companies in New York, Joan Skinner ruptured a spinal disc. She began practicing the Alexander Technique to correct and heal her injury. When the University of Illinois invited her to teach modern dance, she began exploring new ways of conveying imagery in the classroom. She asked her students to imagine being suspended by marionette strings, but they seemingly forgot about the image as they moved in space. So she put them on the floor with the image. They became so involved in the visualization and the sensations it produced that Skinner realized imagery was a powerful way of generating a profound kinesthetic experience and expressive movement. Integrating her teaching experiences, dance training, understanding of the Alexander Technique, childhood experiences of interpretive dance, dance improvisation, and her own experiments with movement visualization, she created the Skinner Releasing Technique.

"The marionette strings: This helps me be in touch with my body and makes me realize the structure of my body, and the interaction and connection between my head and tail. This inspires me as I can feel my body and I can really imagine my head and body being pulled up, this restricts my movement, making my movement more interesting as I can imagine the strings pulling on my body. Whilst the strings are pulling me from beneath this allows me to connect to surfaces and the floor."

Excerpted from dancernikki9.blogspot.com (written by a student at Coventry University)

Joan Skinner (below) realized that visualization could help release dancers from habitual movement patterns.

7
CHOREOGRAPHY, EXPRESSION, ARTISTRY

The word *choreography* is French (*chorégraphie*), derived from the Greek words *khoreia*, meaning "to dance," and *graphein*, which translates as "to write." The word *choreographer*, then, actually means one who writes with dance. The choreographer's lexicon isn't words, but rather movements. Hence the common use of the phrase *movement vocabulary* to describe the distinctive style, technique, movements, phrasing, shapes, and compositional strategies that characterize a choreographer's work. This chapter introduces aspects of the choreographic process, the creative work through which a dancer learns, practices, and executes a dance piece. From the point at which a dancer begins working with a choreographer on a piece or routine, the dancer must also regularly practice what they've learned, discover how to express the choreographer's intention, and aspire to achieve a level of artistry that distinguishes their dancing. "Good choreography fuses eye, ear and mind," wrote dance critic Arlene Croce. The dancer transforms such coalescences into art.

THE CHOREOGRAPHER

When creating an original dance or routine, the choreographer generates the movement material alone or in collaboration with the dancers. The material ranges from steps, combinations, and sequences to creating a structure for the dance. Choreographers may audition dancers, especially if they have specific characters, a movement style, or an overall attitude in mind for the work.

Choreographers setting an existing work on a company may have video of past or original performances they can refer to and study with the dancers. Folk, African, South Indian, and Polynesian choreographers restaging or creating new interpretations of traditional works may provide dancers with archival images of the original dances for inspiration.

Most of the time, because few dances are written down or notated (as with Labanotation, see page 100), choreographers instruct performers both verbally and through demonstration on what to do and how to do it. The choreographer may work with any number of performers, from a solo dancer to the entire company. As the work progresses, the choreographer spends more time editing and refining sequences, and having the dancers practice sections of the work to perfection.

A work may take weeks or months to complete, as the choreographer continues to rehearse, rearrange, edit, change, and even generate new material. Choreographers also choose the costumes, work with the lighting designer, name or title the dance piece, and select a composer to write the music or select/create the music/sound score.

Choreographers need to …

- be creative, inventive, and innovative;
- be resourceful, open minded, and problem solvers;
- be observant and perceptive;
- have the flexibility, technique, and stamina to demonstrate steps and moves;
- have patience and perseverance;
- have good communication skills;
- exhibit a sense of humor;
- work outside of or disregard stereotypes;
- motivate and encourage;
- critically evaluate and edit their work;
- remain calm under pressure;
- have self-discipline;
- have a take-charge attitude.

Where and for whom choreographers work

- On staff or under contract with dance companies as a choreographer-in-residence
- On staff or under contract at theater and musical-theater companies as a choreographer and/or movement coach for actors
- As a guest artist creating choreography for an opera company
- As the artistic director and choreographer of their own dance company
- As a commissioned choreographer hired to create a new work for a dance company
- As a guest choreographer making a new work or setting/staging a previously choreographed work for a group of dance students at a college or university
- As a dance studio choreographer who creates and teaches routines for student competitions

A choreographer should work closely with the dancers to enable them to fulfill his or her vision.

- As a freelance specialist who choreographs routines for ice skaters, cheerleaders, synchronized swimmers, gymnasts
- As a freelance choreographer hired for such special events as a festival or fashion show, and/or to choreograph singers and dancers for music videos or live concerts, dancers for television shows and/or reality-television competitions, or martial-arts sequences for movies

"The choreographer cannot deliberately make a ballet to appeal to an audience; he has to start from personal inspirations. He has to trust the ballet, to let it stand on its own strengths or fall on its weaknesses. If it reaches the audience, then he is lucky that round!"
Gerald Arpino, dancer, choreographer, and artistic director and cofounder of the Joffrey Ballet

CHOREOGRAPHIC APPROACHES

Choreographers are hired to create a new dance work, competition routine, or movement sequence for a stage show, or task themselves with creating a new work for their companies.

The choreographer often starts by
1) finding a source of inspiration, such as
- a piece of music, song, or sound score;
- a story, poem, or myth;
- an event (familial, political, historical, cultural);
- a building or site, and its history (architectural, historical, cultural);
- an emotion, feeling, or mood;
- a situation or relationship;
- an idea, thought, or concept;
- a particular dancer or dance company;
- exploring the kinetic potential of a movement idea;
- nature, natural systems, and the environment;
- during improvisation, either alone or with other dancers; and
2) deciding on a goal or intention to
- communicate an idea;
- interpret another art form/object through dance;
- express a feeling, concern, or concept;
- celebrate an occasion;
- explore ways the body can move;
- win a competition;
- showcase a particular dancer;
- tell a story; and
- entertain.

Choreographic inspiration can come from any source—from a pivotal historical event to a fleeting emotion. The image above shows *After Eden* by the Heidi Duckler Dance Theater.

"WE COME PRETTY OPEN AND SPEND TIME WORKING IN A PLACE AND LIVING IN A PARTICULAR ENVIRONMENT OVER A NUMBER OF DAYS OR WEEKS, AND BUILD UP A RELATIONSHIP TO THAT PLACE WHILE CREATING MATERIAL AND IMAGERY AND COLLECTING SOUNDS. IT'S ALL DONE LARGELY FROM A BODY-MIND CENTERING PERSPECTIVE AND OTHER IMPROVISATIONAL PRACTICES."

Site choreographers Olive Bieringa and Otto Ramstad, cofounders of the BodyCartography Project

In creating *Subversions*, which occurred inside an abandoned subway station, the choreographer and dancers collaborated on finding innovative ways to use props and movement to convey the meanings behind the work.

Before entering the studio

Before entering the studio to meet and work with the dancers, choreographers may spend time researching their ideas and developing their intention. If a dancer is choreographing to a specific piece of music or score, they'll listen to, study, and notate its melody, rhythm, structure, and phrasing. If they're creating a folk, Spanish, Mexican, or southern Indian dance, they travel to research the dance form and its practitioners, traditions, music, and costumes. Site-based choreographers often spend time exploring the site or building, talking to people there, and improvising.

"I PRAY FOR WHAT THE BUDDHISTS CALL THAT 'DON'T KNOW MIND.' I TRY NOT TO KNOW WHAT THE PIECE WILL BE. I CAN START WITH AN IDEA AND I'LL STUDY FOR YEARS ACTUALLY TO THINK ABOUT SOMETHING, BUT WHEN I GO INTO THE STUDIO I WANT TO BE ABLE TO SEE WHAT IS IN FRONT OF ME, I WANT TO NOT HAVE ANOTHER IDEA.... I TRY TO DEVISE METHODOLOGIES THAT ARE COMMENSURATE WITH THE PROJECT. THE PROJECT USUALLY HAS SOME FORM AS AN IDEA, BUT THOSE IDEAS HAVE TO BECOME METHODOLOGIES, AND I HAVE TO LOOK AT WHAT THE RESULTS ARE, I HAVE TO LOOK AT DANCERS, AND THAT I THINK IS THE BIGGEST CHALLENGE, IS NOT SEEING WHAT I WANT TO SEE BUT SEEING WHAT'S ACTUALLY IN FRONT OF MY EYES."

Dancer and choreographer William Forsythe, former artistic director of Ballett Frankfurt and artistic director of The Forsythe Company

CHOREOGRAPHIC COMPOSITION

Choreographic or dance composition is the process of translating inspirations, research, and goals into physical expression and meaning. Choreographers generate steps and movements; connect these building blocks together via transitions to create phrases, sequences, and sections; then edit and arrange these components into a dance work. While composing a dance, choreographers are concerned with compositional elements, themes or motifs, form, structure, number of dancers, and the technique used.

Compositional elements

- Shape: whether movements are symmetrical on each side of the body or asymmetrical; scale (small as in folded or contracted, large as in big, open, or extended); direction of the shape or movement
- Space: paths and patterns (geometric, spirals, clockwise or counterclockwise, vertical or horizontal, changes in direction, lines or rows); placement of dancers and groups on stage; the level at which a movement is performed
- Timing: speed or tempo; meter or rhythm; counterpoint and syncopation
- Dynamics: type of energy; amount of effort; quality or style; stillness; dancers' focus (inward, forward, backward, toward another dancer)

(Also see Elements of Dance in Chapter 2.)

One choreographic or compositional strategy choreographers use is having part of the dance company perform movements as a unified group, as the corps de ballet does.

Creating themes or motifs

- By combining compositional elements
- By variegating combinations by altering direction, level, size, focus, plane, pattern, or tempo
- By breaking up and remixing phrases
- By reversing the order of movements in the motif

Compositional forms

- ABA: the opening choreographic theme transitions to a different yet corresponding theme, then returns to the opening theme
- Rondo or ABACADA: expands on ABA by using a recurring theme interspersed with contrasting themes, which converge at the conclusion
- Theme and variation, or A, A1, A2, etc.: a key movement theme or motif is presented, and then altered in diverse ways (via tempo or mood, quality or style, number of dancers)
- Round: a sequence is repeated as dancers join in on different counts, at different levels, or in varied directions
- Chance: the order of movement sequences or sections is determined by a toss of the dice or I-Ching.

Methods for creating structure

- Defining beginning, middle, and end
- Adhering to number sequences or time constraints
- Adopting the rules of adult or children's games or sports
- Using collage, cutups, lists

Number of dancers

- Soloists (focus of dance)
- Duets, trios, quartets, quintets (arranged throughout a space to create multiple points of interest)
- Full company (unison choreography or scattered for diverse points of interest)
- Corps de ballet (frames soloists or small groups)

Technique to be used

- Adhering to a specific codified technique, whether Cecchetti ballet, Graham modern, Giordano jazz, or Kathak
- Creating a movement vocabulary for a specific dance work and teaching/communicating it to the dancers
- Melding several styles, such as modern, African, and ballet
- Avoiding technique for a focus on everyday, nonvirtuosic movement

"I use dancing to embellish, extend or enlarge upon an existing emotion."
Gower Champion, dancer and choreographer for Broadway and film

WORKING WITH A CHOREOGRAPHER

When a choreographer enters the studio, ready to create a dance on an individual or group of dancers, you'll use all of your training and artistry to manifest the choreographer's creative vision. They often experiment as they choreograph, and convey their movement ideas through verbal description, by demonstrating what they want, and/or by asking you to improvise and then providing feedback.

Whether the dance you're learning is for the stage, a site, the video or television screen, or a competition, practice and dedication are necessary to fully realize a choreographer's intent. Whereas dancers spend years developing their technique and movement abilities, most choreographers need decades to explore, define, and refine their choreographic purpose.

Some choreographers create works that are strong, bold, and abstract, which may suggest a keen intelligence. Others make dances that are light, soft, and lyrical to evoke such qualities as romance or harmony. Most choreographers have refined their physicality and artistic vision into a distinctive movement aesthetic, which becomes a starting point in their choreographic approach. Dancers and choreographers, working together, make such artistic ambitions a physical reality.

The choreographic process

1. Gathering movement material.
2. Developing the movements into phrases and building the phrases into sections.
3. Refining phrases and sections through revision.
4. Generating the work's final structure.

Generally, choreographers work with dancers in one of three ways:

1. **Setting an existing dance.** The choreographer teaches the dancers a work that's already been choreographed. The dancers are asked to perform the work as it was created, with the same movement qualities and expression as the original.
2. **Give and take.** The choreographer is setting an existing piece on the dancers, but asks for their individual input and unique perspectives on the material.
3. **Improvisation.** The choreographer gives the dancers an idea or image and asks them to generate the movement material, which the choreographer then edits and arranges into phrases and sections.

"The choreographic process happens on one's feet after hours of work, and the energy required is roughly the equivalent of writing a novel and winning a tennis match simultaneously."
Agnes de Mille, choreographer

PROFESSIONAL DOS AND DON'TS WHEN WORKING WITH A CHOREOGRAPHER

- **Don't** start cold. Arrive 20 minutes before class or rehearsal to warm up sufficiently.
- **Don't** come ill-prepared. Know when you'll be learning new choreography, and ready your mind and body so you're open to the learning process.
- **Do** come with a clear understanding of your learning processes. Know how you take in and process new information, so you can quickly learn new steps and combinations.
- **Don't** let yourself be distracted by other dancers, people entering or leaving the studio, or outside noises.
- **Do** ask the choreographer questions if allowed; otherwise wait until after class or rehearsal.
- **Do** watch the choreographer closely as they demonstrate the steps. Don't try the steps yourself until the choreographer is finished demonstrating.
- **Don't** watch yourself in the mirror. Work out the steps or phrasing away from the mirrors, to focus on what your body is doing rather than what it looks like.
- **Do** be patient with yourself.
- **Do** keep up with your technique. After class or rehearsal, practice honing and perfecting your technical skills, and any particular steps or phrases in the new dance that are difficult.

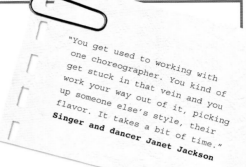

"You get used to working with one choreographer. You kind of get stuck in that vein and you work your way out of it, picking up someone else's style, their flavor. It takes a bit of time."

Singer and dancer Janet Jackson

Singer Janet Jackson has hired various choreographers to help her devise routines that provide a kinetic element to her performances onstage.

LEARNING CHOREOGRAPHY

Whether you're learning a new combination from your dance instructor during class, or are developing and practicing dance material with a choreographer in anticipation of a finished piece, you'll need to quickly understand, learn, and retain the choreography. Choreography depends on the dancer's unique ability to memorize and recall movement, and dancers use their artistry, intelligence, and "muscle memory" (embedding choreography into your body's muscles through repetition) to do so. Dancers need to engage the mind, the neuromuscular system, and memory to accurately perform a routine, and different techniques work for different dancers. Here are some suggestions for learning, recalling, and performing choreography.

Dance map

While the choreographer is demonstrating, mentally note the lines, shapes, levels, speed, and direction of the movement. Draw a mental map of the choreography, adding movement sensation as you practice the sequence. After class, draw a physical map of the combination on a piece of paper. Along pathways that outline direction, use symbols, numbers, or colors to designate such specifics as step, level, speed, body part, type of motion, spacing, and placement of other dancers. (Don't forget to make a key.) Practice the sequence with the map, marking the places you experience difficulties. Alter the map if your body remembers a movement quality your mind doesn't.

Correction is an essential part of the learning process. Don't be disheartened when an instructor provides you with a correction; instead, see it as an opportunity to improve.

Words

Some dancers use the names of steps and movements to remember them in combination. Others title sequences or sections with words that serves as cues, such as *twisty combination, group unison*, or *flowing trio with abrupt ending*. Another strategy for remembering choreography is to keep a notebook or journal in which you write down word associations for various sections of a dance. The journal strategy and the dance map are excellent tools for rehearsing choreography while using performance visualization techniques (also see pages 136–137).

Music

If the routine is choreographed to music, use such musical cues as rhythm, key changes, tempo, lyrics, verses and chorus, structure, and pauses to help remember movements. By linking a step or turn to a point in the music, you can anchor a whole sequence in your memory. Note: In many competition routines, the same sequence occurs every time the chorus is played.

Chunking

Chunking is a term used to describe the process by which an individual, when memorizing material, groups it together into chunks for better recall. Dancers start with separate, individual chunks of choreography, and gradually assemble them into a whole structure.

Dancers chunk differently. Some can assimilate short sequences, others longer combinations. Some use musical beats or mental counts to anchor chunks. Others use spatial configurations, stage location, or a physical position as cues. Musical verses and rhythms can trigger chunks.

ACCEPTING CORRECTIONS

Hearing, accepting, and incorporating corrections is an integral part of a dancer's training. Instructors and choreographers consider giving corrections part of their job description, as only by being shown how to improve can a dancer progress. Whether you're receiving constructive feedback from a dance teacher in class or a choreographer during rehearsal, applying corrections will enhance your technique and performance.

To make the most of corrections,

- acknowledge and incorporate the correction, even if you're not in the mood;
- respond positively to receive more constructive feedback;
- don't be offended by corrections; they're a part of the learning process;
- pay attention to the feedback given to others, and incorporate those corrections into your own work;
- learn to want constructive feedback;
- seek out corrections or feedback on your dancing from other teachers.

DANCE EXPRESSION

Expression is an aspect of dance that can be challenging to define, teach, and critique. Dancers' individual expressive qualities can take years to develop, until they've reached a level of performance artistry that distinguishes them from other dancers.

Expression in dance is subjective; what dancers feel they're expressing can be read or interpreted differently by people in the audience. Even in Indian dance, where movements and their associated emotions are codified, one dancer's performance will vary from another's in terms of expressive nuance and artistry. Whether abstract or emotional; an interpretation of music, literature, art, or place; a reflection of memory; the celebration of a culture; or purely entertainment—expression in dance can mean different things to different teachers, choreographers, dancers, and audience members.

When learning choreography, keep in mind that the steps, phrasing, and combinations—the building blocks of the dance—are already forms of expression. The choreographer has sequenced the movements in order to communicate an emotion or meaning, and will add movement qualities to further enhance the effect they're attempting to create. The ways in which the choreographer directs those movement sequences, using pathways, speed, level, groupings in space, and such qualities as soft or sharp, fluid or abrupt, compressed or expansive, flat or pointed are intended as means of expression. The direction in which the choreographer asks you to glance or focus, as well as the expression or body posture they suggest, are also expressive indicators.

Techniques for expression

In his book *Dance Imagery for Technique and Performance*, Eric Franklin suggests these strategies for developing your capacity for expression:

- "Endowment": Franklin defines this strategy as "the ability to take an object and transform it." In other words, endow an object, prop, or body part with enlivening, animating, or alchemical

"ALL DANCE HAS EXPRESSION. IF THERE IS NO EXPRESSION, I PREFER THE CIRCUS. THE PERFORMERS DO MORE DANGEROUS, MORE DIFFICULT TECHNICAL THINGS THAN WE DO. BUT WE ARE DANCERS. WE HAVE TO EXPRESS AND WE HAVE TO PROJECT."

Luis Fuente, principal dancer with the Joffrey Ballet, Holland's Het Nationale Ballet, Ballet Clasico y Contemporaneo de Madrid, and other companies

Movements and their associated emotions are largely codified in Indian dance. Still, dancers vary widely in their expressive nuance and artistry.

- "With or Without the Audience": How are you communicating with the audience? Has the choreographer directed you to ignore them, play to them, converse with them, confront them, entertain them, tell them a humorous or horrific story?
- "Your History": Create a backstory for yourself to deepen and broaden your expressiveness as a dancer; also an excellent strategy for developing a character.

qualities, to make it something other and more extraordinary than what it actually is.

- "The Magical Outfit": While in rehearsal and before donning your actual costume for a performance, imagine yourself in clothing, shoes, hats, and other accoutrements you've selected to enhance the expressive qualities of your dancing.
- "The Performance Environment": Create imaginary scenery, curtains, and scrims, or sets for the dance you're rehearsing. Let this fantasy stage inspire your dancing; use your senses to transform the fantasy into a real environment alive with smells, sounds, and images.

EXPRESSION IN INDIAN DANCE

Indian dance, such as Bharatanatyam, is profoundly and poetically expressive. The center of choreographic expression is the dancer's face, specifically the eyes, from which emotion originates; the rest of the body enhances and emphasizes the emotion conjured on the face.

According to the *Natya Shastra*, the ancient Indian treatise on dance, music, and dramatic arts, *rasa* is an emotion, mood, or expression inspired in audience members by a performer. The *Navarasa* (*Nava* = "nine") in the dance scriptures refer to the nine basic human expressions: love (*shringaara*), laughter (*haasya*), compassion (*karuna*), anger (*roudra*), courage (*veera*), fear (*bhayaanaka*), disgust (*bheebhatsa*), wonder or surprise (*adbhutha*), and peace or tranquility (*shaantha*). The rasas are communicated through *bhavas*, the gestures and facial expressions of the dancers or actors.

> Learning to walk sets you free. Learning to dance gives you the greatest freedom of all: to express with your whole self the person you are.
>
> Melissa Hayden

DANCE ARTISTRY

For dancers, the skills needed to become an artist include not only virtuosic technique, interpretive sensibility, mind–body intelligence, musicality, expressiveness, and flawless performance, but also creativity. Dance artistry is the process through which dancers synthesize their abilities in order to assimilate the choreographic work—and transcend it in performance.

Sometimes, dance artistry is referred to as "soul," or expressing the deity within. A dancer's artistry is always an expression of their creativity; their ability to transform their abilities into a wholly original work of art. Artistry comes more naturally to some dancers than others. Still, the desire to strive for, cultivate, and create artistry is an integral part of being a dancer.

Tips for cultivating dance artistry

- Attend as many professional performances as possible. Study the soloists, principals, and other dancers whose unique artistry catches your eye. What are they doing to create such artistry? Why is their dancing particularly dazzling? How have they gone behind dancing to performing with artistry?
- Engage your own possibilities for artistry. Having learned to dance a movement phrase with an expressive quality, refine the phrase to the point where you stop thinking about it and dance with self-confidence, experiencing the pure joy of dancing.
- Explore your creativity. During private practice, experiment with dancing a few steps or a longer combination with different emotions, movement qualities, or ideas in mind.

During a performance, many dancers experience a sense of total and transcendent immersion in what they're doing, a sensation Mihály Csíkszentmihályi has popularized as "flow."

Csíkszentmihályi's "flow"

When someone becomes completely absorbed in their creative task, to the point of transcendent immersion, they're in "flow." Proposed by Mihály Csíkszentmihályi, a Hungarian psychology professor who immigrated to the United States and headed the department of psychology at the University of Chicago, flow is a mental state during which energy, focus, body, mind, and emotions are aligned in the complete involvement and successful outcome of the task at hand. A signature of flow is experiencing a sense of rapture.

According to Csíkszentmihályi, these characteristics may accompany flow:

- Clear goals for accomplishing the challenge (levels of ability and difficulty are balanced and achievable)
- Pure concentration or singular focus (action and awareness merge)
- Loss of self-consciousness
- Altered or "lost" sense of time
- Sense of personal control over the task
- Sense of effortlessness
- Lack of awareness of bodily needs (such as pain, fatigue, or hunger)

"CREATIVITY IS A PRIVATE AFFAIR. IT IS THE PROCESS OF RUMMAGING THROUGH AND PENETRATING THE INTIMATE WORLD OF ACCUMULATED MEMORIES, THOUGHTS, AND SENSATIONS DOWN TO THE VERY NATURE OF BEING. IF THE PROCESS OF CREATING DOES NOT BEGIN AT THE SOURCE, IT STANDS THE DANGER OF BECOMING A SURFACE EXPERIENCE RESULTING IN A SUPERFICIAL DISPLAY."

Murray Louis, dancer, choreographer, and cofounder of the Murray Louis Dance Company, from the foreword to *Moving from Within: A New Method of Dance Making* by Alma M. Hawkins

ACTING FOR THE DANCER

One way in which dancers deepen and broaden their capacity for expression, and develop their artistry, is by studying acting. Learning how to better connect with and express ideas, emotion, and choreographic intention is just one benefit of acting classes. Acting also teaches dancers how to infuse a role with character, create and embody a character, and project to an audience. In addition, learning how to act makes dancers more versatile and well-rounded performers.

Acting exercises include the following:

• Mirroring or reflecting a partner's movement, to develop and deepen relationship skills while dancing

• Differentiating between "indicating" (pretending, emotionalizing, or playing at an emotion), and actually embodying and conveying an emotion

• Working without mirrors, to access internal motivations rather than simply "wearing" an emotion or idea

• Reading texts aloud to develop vocal techniques and intonation

• Using breath and space to develop dramatic tension

• Developing intention and motivation

• Improvisation to explore creativity and spontaneity

• Experimenting with specific techniques, such as the "magic if" technique pioneered by Russian director Constantin Stanislavski's (and advocated by Lee Strasberg as part of method acting), through which actors ask themselves, "What if this situation happened to me?" in order to identify with and think like the character, rather than impersonating them.

SINGING FOR DANCERS:
THERE'S AN APP FOR THAT

Dance is a largely silent art form, in which the body does the talking. But more dancers, whether performing in multidisciplinary postmodern work, dance-theater, or musical theater, are integrating not only acting but also singing lessons into their schedules. Liz Caplan, New York vocal coach and founder of Liz Caplan Vocal Studios LLC, has also created an iPhone and iPod app specifically for dancers. Innovated and launched in collaboration with *Dance Spirit*, the "Singing for Dancers" app includes Caplan's own exercises and videos, which range from warm-ups that combine movement and song, to beginning voice lessons.

"IN ANY KIND OF PERFORMANCE, I'M ALWAYS LOOKING FOR MORE THAN JUST STEPS. YOU CAN HAVE ALL THE TECHNIQUE IN THE WORLD, BUT IF YOU'RE JUST A ROBOT AND YOU AREN'T CONNECTING WITH THE REASONS OR THE EMOTIONS OF THE PIECE, THEN YOU'RE REALLY NOT CONNECTING WITH YOUR AUDIENCE. IT'S ALL ABOUT STORYTELLING AND COMMUNICATING WITH YOUR AUDIENCE … THE BRIDGE BETWEEN THE DANCE AND THE AUDIENCE IS THE ACTING. AND IF IT TRULY COMES FROM YOUR SOUL, LIKE THE BEST ACTORS IN THE WORLD, THEN YOUR AUDIENCE WILL FEEL WHAT YOU FEEL."

Charles "Chucky" Klapow, choreographer for several versions of *High School Musical*, television commercials, music videos for Ashley Tisdale and Vanessa Hudgens, as quoted in an article in backstage.com

Dancers interested in musical theater also need to cultivate their technique and artistry in singing and acting.

Where to find acting classes

- Dance studios
- Performing arts schools and conservatories
- College and university dance and theater programs
- Local theaters
- Community education programs
- Dance centers
- Film schools
- Summer arts camps, intensives, or workshops
- Acting schools

8
THE PERFORMANCE

Modern-dance icon Paul Taylor, artistic director of the Paul Taylor Dance Company, once said, "For a dancer, to be able to perform well, most of his waking hours must be devoted to preparing for the holy white instant of performance." When the audience has taken its seats and the lights fade to black, the dancers poised in the wings or ready on stage are well aware of the intense preparation that has gone into that moment just before the curtain rises—and all the moments that follow. The first stage picture that audiences see, with sound, lights, décor, and costumed dancers coordinated as planned, is one eagerly anticipated by the dance company and its audience alike. This chapter surveys the artistic staff and collaborators also working toward that moment, from the roles of the dance company administration and theater staff in organizing and producing a performance, to the last onstage rehearsals before opening night, as well as post-performance realities such as receptions and audience discussions, and what to expect from the dance critic.

WHO'S WHO? THE DANCE COMPANY

Within a dance company (or troupe), not only does a group of dancers work with a choreographer or choreographers, but the dancers and dance makers are also responsible to the group's artistic director—who may be its founder and/or choreographer too.

In smaller companies, individuals may assume a variety of responsibilities. In addition to dancers, the dance-company personnel include the following:

- Artistic director: He or she establishes the company's aesthetic, and oversees all of its artistic aspects, including performances and productions. The artistic director also hires other staff, decides the repertory, programs the season, and oversees the business of running the dance company.
- Managing director (general manager): an arts administrator who supports the artistic director, directs the company's administrative staff, manages its business and financial activities, and reports to the board of directors.
- Choreographer: may be the artistic director, the choreographer-in-residence, or commissioned to create a new or reset an existing work; specifies music or sound scores for their works, and collaborates on costumes, lighting, and décor.
- Apprentice/intern: young or pre-professional dancers who learn new choreography and rehearse with the company as understudies.
- Dancer representative: a company member, usually one with seniority, who acts as a liaison between the dancers, company administration, and the board of directors, representing the dancers' point of view.
- Rehearsal director/ballet master or mistress: usually a former company member, or a dancer familiar with a specific choreographer's work; schedules and directs rehearsals, and provides notes and corrections after.
- Accompanist/rehearsal musician: usually accompanies the dancers on piano, but could be, for example, a cellist or drummer.

Other creative roles

- Dance captain: Dance groups in musical-theater productions, and competitive dance teams, often have a dance captain. An experienced or senior dancer in the group, the dance captain coaches other dancers, directs rehearsals, substitutes for injured dancers, and provides corrections after rehearsals and performances.
- Composer: Sometimes choreographers or artistic directors will have the funds to commission a composer to write a musical score specifically for a new dance.

The number of performers in a dance company or dance squad can vary from 2 to 52 (for large ballet companies).

- Conductor: Large ballet companies, and smaller companies dedicated to performing with live music, have a conductor who directs the orchestra or other musical group. The conductor may consult with the choreographer or artistic director while arranging the music.
- Choreologist: Trained in a method such as Labanotation, the choreologist notates and documents a finished piece of choreography.
- Repetiteur: Considered an expert on a specific choreographer's work, the repetiteur may travel from one company to another, setting or remounting authorized works. They may teach or set the work on behalf of the choreographer, functioning as a rehearsal director as well.

THE DANCE TEAM OR DANCE SQUAD

In contrast to the dance company, the dance team or squad is a sports group that performs on the competitive-dance circuit, and sometimes during pre-game and halftime sporting events. The routines may incorporate elements of hip-hop, jazz, or lyrical dance choreography, as well as gymnastics, synchronized motions, and group formations. Such groups exist in youth associations, middle and high schools, colleges, and as professional teams. They may participate in local, regional, state, and national, as well as international competitions. Staff leading the dance team may include a head coach, and one or two co-captains, who audition performers and lead the group, create and rehearse choreography, plan and produce performances, and schedule competitions.

The ballet company hierarchy and its titles can vary according to the company, but the corps de ballet is traditionally where new dancers begin their careers. Along with the stature associated with a company promotion come increases in salary.

- Prima ballerina: a female dancer with extensive experience, technical prowess, and signature artistry; performs the repertory's lead roles, and is partnered by and performs pas de deux with the danseur noble.
- Danseur noble: the male equivalent of the prima ballerina, whom he partners; also performs the lead male roles.
- Principal dancer: performs starring and leading roles, and may dance with other companies as a guest artist.
- First soloist: performs a particular solo in the repertory, part of the first cast and may function as a principal's understudy.
- Second soloist: performs solos, duets, and trios as part of the second cast.
- Coryphees (first artists, junior soloists): members of the corps of ballet who have achieved a higher rank.
- Corps de ballet: the supporting ensemble; may perform in unison as backdrop for a principal dancer, or perform such background roles as party guests, swans, or fairies.
- Character artists/dancers: respected senior members of a company who fulfill roles that require more acting than dancing.

Who's who? Dance company administration

From ensuring financial liquidity and paying dancers, to securing bookings for tours, to managing day-to-day operations, large dance companies (and many medium to small troupes) wouldn't survive without enthusiastic and professional support. Members of a dance company's administration are often helped themselves by volunteers, dance patrons, and company supporters. The administrative staff is also key to the planning and production of a dance concert. In coordination with the artistic director and managing (or executive) director, administrative staff assist with securing venues for performances, producing and signing contracts, and issuing technical riders that specify performance needs and dressing room requirements, and ensure the safety and well-being of the dancers.

Administration also oversees financials and fund raising (or development); touring and booking; the design and printing of publicity materials for the performance; the writing, design, and printing of the performance program; media contacts and requests; coordination of costumes, sets, and props; and equipment rental.

In small companies, the managing director will handle many of these tasks. In larger companies, other staff fulfill these needs and report to the managing director. Some of these positions are as follows:

Administrative staff are crucial to the smooth running of any dance company.

- Business manager: responsible for the company's finances (including documenting fund raising/donations, accounts payable and receivable, payroll, bank deposits); reports to the managing and/or artistic director and the auditor
- Scheduler: negotiates and coordinates class and rehearsal schedules, and studio and stage space, for dancers, choreographers, rehearsal directors and repetiteurs, and accompanists (as well as production and technical crew, costumers, and set designers)
- Development director: initiates and oversees fund raising; researches and writes grants; cultivates and nurtures corporate and individual donors; secures donor commitments and contributions; creates and directs fund-raising events; creates and oversees direct-mail campaigns; manages donor database
- Marketing director: oversees and coordinates public image and perception of the dance company; brands the organization with graphic identity; creates strategic marketing plans; institutes policies for technology-based or social-media marketing; designs and implements web site; designs, issues, tallies, and reports on audience surveys; books advertisements in broadcast and print media; creates and distributes posters, postcards, flyers
- Public relations/media relations/ communications director: publicizes and promotes a show, concert, or tour by communicating and establishing relationships with journalists/critics in print, broadcast, and social media; creates and distributes press kits, media releases, touring brochures, photos; sets up photo shoots; answers and fulfills media requests; liaises with artistic and managing director on media requests; documents reviews and other press; reserves complimentary tickets for media
- Tour manager/representative: books, organizes, and schedules touring dates for the company; reserves accommodation and transport; confirms

signing of performance contracts and technical riders; liaises between company and presenter/producer

- Company manager: travels with a touring dance company to ensure dancer safety and well-being, maintains everyday travel schedules and arrangements, oversees performances, collects payment for performances
- Archivist: assembles, records, preserves and stores dance company programs, press, marketing materials, photography, and video

On the road

Around the world, various festivals, centers, and theaters have a dance series, season, or component led by a presenter or curator. This person travels internationally to see new and established companies and dance works, cultivate relationships with artistic directors and choreographers, and gather information for programming or curating upcoming seasons in their venue.

The presenter or curator plans seasons several years in advance. They invite companies that fulfill the festival, center, or venue's mission and will appeal to their audiences, donors, and patrons. A season or series may have a theme, or focus on a particular genre or style of work. The presenter or curator may also commission a new work from a company (often in collaboration with other similar venues around the country), which they then co-present.

THE BOARD OF DIRECTORS

All nonprofit dance companies are required to have a volunteer board of directors. The members of the board of directors are executives from the business, legal, financial, communications, and creative communities, who bring their knowledge, expertise, resources, and community connections to the dance company to ensure its stability, vitality, and growth.

The board is responsible for the company's governance, management, and ethics, and its legal, business, and fiscal practices. The board instigates, oversees, and manages the company's long- and short-term strategic planning. In some cases, the board has the power to hire, fire, and advance members of the artistic and administrative staff— including the artistic director, managing director, and dancers.

Individual board members may also lead committees in charge of fund raising or development, event planning, and marketing and public relations. In addition to a board of directors, some dance companies also have advisory committees of high-profile dancers, choreographers, artists, and executives who lend their professional expertise and advice to the company.

ARTISTIC COLLABORATORS: LIGHTING, COSTUMES, DÉCOR

Costume design

The costume designer works with the choreographer and artistic director to clothe the dancer in a costume that enhances both the dancer's body, and the choreographer's ideas or concepts about the work. The costume can also transform the dancer, by putting their mind, body, and emotions more deeply or comfortably into the mood or tone, character, or personality of the work. Accessories such as hair, shoes, earrings, or shawls are also part of the dancer's costume, as is makeup. Costumes vary depending on the genre of dance. In such styles as African dance, Bharatanatyam, Kathak, and many European folk dances, the traditional (or historic) costumes are decorative and colorful, and may include ankle bells, wrist bangles, headdresses, and props such as swords or drums. In contrast, the traditional costume of the classical ballet dancer is tutu, tiara, tights, and pointe shoes for the women; tights, snug tunics or jackets, and ballet slippers for the men. In traditional Butoh, conversely, the costume may simply be rice powder patted over the entire body.

Whereas modern-dance pioneer Isadora Duncan wore loose Grecian-style tunics to dance in, Martha Graham wore tight fabrics and long snug dresses that displayed the body (and even enveloped it, as in *Lamentation*). Merce Cunningham and his dancers usually wore full-body leotards. But modern, postmodern, and dance-theater performer dancers today wear everything from street, used or vintage, and new ready-made clothes to especially designed costumes to nothing at all.

Although most modern and postmodern dancers perform in bare feet, dancers in the worlds of hip-hop, ballroom, flamenco, jazz, and lyrical wear special shoes designed for

Stage costumes can be simple or highly elaborate, such as the Lebanese pants, tunics and headdresses worn by these Ethnic Dance Theatre performers.

Costumes, lighting, and sets are all a part of a dance work's "décor" (as Merce Cunningham put it), and are designed by professionals to manifest and enhance particular aspects of a performance.

their dance form, as well as specially designed clothing for their performances. Whoever is designing or assembling dance costumes needs to remember the following:

- the costume should relate to and enhance the overall tone, concept, or personality of the dance.
- the dancer needs to move in the costume; the clothing should not restrict, hamper, or endanger their movements (unless that's the intention), but should accentuate the dancer's shape and motion.
- the costume should enhance the overall design of the dance work, by adding color, texture, pattern, and/or motion.
- the costume should be easy to put on and take off.

Large dance companies usually have their own in-house wardrobe department, with a costume designer, sewer (sews, alters, repairs, and otherwise maintains the costumes), milliner (hat and headdress maker), and shoe coordinator (finds, buys, fits, stores, and maintains dancers' footwear). In smaller companies, the artistic director may take on some of the costume responsibilities, or commission a costume designer to create, fit, and sew the dancers' clothing.

Lighting design

The lighting designer collaborates with the choreographer and artistic director to further communicate the choreographer's intention, by creating a lighting design that will augment the choreography's structure and the sculptural qualities of the dancers' bodies and movement, enhance the dramatic tone or mood of the dance, and transform the stage space into a unique setting for the dance taking place.

After deciding on the type and number

of lights, their positioning and color, the designer plots the cues on a diagram. After the lights are hung and adjusted, the plot is programmed into a computerized light board.

Lighting is generally referred to as a path (a light pattern from upstage to downstage), a plane (a light pattern across the stage), or a wash (full stage illumination). These types of light are used in dance:

- sidelight: highlights the dancer; lights hung on a boom (vertical pipe) on the sides of the stage; standard hanging positions are shin buster (just off the floor), knee (3 feet off the floor), and head (about 6–8 feet off the floor)
- striplight: placed along the front of the stage to create a wash of light
- spotlight: highlights the dancer; types of spots include the fresnel (wide, even field of light with soft edges), ellipsoidal (more focused beam of light), scoop (throws broad light over a specific area), PAR can (harsh oval beam of light with soft edges)
- backlight, toplight: strategies for lighting the stage with shadows, colors, and patterns.

The lighting designer may also incorporate lighting effects to create pattern, shape, or a scenic effect, alter intensity and brightness, or switch colors. Such tools include the following:

- gels: thin colored plastics placed in front of lights to change colors or glows
- gobos: flat pieces of metal with cut-outs placed over lights to create pattern, a streetscape, a window, etc.

Sets and props

The set or décor designer collaborates with the choreographer and artistic director to research and create drops, scrims, sets, scenery, props, and other aspects of stagecraft that will complement, respond to, or enhance the choreography—whether the work is abstract modern, neoclassical ballet, folk dance, postmodern, or a classical Romantic story ballet. Whereas some large dance companies have an in-house production workshop where scenic artists, electricians, and carpenters create and build décor, others commission set designers, architects, and artists to create décor for dance works.

Sometimes the décor is considered a work of art in itself. The Walker Art Center recently purchased more than 1,000 items created by such artists as Robert Rauschenberg, Jasper Johns, Andy Warhol, and Bruce Nauman for the Merce Cunningham Dance Company. Martha Graham famously worked with sculptor Isamu Noguchi, who created iconic set pieces for her works. Impresario Serge Diaghilev had such artists as Marc Chagall, Georges Braque, Henri Matisse, and Pablo Picasso design sets and costumes for his Ballets Russes.

> So many dancers rely on some sort of magic happening on the stage. They never, for various reasons, work full out in rehearsal. That's very uncreative. They don't discover the kinds of things that add up to a remarkable performance.
>
> Melissa Hayden

BEFORE THE PERFORMANCE

Between studio rehearsals of a dance work or program of works, and the opening-night performance with an audience, are the pre-performance rehearsals. These rehearsals, which occur on stage (or on-site) at the theater (or venue), are sequenced according to increasing technical complexity, to ensure all details—from spacing to lighting and costumes—have been correctly prepared, coordinated, and tested.

- Blocking/spacing rehearsals: The choreographer and/or artistic director determine entrances and exits, and where the dancers stand and move to and from during a dance piece; "windows," the visual spaces between dancers, are unblocked and clarified; the lighting crew watches and learns how to better light the action on stage.
- Tech rehearsal: tests and coordinates the technical aspects of the dance, including lighting, sound, music, projections; dancers are often in costume and props

Tips for pre-performance rehearsals
- Arrive early to warm up.
- Bring shoes, props, and costumes needed for the rehearsal.
- Take notes on your blocking and spacing directions.
- Pay attention and concentrate, even if you're waiting your turn.
- Snack before (not during) the rehearsal.
- Stay hydrated.
- Maintain a positive and can-do attitude.

and scenery are on stage to change and/or fine-tune lighting (hotspots, follow spots, gels, etc.).

- Dress rehearsal: the night before opening night, with dancers performing the dance or program full-out and in costume with all tech in place.
- Open/public rehearsal: a performance for press, donors, or other selected members of the public to create interest in the upcoming performance; sometimes occurs in the studio before onstage rehearsals, or can occur during the dress rehearsal.

Dancer makeup

Dancers almost always do their own makeup. The type of makeup depends on the venue, lighting, location of the audience, and type of dance being performed. Whereas the makeup of South Asian dancers is quite elaborate—with layers of foundation and blusher, exaggerated eyes, and attached hair and headdresses—hip-hop dancers wear very little makeup. Following are some general rules for dance makeup:

- Enhance the bone structure and features of the face so it can be seen from a distance by the audience.
- Shadow the jaw line and cheekbones to highlight structure.
- Emphasize the eyes to make them appear larger and more expressive.
- Balance the eyes with lip and skin color.
- Make sure lip color complements skin and costume color.

THERE'S AN APP FOR THAT

An interdisciplinary group of students from the Herberger Institute at Arizona State University has developed Rehearsal Assistant, an application for Android phones that digitally records dance rehearsals. Stjepan Rajko, a graduate student in dance, initiated the app's development after imagining software that would allow a dancer to play music and record a rehearsal in response to voice commands. The app coordinates video recording and playback with time-stamped audio annotations, so dancers can easily review their rehearsal. The app eliminates the need to run back and forth to stop and start music playback or video recording. For more information go to urbanstew.org/rehearsalassistant.

In most companies, the dancers do their own makeup (per the artistic director or choreographer's instructions); costumes may be designed and constructed by a professional specifically trained in that field.

KNOW THE STAGE

Perhaps the most common stage on which dancers perform is the proscenium, with its signature "picture frame" or arch around the front of the stage, which separates the dancers from the audience.

The choreographer, artistic director, and technical and production staff give stage directions from the point of view of the on-stage dancer facing the audience:

- stage left and stage right: the dancer's left and right
- downstage: toward the audience
- upstage: toward the back wall
- plaster line: runs from the back of one proscenium arch to the other
- center line: runs upstage/downstage halfway between prosceniums and perpendicular to the plaster line

The wings (or wing spaces) are on either side of the stage; the fly loft is the space above the stage; and backstage is the area out of sight of the audience. In front of the closed curtain of the proscenium arch is the apron. The audience is seated in the theater or the house. The audience faces the stage, which is usually higher, by several feet, from the front row of audience seating.

Other styles of theaters

- Theater in the round (arena theater): The stage is in the middle of the theater with audience seating surrounding the stage.
- Thrust stage (platform or open stage): The stage extends into the audience.
- Black box theater: a simple performance space, with a flat floor, that is easily reconfigured to accommodate varying productions and audience viewpoints

The production staff

All dancers—whether performing in a major dance company with its own house (theater), or with a troupe that performs in various venues while touring or by renting the space—need to be aware of the house (behind-the-scenes or production) staff. These people manage the house, ensure performances go smoothly, and take care of the audience.

- Production manager: in charge of the production while keeping it on schedule and on budget; creates the production schedule with designers, choreographer, and artistic director; hires technicians; resolves issues and problems
- Stage manager: calls the technical cues (lighting, sounds/music, curtains, sets); calls dancer entrances and exits; makes sure props and sets are in place; and oversees performer and crew safety
- Assistant stage manager: supports the stage manager with cues; readies

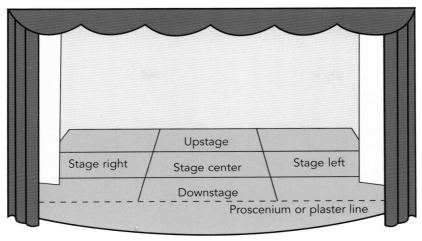

Upstage

Stage right | Stage center | Stage left

Downstage

Proscenium or plaster line

dancers; works with stagehands on placing props and sets

- Technical director: decides facilities and equipment needed for show; oversees lighting, music/sound, and rigging; problem-solves technical challenges
- Head of properties: in charge of sets and props (building, using, storing, maintaining)
- Dresser: helps dancers with quick costume changes; assists with hair, makeup, headpieces, footwear, handheld props
- Front-of-house manager: works for the theater and coordinates the use of and flow of people in entrance, lobby, concessions, and seating in the theater; supervises ushers, coordinates show start with stage manager, documents size of audience;

takes charge during fires or other emergencies

- Box office manager: works for the theater and sells, tracks, manages, and reports ticket sales
- Usher: works for the theater and takes tickets, hands out programs, helps audience members to their seats, disciplines bad audience behavior, helps audience members in case of emergency

"THEN COME THE LIGHTS SHINING ON YOU FROM ABOVE. YOU ARE A PERFORMER. YOU FORGET ALL YOU LEARNED, THE PROCESS OF TECHNIQUE, THE FEAR, THE PAIN, YOU EVEN FORGET WHO YOU ARE YOU BECOME ONE WITH THE MUSIC, THE LIGHTS, INDEED ONE WITH THE DANCE."

actress, singer, dancer Shirley MacLaine

Dancers can reduce pre-performance anxiety by relaxing and focusing on positive thoughts.

PERFORMANCE ANXIETY OR STAGE FRIGHT

Performing is the highlight of any dancer's career. After years of training and months of rehearsal, dancers are more than ready to perform full-out onstage for an admiring audience. But often, along with the thrill of performing, comes performance anxiety or stage fright—even at the professional and elite levels.

Performance anxiety can begin long before the show, as a dancer prepares to dance onstage for the first time or rehearses a new role. For many dancers, stage fright happens before every performance, and can manifest as thoughts, emotions, or physical symptoms.

This form of anxiety, which can affect classroom learning and onstage accomplishment, occurs when a dancer feels at risk of not performing to expectations. The mind and body respond in a primal way, and enter a physiological state of alertness.

"WE TALKED ABOUT WHAT HAPPENS IN OUR BODIES WHEN NERVES GET THE BETTER OF US, BUT WE ALSO TALKED ABOUT HOW THIS 'FLIGHT OR FIGHT' REACTION IS ACTUALLY A POSITIVE, BUILT IN RESPONSE THAT HELPS US MOVE FASTER, SEE AND HEAR BETTER, JUMP HIGHER, STRETCH FARTHER, AND GENERALLY REACT WITH GREATER AGILITY, SPEED, AND STRENGTH. WE ALL AGREED THAT THIS WAS A 'GOOD' THING; IT IS A FORM OF 'PHYSICAL INTELLIGENCE,' A WAY OF PROTECTING US FROM POTENTIAL HARM. THIS WAS A FIRST STEP TOWARDS VOCALIZING, SHARING, NORMALIZING, ADDRESSING, AND ULTIMATELY REFRAMING OUR EXPERIENCES OF STAGE FRIGHT AND PERFORMANCE ANXIETY."

Dr. Chantale Lussier-Ley, a registered member of the Canadian Sport Psychology Association, from her article "Stage Fright & Performance Anxiety: Dancing With the Butterflies" on one of her workshops with dancers, published in *Physical & Health Education Journal*

Under everyday circumstances, this state of anticipation is normal and fairly neutral. It allows us to prepare for and digest a meal, get ready for a night out with friends, or complete work on deadline. But before a performance, the alert state is heightened. As adrenaline enters the bloodstream, a dancer may feel excitement and eagerness to get onstage, or a surge of anxiety and fear.

Cognitive (thoughts, emotions) symptoms
- Worry
- Self-doubt
- Fear
- Nervousness
- Feeling overwhelmed
- Mind goes blank

Somatic (physical) symptoms
- Sweaty palms
- Shaking
- Muscle tension
- Stomach butterflies and nausea
- Frequent urination
- Pacing
- Sleeplessness
- Dry mouth
- Heart races, blood pressure rises

RESEARCH FINDINGS

Drs. Imogen Walker and Sanna Nordin-Bates, of Trinity Laban Conservatorie of Music and Dance, researched ballet dancers' performance anxiety in relation to:
1. "symptom type, intensity, and directional interpretation"
2. "experience level (including company rank)"
3. "self-confidence and psychological skills"
They surveyed 15 ballet dancers of all ranks from the same company. The researchers found that "cognitive anxiety was more dominant than somatic anxiety, and was unanimously interpreted as debilitative to performance. Somatic anxiety was more likely to be interpreted as facilitative, with the majority of dancers recognizing that a certain amount of anxiety could be beneficial to performance." The results also indicated that principals experience more performance anxiety, and feeling out of control, than members of the corps de ballet.

Tips for managing performance anxiety
- Set realistic goals for each performance based on skill level, onstage experience, choreographic difficulty
- Neutralize the intensity of the symptoms by thinking of them as a normal part of performance
- Reframe symptoms as a natural part of psyching-up for a performance
- Work on neutralizing negative thoughts or inner commentary
- Focus on positive thoughts and commentary
- Become aware of and try to eliminate stressors that heighten anxiety
- Try to minimize outside distractions
- Practice mind-body centering and deep breathing (see pages 140–141)
- Practice visualizing perfect performance (see pages 136–137)

THE PERFORMANCE

After years of training, weeks or months in the studio, and such final preparations as the tech and dress rehearsals, dancers ready themselves for that moment when it's their cue to get on stage and perform. In performance, the main objective is to dance the part, routine, or dance piece perfectly, which requires energy, focus, and self-confidence.

To ready yourself, consider these tips:

- Know the choreography so you can perform it, not simply dance it. Through rigorous practice, and use of mind–body connections and performance visualization techniques, you'll have embedded the movements into your neuromuscular system and memory.
- Be well rested. A good night's sleep will do wonders for your performance.
  - Be well nourished and well hydrated (see pages 90–91).
  - Organize your packing. Assemble accessories in plastic bags and label according to dance piece. Be sure to include extras (hair ties, tights, etc.) in case of loss; body care items (bandages, toe pads, foot wraps, etc.) in case of injury; and repair kit (tape, needle and thread, scissors, glue) in case of a costume mishap.
  - Arrive at the venue before the artistic director's call to fix hair and makeup, warm up your body, do breathing exercises, and visualize your movements on stage.

Even if you're dancing a solo, don't dance by yourself. Extend your awareness and energy beyond yourself, to engage the audience in your performance.

PERFORMANCE TIPS

- Don't dance by yourself. Even if you're the only one on stage, dance in relationship with the other dancers in the company, the space, the choreographer, and the audience. Extend your awareness and energy beyond yourself, to engage others in your performance.

- Project yourself and your energy. Eric Franklin, in his book *Dance Imagery for Technique and Performance*, suggests imaging yourself with an aura or atmosphere around your body (choose a color, a pattern, a vibration that augments the choreography), as if a spotlight is beaming through the center of your body, or as if you're sparkling or glowing.

- Sustain the energy and engagement. One mark of an immature or unprofessional performer is allowing the spaces or moments between shapes, steps, phrases, action, or dancers to lose energy and go slack. Experienced dancers sustain energy levels whether dynamic or quiet, and whether or not they're the center of attention onstage at that moment.

- Engage your face. Not all dance styles emphasize or require a facial expression (in some modern and postmodern dance, the face is to remain nonemotional or even blank). When facial expression is required, keep it sincere and real, which means emoting more with the eyes than with the mouth, and keeping the face open and relaxed rather than broadly smiling.

- Radiate confidence. This doesn't mean acting self-absorbed or disinterested in what's happening around you (unless that's what the choreographer called for). Rather, self-confidence comes from knowing and believing in yourself, trusting yourself and the other dancers, and having thoroughly prepared for your performance.

- Be ready to adapt. What if another dancer is suddenly injured, misses their cue, or performs a phrase incorrectly? Or a set or prop falls? Or part of your costume tears or flies off? Be ready to tap into all of your preparation and professionalism to overcome such mishaps. Be ready to fill in or account for the gaps, without breaking character or losing the momentum of your own performance, with appropriate energy, improvisation, and flow.

Stepping onstage

A dance company will often do its warm-ups on stage before the curtain rises, then retire to the dressing room to put on costumes and wait for cues to take their places in the wings. While on the stage, refamiliarize yourself with the space, where the audience will be, and the location of your places and pathways. When it's your time to perform, enter the stage performing with concentration, confidence, and charisma.

AFTER THE PERFORMANCE

Just as ballet classes end with a reverence (male students bow and female students curtsy to each other and to the teacher and accompanist) and yoga classes conclude with Namaste and a bow, dancers take bows at the conclusion of a concert.

During moments of spectacular solo dancing and pas de deux in the classical ballets, dancers bow as well. Individual dancers and ensembles also may bow after performing each dance piece in a concert. But usually, after the curtain closes on the final dance piece and opens again to audience applause, the entire dance company bows in unison, then sweeps arms out or up to acknowledge the musicians and technical staff.

In dance, the bow may be as simple as inclining the head, or bending the head and upper part of the body. Or the head and upper body may bend as one knee bends, as well. In ballet, the dancers' graceful walk to center stage to take a curtsey or bow is called a pas marché; ballerinas do a slight curtsy with the back leg slightly bent without going down on the knee, and the male dancers bow.

Most often, the dancers leave behind the world they've created onstage when they take their bows, but some stay in character. Choreographers also may create their own bows for dancers at the conclusion of a performance, almost as a brief extension of their work. During full-company bows, soloists will step out of the line for their own bows.

MEETING THE AUDIENCE

After selected concerts or shows, many dance companies hold post-performance discussions during which the audience can address the dancers and choreographer/artistic director. The format might be a question-and-answer session between audience members and performers facilitated by a local dance writer or administrator of the theater. Other formats include a discussion on a particular cultural, political, or social topic raised by the performance; or a behind-the-scenes talk about the creation of the work, choreography, costumes, and sets.

Post-performance meet and greet
Following an opening night performance, companies often hold a reception where dancers, company staff, board members, and audience members can meet each other and talk about the concert. These events may be open to the public, or to a select group of supporters and patrons. During such events, dancers are encouraged to mingle and talk about their roles and performances with donors, benefactors, and other audience members. This builds relationships between performers and patrons, and establishes openness, accessibility, and goodwill between the company and its public.

Critics and reviews

Before a performance, the publicist for the dance company will work with media representatives to arrange press coverage prior to the show.

The previews might profile a particular dancer in a milestone performance, new dancers, or a visiting choreographer. Articles or radio interviews may also focus on the creation of a new work having its premiere, the company itself and its style of work or choreography, or why a specific work might appeal to a particular audience. The purpose of previews is to generate public interest in the upcoming performance, in order to sell tickets and increase audiences.

On opening night, local dance critics will review the performance. In general, the purpose of a dance review is to analyze,

describe, evaluate, and contextualize the performance for readers. Every dance critic approaches the watching and analysis of a performance in a different way, while drawing from their knowledge (whether vast or scant) of dance and the arts; the company, choreographer, and dancers under review; and the journalistic practice of criticism.

Nevertheless, a dance critique can sway public opinion about a production and affect how dancers perceive their work. Some dancers avidly read reviews of their work (particularly if they trust the insights of a specific critic); others avoid reading reviews altogether. Administrators and directors within a dance company, however, anticipate reviews and will use positive comments to further public interest in and discussion about a show.

What turns critics off?
- marking or "calling it in" rather than dancing full-out
- overacting, overselling, or "indicating" rather than honest expression
- underdeveloped or flawed technique
- unison passages not performed in unison
- lack of sustained energy (dead spaces within and/or between dancers)
- tense or nervous dancers
- absence of kinetic energy between dancers onstage and people in the audience
- lack of clear choreographic intention

Some dancers seek out critiques, particularly if they trust the insights of a specific critic; others avoid reading reviews.

DANCING FOR THE CAMERA

Since the invention of film, video, and digital technologies, dancers and choreographers have used the camera to expand the possibilities of dance performance. In the early days of Hollywood, such innovators as Busby Berkeley, Fred Astaire and Hermes Pan, and Gene Kelly, and Stanley Donen experimented with making the camera dance to better capture the kinetic qualities of dancer and choreography.

In the 1980s, the advent of MTV and the music video popularized the power of dance to help sell promotional videos for bands. Michael Jackson and his choreographer Michael Peters advanced the music video with the groundbreaking creation of the 13-minute video *Thriller*, showcasing Jackson's signature moves. Since then, dancers and choreography have become an integral part of the stage and screen in the selling of pop singers, from Madonna to M.C. Hammer, Britney Spears, and Lady Gaga.

Dance companies also use cameras to record rehearsals to study and improve technique and learning; to document concerts for company archives; to film sequences that are projected during multimedia live performances; and as a form of artistic expression to create new modes of dance presentation and performance.

Choreography for the camera

Around the world, some choreographers, in addition to creating works for the stage, have created dance films in which in-camera and post-production (such as editing) techniques are deployed to skew narratives, generate dramatic tension, cross the dimensional boundaries of time and space, and blur realities. Here are some examples:

- DV8 Physical Theatre, directed by Lloyd Newson. Works include *Enter Achilles* and *The Cost of Living*.

- The Physical TV Company, directed by Richard James Allen and Karen Pearlman. Works include *Entanglement Theory* and *Thursday's Fictions*.
- The BodyCartography Project, directed by Olive Bieringa and Otto Ramstad. Works include *Seawall* and *Holiday House*.
- Merce Cunningham Dance Company, directed by Merce Cunningham and Eliot Caplan. Works include *Beach Birds* and *Changing Steps*.

Approaches

- Pre-made choreography. The dancers perform choreography learned in the studio or during rehearsal in front of a camera. The director decides on camera placement and angles, and how the film will later be edited. The director may also watch and study the choreography before the shoot, to create a storyboard (using lists, notes, or snapshots) of the portions they want to be sure to capture on camera. This information can be shared between the director, dancers, choreographer, and camera technicians, and can also guide the editing process.
- Improvisation. Often used during the making of dance films in locations other than the concert stage, improvisation can generate a unique relationship between dancer(s) and camera. Because improvisation is inherently organic and in-the-moment, dancer and camera can use their symbiotic relationship to deepen their exploration of movement in a particular place and frame specific movements.

Maintain a good working relationship with a videographer who specializes in performance in order to have fruitful experiments with dance on film and video.

9
THE BUSINESS OF DANCE

Whether studying dance since the age of three, thirteen, or twenty-three, a dancer who has successfully performed for an audience and acquired an unquenchable thirst for more knows it's time to transition into the next stage of life as a dancer: a professional career. To create a career in dance as a performer, a dancer needs to continue training and honing his or her unique talents. Dancers also must find and fulfill a niche, and seek out opportunities for work. This chapter compiles the basics of a dancer's self-marketing tool kit. Along with creating a marketing or application package that includes CV, photos, and demo reel, dancers can brand themselves in the dance world by creating a website, becoming proficient at social media, and employing the help of an agent. By assembling the right marketing tools, a dancer can gain a leg up in the competitive world of professional dance.

AN INTRODUCTION TO SELF-MARKETING

When looking for work, a dancer needs to become his or her own best salesperson. Before seeking out audition notices, starting on an audition application package, figuring out your "brand," looking for an agent, or setting up a Twitter account, put yourself in the right frame of mind.

Self-marketing is about knowing who you are, recognizing why you're unique, and believing in yourself. Begin by listing
- the talents and abilities you have to offer;
- your accomplishments and how they've brought you to this point as a dancer;
- your strongest assets as a performer;
- where and with whom you want to dance

Part of the business of dance is maintaining an engaging online presence, as well as knowing your "elevator speech" when you meet new people in person.

What is self-marketing?

Marketing is a process by which a company learns how and why its products or services are of interest to customers, and promotes those products and services, and their value, through sales and communications. Self-marketing for dancers, then, is the process of discovering one's distinctive abilities, and communicating that value to the people in the position of hiring dancers.

Mastering the ability to sell yourself on paper (via a résumé and cover letter), online or virtually (via social media), and visually (through video and photography) is the key to self-marketing—and getting those first auditions. Begin preparing:

- Write and practice the "elevator speech." Every time you meet someone new in the dance world, you have a few seconds to "sell" yourself. Start thinking about who you are and who you want to be as a professional dancer. Practice your 30-second-long introduction with passion and enthusiasm. Think of your "elevator speech" as a verbal calling card and a way of leaving an impression of yourself with others.

- Research dance communities, trends, companies. Where do you want to work? Who would you like to work with? Where are dancers being hired and for

Tips for meeting the self-marketing challenge
- Deadlines. They're real and serious. Always meet them. Never ask for or think you can get an extension.
- Personality. Bring it to the floor, to the page, to the photo shoot, to the audition. Your personality is a tremendous asset in marketing, and will help you stand out. It's also a great way to begin forging relationships with artistic directors, producers, and agents.
- Don't get discouraged. The next day is a new day to start again.
- Have fun. Self-marketing entails learning about yourself and sharing what you've learned.

what types of jobs? What are cruise ships, modern-dance choreographers, musical-theater producers and music-video directors looking for in their dancers?
- Get feedback and advice. Put your ego aside, and ask dance teachers, fellow students, colleagues, and other artists about your strengths and weaknesses so you know what to improve upon.

"TRAIN! PUT THE TIME IN TO REALLY STRENGTHEN YOUR TECHNIQUE—DON'T TAKE SHORTCUTS, IT SHOWS IN YOUR DANCING. KEEP FOCUSED AND STAY MENTALLY STRONG WHEN APPROACHING THE DANCE WORLD AS YOUR CAREER— YOU'LL TAKE A LOT OF HITS, IT'S PART OF THE BUSINESS. BE PREPARED, REMEMBER THIS IS A BUSINESS LIKE ANY OTHER— DO YOUR HOMEWORK ON AUDITIONS, DRESS APPROPRIATELY, HAVE A SONG READY FOR BROADWAY AUDITIONS, ETC. AND KEEP LOVING WHAT YOU DO!! IT HELPS YOU GET THROUGH A LOT OF THE DISAPPOINTMENTS."

Suzi Taylor, a founder of lyrical dance

THE AUDITION PROCESS

Although nerve-wracking and intimidating, auditions are a necessary part of a dancer's career. Open auditions are invitations for anyone to attend, often without pre-screening. A scheduled audition is more like a job interview, in that an application and other self-marketing materials are required in order to pre-select dancers.

Depending on the type of audition, an agent, choreographer, artistic director, producer, casting director, competition judge, or event planner may conduct the "call." They're often accompanied by an audition panel, which provides additional insights and opinions on the applicants. Even before the audition begins, as the dancers walk through the door, the employer is already appraising each applicant's attitude and poise.

During the audition, which usually involves quickly learning and performing choreography, the panelists assess each person's ability to take direction, learn, adapt, progress, and perform. Sometimes an applicant may be asked to also perform a minute or two of prepared choreography. The applicant may be asked to answer a few questions after the audition.

Pre-audition requirements

Before an audition, the choreographer, competition planner, event producer, or dance company artistic director will require that specific information be e-mailed or mailed to their offices. Read the requirements carefully. Is the audition for a company, production, or event in which your talents and abilities would be an asset? Do you or can you fulfill all of the requirements? Before submitting the application be sure to include all the information requested; leaving a line blank or forgetting to include a reference could mean the end of the audition before it begins.

Always arrive early at your audition and use the extra time to stretch, relax, and prepare yourself for your performance.

Audition tips

1. Do your research. Read the audition notice thoroughly (see pages 192–193). Then learn about the choreographer, company, or organization for which you're auditioning. Research choreographic methods, dance style, personalities, previous work, interviews, and reviews to educate yourself about your potential employer. Arrive informed and dressed appropriately. Don't wear too many layers; the panel wants to clearly see your body in motion.

2. Be prepared. Gather together everything you'll need ahead of time, including the appropriate apparel (wardrobe changes if necessary) and shoes, hair accessories, foot and injury protection (bandages, moleskin, ankle and knee support), water, and snacks. Bring an extra copy of your demo reel (on DVD or flashdrive), CV, and references.

3. Arrive early. Figure out, the night before, how to get to the audition. Then arrive 30–45 minutes early, in order to become familiar with the space and have plenty of time to relax, warm up, and focus.

4. Show yourself. If possible, stand in front of the room. Demonstrate your ability to follow directions, learn combinations quickly, and retain choreography. Show your respect for the choreographer and other dancers around you, your comfort with performing, and your commitment to and passion for dance.

5. Remain positive. Every audition panel is different. One panel may be looking for specific qualities you have; another may not.

Depending on the type of audition, the panel may go through a serious of "cuts" during which applicants are eliminated. If you're cut, exit the stage with a positive attitude and thanks for the experience. Always dance to the best of your ability, and never take rejection personally.

MUSICAL-THEATER AUDITIONS

Dancing and singing are required for most musical-theater opportunities. Be ready to do the following:

- Sing at least two prepared songs. The songs should be about 32 bars in length, and showcase your versatility in song style, vocal range and dynamics, and character creation through song. One song should be similar in style to what you'd be singing if you win the role. Bring the sheet music for the accompanist.
- Perform a prepared dance routine, or learn and perform one during the audition.
- Read for the acting portion of the role, using a text you've prepared that displays your ability to create and express a character.

Where to find audition notices:
- Dance, cheer, and competition magazines (in print and online)
- Audition websites (including dance.net, danceplug.com, stagedooraccess.com, article19.co.uk, en.stagepool.com, starsearchcasting.com)
- Dance service organization websites (including danceusa.org)
- Dance school and dance company websites, bulletin boards, blogs

Types of dance auditions:
- For admission into a college, university, or conservatory dance program
- For a student or professional dance company
- For traditional musicals and contemporary dance musicals

- For entertainment revues at casinos and resorts or on cruise ships
- For live concerts and music videos
- For movies and television

SAMPLE AUDITION NOTICE

Carte Blanche (Norway)

Carte Blanche's annual audition takes place on December 3rd 2011 from 10:00 am to 6:00 pm. Registration opens at 9:00 am. Applicants should be available for a call back on 4th December 2011. The audition takes place at Carte Blanche's home Studio Bergen, Nøstegaten 119, 5011 Bergen, Norway.

Applicants must have a solid ballet and contemporary dance technique and be experienced in improvisation. Applicants should send their CV including headshot and letter of motivation to the company by post or e-mail audition@ballet.no by 27th November 2011.

Contracts available: Female dancers, one regular contract and one production contract; Male dancers, one production contract.

Carte Blanche consists of a twelve dancer strong ensemble acknowledged for its technical abilities and powerful stage presence. This season they are joined by three apprentices. The company produces two to three new choreographic works a year and presents an average of four to six different productions per year. Carte Blanche tours both nationally and internationally and has an average of 65 performances annually.

Carte Blanche's repertory includes works by some of the best Norwegian and internationally known choreographers. The company equally puts a strong emphasis on commissioning work by a new generation of contemporary dance makers.

SAMPLE AUDITION NOTICE

Dutch National Ballet (Amsterdam)

Artistic director Ted Brandsen will be auditioning for strong classical male and female dancers (min. height: female 1.65 m; male 1.80 m) on 21 January 2012 at Het Muziektheater, Amsterdam (registration between 12:00 and 13:00). To apply for the audition go to www.ballet.nl.audition and fill out an application form online. Application deadline: 27 December 2011. Participation by pre-selection only. Selected dancers will receive an invitation before 1 January 2012.

Application materials: cover letter

Many pre-audition requirements include submitting a cover letter in conjunction with a completed application and résumé. These materials are part of the pre-selection process, and reflect your progress, experience, and intentions as a dancer. They're an integral part of your marketing campaign on the audition circuit.

In these written materials you make first contact with the audition panel, and a first impression. Because the cover letter is the first item the artistic director or producer sees (as it usually "covers" or precedes the application and résumé or CV in the sheaf of documents), a well-written cover letter can significantly improve your chances for an audition. The cover letter

- is formal and formatted like a business letter, with your return address, date, the address of the person or company, and personal salutation.
- has a strong introductory paragraph, in which you state your interest and intention (e.g., you saw the audition notice at x or heard about it from y [a mutual acquaintance], are experienced in a and b, and would like to audition for the opening at d or e).
- continues with a paragraph highlighting the unique experience, talents, and value you will bring to the position (the highlights should correspond with the background and dance styles required in

the audition posting).
- continues with a paragraph summarizing your educational background and performance experience.
- wraps up with an action statement ("I would appreciate/welcome the opportunity to audition for xxxxx").
- concludes with appreciation ("Thank you for your time in reviewing my materials. I look forward to hearing from you").
- closes with Best Wishes or Sincerely, your signature, and your name and contact information.
- is well written and free of misspellings, incomplete sentences, and other grammatical errors.
- reflects your personality and an understanding of the company, group, event, or production for which you are auditioning.

CV or résumé

Your CV or résumé is the document in which you unpack and detail the highlights in your cover letter. But it's not an all-inclusive list. Information in the CV is mindfully selected and well organized to present your background, experience, and abilities in the best possible light. Research résumé templates on the Internet or study what other dancers have done. Then include your

- name, address, phone numbers (land, mobile), and e-mail address;
- date of birth, citizenship, height, and weight;

- education: schools, workshops, and residencies attended, degrees or certificates earned, with dates;
- companies or organizations worked with, and dates, locations;
- outstanding roles, dances performed, choreographers/producers/directors worked with and dates, locations;
- awards, recognitions, and medals received, with dates.

Depending on the type of audition, the CV may also include choreography created and for whom, acting and singing experience, collaborative work, competitions entered and won, and/or screen credits. If at all possible, keep your résumé to one page.

References

Many pre-audition requirements include providing a list of two or three references. Your references could be a choreographer with whom you've closely worked, a dance teacher, or a dance company artistic director. Before compiling your list, make courtesy calls. Contact each potential reference to ask whether they'd be willing to speak on your behalf. Discuss with them the audition and its specifications, to determine whether they're comfortable lauding your experience and abilities to the audition panel. If they agree, add their name, title, relationship to you, address, phone numbers, and e-mail address to the reference list.

Photos

A nonreturnable photo is often required as part of the pre-selection audition package. Two types of photographs may be required:

- Headshot: helps the audition panel associate a face with your cover letter and résumé. Dancers usually get two headshots: a commercial shot infused with personality and a smile, and a headshot that's a more aesthetic or artistic reflection of personality.
- Bodyshot: displays clean lines and physical attributes to best advantage. Some bodyshots are executed in motion, as during a leap; others are stationary, to exhibit the dancer in a perfect pose.

To get the best pictures, find a photographer with experience shooting headshots and dancers in motion, whose work you admire. Study other dancers' photos and find examples of what you'd like to achieve to share with the photographer. Arrive at the photo shoot in hair and makeup, and with wardrobe that flatters your physique and suits the style of dance for which you're auditioning. Relax and smile during the shoot.

Demo reel/DVD

A demo or presentation reel is a résumé-in-motion or movement portfolio: a collection of performance highlights that showcases your technique, artistry, special abilities, personality, and appeal. A demo reel may be required as part of the pre-audition package, and sent on DVD or a flashdrive. Demo reels can also be uploaded to your website, MySpace page, or Facebook account (also see pages 200–201), and the links to the performance videos provided to audition panels as part of online auditions.

Dancers collect and create demo reels in a number of ways:

- By editing solo or featured footage out of a dance performance tape and editing it into the demo reel.
- Having a professional video photographer or another dancer shoot them in performance or in the studio.

For optimal footage, remember to

- shoot in a place that reflects your dance style (stage, street, studio);
- dance in front of an uncluttered, bright background;
- dance in balanced lighting;

- shoot in a high-definition format;
- perform in the style(s) for which you're auditioning;
- look at the "rushes" (the footage just shot) to see whether the footage is clear and you're happy with your performance.

For students, the demo reel shouldn't be more than a minute long; professionals keep their reels to about five minutes. After editing the footage into a compelling portfolio, transfer it to DVD or flashdrive (read application requirements), make copies, and label each copy with the date, and your name, address, phone number, and e-mail.

When working with a videographer on a demo reel, always look at the "rushes" (the footage just shot) to make sure you're happy with your performance onscreen.

BRANDING YOURSELF

Today, anyone in the business of selling themselves and their unique talents—including dancers—seeks to brand themselves in order to stand out from the crowd.

According to the American Marketing Association, a brand is a "Name, term, design, symbol, or any other feature that identifies one seller's goods or services as distinct from those of other sellers." For dancers, creating a personal brand is a marketing strategy that involves deciding on and highlighting your best and most singular characteristics.

As young and new dancers progress in their careers, finding a personal brand becomes easier. With more experience comes deeper understanding of individual style, abilities, and personality, and how to best market those assets to a potential employer.

Once you've created a personal brand, all of your marketing materials—from CV to status updates on Facebook—should incorporate your brand. The more people

When developing a personal brand based on your dance style and performance personality, be sure to focus on what differentiates you from everyone else.

"BEING A PROFESSIONAL DANCER WHO CHOOSES TO SUBSIST BY LIVING AND WORKING AS A DANCER, YOU MUST THINK OF YOURSELF AS A PRODUCT—A BRAND. WHO ARE YOU? WHAT DO YOU HAVE TO SAY? WHAT TYPE ARE YOU? HOW DO YOU STAND OUT? THIS MEANS THE WAY YOU PRESENT YOURSELF IS REALLY BRANDING WHO YOU ARE. DANCERS, ACTORS, MODELS AND SINGERS NEED TO HAVE A SENSE OF WHO THEY ARE AS PRODUCTS IN A MARKETPLACE, NOT JUST AS ARTISTS."

Michelle Zeitlin, dancer, choreographer, director, producer

Use your brand to
- remind you of your intentions, progress, and goals as a dancer;
- develop and refine your audition materials (cover letter, CV, demo reel);
- help you develop an artist's statement and bio;
- promote yourself on your website, blog, and through social media;
- keep your self-marketing consistent;
- confirm your identity throughout your dance communities; and
- create a community of dancers (across the world and the Internet).

who see it, the more recognizable you become, and the more your particular skills, talents, and abilities become valuable.

Your personal brand is you: who you are, what you value and believe, and what you can offer others. One problem with branding is that people often inflate their abilities, to the point where ego overshadows reality. Some marketing professionals equate personal brand with "reputation" or "image." Just remember: When building a personal brand, keep it real.

Techniques for developing a personal brand

Address the following questions. Also ask other dancers, instructors, and choreographers for their opinions.

- Identify your niche:
  What is unique about you? What are you known for? What makes you different? What is unique about your dancing? Define your "voice" or singular qualities. In what style or technique do you specialize? Or in what ways are you multifaceted?
- Identify your "customer": Who do you want to work for or with? What can you offer that no one else can? What value do you bring to a company, choreographer, director, or producer?
- Identify your character: What is your persona as a dancer? What kind of energy and personality do you project? Do you have a signature haircut or hairstyle, fashion sense, or wardrobe color or accessory that complements your personality or character?
- Identify your values: What about dance is most important to you? What communication or interpersonal strengths do you bring to the studio, stage, and/or screen? What is essential to your work process that benefits others?

Condense your answers into a list of words, and a mental picture of yourself, that encapsulates a potential brand in words and images.

CREATING A WEBSITE

An integral part of a dancer's self-marketing plan, and branding strategy, is to create and maintain a website. A high-quality and engaging personal website is a 24/7 advertisement that's accessible the world over. No dancer should be without one.

Domain name

Choose a domain name—the URL people type into the search line to find your site. Your domain and website name should be your name. Avoid using punctuation or symbols that will make finding or typing in your name difficult, unless your name is already taken. Prices for domain names vary, and they must be renewed annually.

Hosting

If you go with a free website, or blogging platform like tumblr.com or wordpress.com, hosting is free. Many other website-creation services also offer free hosting, and some have a nominal fee.

Designing and maintaining a website is a way of ensuring your brand and your information is available around the world 24/7.

Design considerations

Options for designing websites include purchasing a kit with software and templates for do-it-yourself design; selecting a blog site and choosing and/or customizing one of its templates; or hiring a professional graphic or website designer. Following are some design considerations:

- Brand: Your personal brand guides and defines the overall design concept (see pages 188–189).
- Style: Clean and uncluttered, with plenty of white space and an emphasis on visuals (headshots, bodyshots, video).
- Color: Choose two or three colors that reflect your brand, and use them for background, accents, and emphasis throughout the website; don't overdo color.
- Type: Choose an easy-to-read font in a large, legible size.
- Navigation: Most people scan web pages, so allow them to quickly access your pages from an easy-to-find and easy-to-use menu.
- Menu: Keep options to a minimum; Home, Contact, About, Press, Photo Gallery, and Media are all you really need.
- Number of pages; see Menu.

Information to include

- Homepage: first impression; introduces you and your brand; clean and engaging design; includes photo and/or video
- About: CV, bio, where and for whom you've danced, upcoming performances
- Photo gallery: headshots, bodyshots, engaging in activities that show range and skills (singing, acting, etc.)
- Press: scans and/or Internet links to articles and reviews of your work; list of reviewer quotes
- Media: your demo reel (see pages 194–195); links to video excerpts on other sites such as MySpace or Facebook
- Contact: your e-mail address and telephone numbers; agent name (if you have one) and phone number

"SETTING UP A WEBSITE IS IMPORTANT BUT, UNLESS THAT SITE IS ALSO BEING USED AS A BLOGGING PLATFORM, IT IS THE EQUIVALENT OF A BUSINESS CARD. SOCIAL MEDIA IS WHERE WE HAND OUT THAT CARD, WHERE WE CAN PROMOTE CONTENT BUT ALSO MAKE KEY CONNECTIONS, SCOUT FOR HOT TOPICS, UNDERSTAND READERS' OPINIONS AND EXPECTATIONS. IT'S WHERE WE CAN ALSO TAKE PART IN INTERESTING CONVERSATIONS."

Emilia and Linda, authors of theballetbag.com (right), from their article "Social Dancing" on dancepulp.com

BLOGGING

For many dancers, blogging on a personal website is a way of extending their brand and their personality to visitors. Dance blogs abound, with bloggers musing on the pros and cons of the dance lifestyle, working with choreographers, finding and landing gigs, and how to buy shoes, do a perfect plié, or wow competition judges.

Bloggers also share their love of dance, celebrate their favorite dancers, and chronicle their own performances. They share and comment on dance-related articles and reviews. Dancers blog to display other skills, including dance reviewing and teaching experiences. Proactive dancers upload video or photography on their blogs, in order to add fresh content about their artistic activities on a regular basis.

Blogs are an important part of the growing online dance community, as well. By blogging, dancers join audience members, teachers, choreographers, critics, students, and other dance professionals in communicating why dance is essential in contemporary art and culture, and is worth celebrating and appreciating.

SOCIAL MEDIA

Blogs are considered a component of social media. So are Facebook, Twitter, MySpace, and YouTube. Each of these Internet-based communication and media sites offers dancers a different format for extending their personal brand, attracting new fans, and retaining current followers.

On any given day, you can find dancers tweeting about their performance during intermission, decrying the difficulty of learning new choreography on their Facebook status update, posting new footage from a demo reel on MySpace, and updating their YouTube channel with video. Not only are the contestants from *Po prostu ta cz!* and *Strictly Come Dancing* tweeting and updating their struggles and successes, but so are internationally famed ballerinas, students on the competitive

Maintaining an active Twitter presence means informing, engaging, and enlightening followers about your life as a dancer.

SOCIAL MEDIA TIPS

- Be consistent: whichever outlets/platforms you choose, post regularly to attract and keep followers.
- Reply: respond to other people's comments and questions, to keep the dialogue going and your presence vital.
- Don't overshare: remember to maintain your professionalism, brand, and identity.
- Mix it up: don't always talk about the same things.
- Be creative: find people with similar interests, projects, and connections to continually expand your network.

dance circuit, modern-dance choreographers, and jazz dancers.

At 140 characters per tweet, Twitter is the outlet for clever and succinct commentary, reflection, and insights. The point is to entice and tease readers into

Between classes and rehearsals is a great time to reinforce your dance brand on such social media sites as Twitter, Facebook, LinkedIn, and YouTube.

becoming your followers. Twitter is perfect for nonwriters with limited time.

Facebook status updates keep "Friends" in the loop about your activities. In addition to your personal page, you can create a professional page to generate a following outside of your Friend network, and post more links, and upload more video and photos than you might on your personal page.

Other social media sites such as MySpace and YouTube let you create a site for posting music and video, which you can also link to your website, Facebook page, and Twitter account (and vice versa). Through social media, dancers can meet and converse in cyberspace, make connections, network with choreographers, and extend their brand.

In creating a lively Internet presence through social media, remember to continually maintain a singular voice that supports your personal brand.

"LOTS OF PEOPLE WILL TELL YOU TO 'BE YOURSELF' IN SOCIAL MEDIA. I'D ADVISE CREATING A PERSONA THAT MIXES WHO YOU ARE AND WHO YOU WANT TO BE. THIS HEIGHTENED VERSION OF YOURSELF ALLOWS YOU TO LOSE THE PERFORMANCE ANXIETY AND MAGNIFY THE PERSONALITY TRAITS NEEDED TO ATTRACT THE RIGHT PEOPLE. WE FALL IN LOVE WITH THOSE WHO ARE BRAVE ENOUGH TO DO WHAT WE THINK WE CAN'T. AS LONG AS YOU'RE BASING YOUR CHARACTER OFF WHO YOU REALLY ARE, YOU'LL BE ABLE TO KEEP IT AUTHENTIC."

Lisa Barone, belly dancer and blogger

FINDING AN AGENT

Once upon a time, the dance agent was sought after by dancers seeking to audition for directors hiring for such commercial ventures as Broadway, film, and musical-theater productions—and, for the most part, agents worked only with stars. Currently, however, most professional dancers rely on agents to find them work, whether dancing with Britney Spears, a touring production of *Movin' Out*, a major ballet company, or in an iPod ad or music video. Agents can also help secure gigs on cruise ships, in theme parks, and as a guest artist with a dance company.

What agents do

- Provide access to "invited calls"; auditions not in magazines or online, but sent directly and only to agencies
- Refine your "look" and brand so it's more marketable
- Make travel arrangements; book accommodations and rental cars
- Negotiate contracts and fees
- Ensure you're paid on time
- Secure details of expectations and working conditions for upcoming gigs
- Resolve disputes that arise
- Take 10 percent of your earnings as their fee

How to find an agent

- Network with dance teachers, choreographers, and other dancers to learn about agents.
- Ask dance teachers, choreographers, and professional dancers to recommend you to an agent.
- Search online for reputable dance agents.

"A GOOD AGENT WILL NOT ONLY GUIDE YOU IN THE RIGHT DIRECTION, BUT ALSO FIND WAYS TO INSPIRE AND MOTIVATE YOU TO BE YOUR BEST. OPEN CALLS CAN BE CATTLE CALLS, DONE MOSTLY FOR PUBLICITY BUZZ. WHEN YOU HAVE SO MANY DANCERS ATTENDING OPEN CALLS, IT'S EASY TO BE OVERLOOKED. MANY CASTING DIRECTORS DO NOT HOLD OPEN CALLS VERY OFTEN. THEY RELY SOLELY ON WORKING WITH AGENTS BECAUSE THEY UNDERSTAND THAT THAT'S WHERE THE TALENT IS. IT SAVES THEM TIME AND MONEY. SO HAVING A GOOD AGENT IN THIS PROFESSION IS A MUST."

Aris Golemi, founder of Xcel Talent Agency

- Prepare and mail out a professional information packet (similar to that for auditions), which includes cover letter, CV, photos, and demo reel.
- Find out how reputable agencies recruit talent.
- Attend auditions held by talent agencies that represent dancers.
- Make appointments to visit agencies that have appointments for auditions.
- Interview agents to make sure he/she has your best interests in mind.
- Make sure you trust and respect the potential agent.
- Be respectful, patient, and persistent: keep honing your technique, practicing your dancing, and resubmitting your application materials for an audition.

Many musical-theater artists use an agent to help them hone their brand, reach out to directors, locate auditions, and land work.

Before signing up with an agent, research their qualifications and client lists, and ask for recommendations from dance teachers and choreographers.

Qualities agents seek
- Professionalism
- Versatility
- Exceptional technique and performance ability
- Audition experience
- Ability to follow directions
- Works well with others
- Self-discipline and a good work ethic

10
LIFE AS A DANCER

Life as a dancer is unlike any other. Ask Mariel Greenlee, who has studied in New York City and Spain, and currently dances in the United States. "We work in one room, no furniture, no cubicles, no privacy, and if you miss a class someone asks if you are OK. There's always personal feedback you get as you work. And we love what we do, despite the low pay and the physical toll it takes," she told indystar.com. "The best part is that I get to do it again tomorrow." This chapter explores some of the everyday ups, downs, and opportunities that fuel such passion and commitment. In addition to outlining the qualities and abilities that make up the dancer skill set, the chapter looks at the goal setting and dealing with rejection that enter into the daily schedule of a professional dancer. As dancers mature, they also begin considering when to expand their creative impulse, whether that means having a family or beginning to choreograph their own works. "Every day is different and always a gift," Greenlee adds. "I'm so lucky to get to do what I do." How many nondancers do you know who can say that?

THE SUCCESSFUL DANCER SKILL SET

What do you dance? Whether hip-hop or salsa, ballroom or ballet, tap or tango, African or Zumba, successful professional dancers share many of the same characteristics and skill sets. Regardless of aspirations—one person's goal may be prima ballerina; another's, backup dancer for Rihanna—dedicated dancers share certain skills, personality traits, and physical and somatic qualities. They also have in common the ability to recognize challenges or deficiencies, and compensate for those in other areas.

Overall, dancers learn, and convey their learning, through movement. They absorb information kinesthetically and through the other five senses—in other words, through the body. Dancers are engaged in a continual feedback loop of reception and response that hones their interactions with self, objects, space, and other dancers.

Because dance is so competitive, not everyone can be an international star. But by cultivating the successful dancer's skill set, anyone can have a starring role in their own dance story.

"You spend years and years at school, trying to make your best frappe, or your développé to the left a bit higher, or your arabesque a bit more extensive. Suddenly you join the company and the first thing is you're acting. You're not being this ballerina you trained for. You are pretending to be a peasant, a whore or a gipsy."
Lauren Cuthbertson, principal, Royal Ballet, London, as quoted in an article in *The Telegraph*

RESEARCH FINDINGS: DANCERS ARE DIFFERENT

Dr. Richard P. Ebstein, head of the Scheinfeld Center for Human Genetics in the Social Sciences at Hebrew University in Jerusalem, studied the genes of eighty-five dancers and dance students in Israel, and found variants of two genes that provide the code for the serotonin transporter and arginine vasopressin receptor. Both genes are involved in the transmission of information between nerve cells. His genetic evidence was corroborated by two questionnaires: one that correlates aspects of spirituality and altered states of consciousness, another that measures the need for social contact and communication. He compared the dancers' data with that of athletes and nonathletes. He found the dancers have genetic and personality characteristics the other groups do not: They're more communicative and spiritual.

When dancers perform the same role night after night, they need to stay focused and disciplined to keep their dancing strong and fresh.

Knowledge areas
- Quick memorization
- Dance and acting techniques
- Anatomy and bodily self-awareness
- Ability to improvise
- Ability to give choreography meaning
- Performance skills
- Creativity
- Expressiveness, artistry

Mental qualities/personality
- Confidence
- Ambition, motivation
- Resilience, adaptability
- Self-discipline balanced with self-respect
- Dedication, commitment
- Detail oriented, yet can envision big picture
- Reliable, responsible
- Collaborator, team member, works well with others

> Someone once said that dancers work just as hard as policemen; always alert, always tense. But ... policemen don't have to look beautiful at the same time.
>
> George Balanchine

Dancers take class every day, whether they feel like it or not. A dancer's body must be continually stretched and strengthened in order to prepare for peak performance.

DAILY LIFE OF A DANCER

For most people, the daily life of a dancer is a mystery. What do they do all day? Prepare for performances, of course, which happen only several times a year. So what are they doing the rest of the time? In addition to taking class, dancers are cross training, tending to injuries, working with choreographers on new works, and rehearsing repertory. Such is a dancer's backstage existence.

Their daily lives, in other words, are all about mental and physical self-discipline, exhausting, sweaty work, and perpetually striving for perfect technique. Professional dancers, in fact, do little else. They engage in these everyday realities whether they feel like it or not, because the dancer's body must be continually stretched and strengthened, challenged and exerted in order to prepare for peak performance.

DAILY LIFE: FREELANCE DANCER

Monday–Sunday
Like full-time dancers, freelancers maintain a rigorous schedule of technique and dance classes, cross training, and visiting health practitioners when necessary. In addition, they may be juggling part-time jobs, teaching at the studio where they take class, auditioning, and/or rehearsing with one or more companies with which they're performing in an upcoming show.

There's a saying that goes: "Miss class for one day; you notice. Miss class for two days; your colleagues notice. Miss class for three days; your audience notices."

DAILY SCHEDULE: SALARIED DANCER IN A PROFESSIONAL COMPANY

Monday—Saturday

Early morning:
Many dancers start their day with swimming, yoga, a run, or a workout at the gym.

Morning:
Company class begins after 9 a.m. The class usually runs for 75 minutes, and includes warm-up exercises and technique. Even in nonballet companies, dancers may spend time at the barre working on ballet technique, which many artistic directors and choreographers consider fundamental to dance practice.

Afternoon:
After company class, the remainder of the day (until 6 p.m. or so) includes additional dance and technique classes, rehearsals with choreographers, and repertory rehearsals. Large companies may have several studios, in which different works are being created or rehearsed. Rehearsals may be short (coaching on a new role or solo) or several hours (to run through, make corrections, and again run though a new work).

Evening:
Dancers may take additional classes with other dance companies or studios, or engage in cross training or somatic practices.

Throughout the day:
Dancers may meet with administrative, production, scheduling, or touring staff; participate in costume fittings and photo shoots; be interviewed by journalists; have sessions with a physical therapist or chiropractor.

Being a professional dancer involves an immense amount of hard physical work and discipline every day.

"ONE OF THE HARDEST THINGS ABOUT BEING A PROFESSIONAL DANCER IS THE DISCIPLINE INVOLVED IN OUR DAILY LIFE. THE DISCIPLINE COMES WITH CONSISTENTLY STARTING YOUR DAY WITH THE STRETCHING AND THE EXERCISES THAT YOU NEED FOR YOUR BODY TO OPEN UP… EVERY MORNING IS BASICALLY A WORKOUT, BECAUSE YOUR MUSCLES ARE ASLEEP AND THEY NEED TO OPEN UP SLOWLY AND CAREFULLY. THAT'S ONE OF THE HARDEST THINGS THAT WE HAVE TO DEAL WITH ON A DAILY BASIS, BUT IT BECOMES REALLY EASY, AND IT BECOMES SOMETHING THAT WE LOVE TO DO, AND IT'S PART OF US."

Fadi, a dancer, in a video on healththeater.com

DEALING WITH DISAPPOINTMENT OR REJECTION

So you didn't make the cut at the audition; the summer workshop didn't accept you; a plum role in a new work went to your competitor; the choreographer decided—last minute—to eliminate your solo. Or perhaps the school accepted you, but at a lower level. Or you love your company, but it's laying off dancers.

A life in dance is full of disappointments and outright rejection. How a dancer handles having their hopes dashed, in order to pick up, dust off, and keep going, is an essential part of living a successful dance life. The best lesson learned from any rejection is how to better deal with the next one. Getting turned down for a part tests a dancer's resolve: Only those with a true commitment to their growth and development as a dancer rally and forge ahead.

Coping strategies

- Acknowledge your feelings. Whether you're frustrated, disappointed, angry, or sad, the first step to moving on is validating your emotions.
- Recognize what you can and cannot change. No one can alter the choices, actions, thoughts, or feelings of another person. The only person you can change is yourself.
- Let it go. There is another workshop, audition, and role on the next bulletin board.
- Consider the ways in which you are

"You are going to be amidst many others doing the exact same thing, and that is exciting. Use that energy as a positive motivation to keep you moving forward. Remember who you are and what you want, but definitely have an open mind and heart to new experiences and avenues that may present themselves. Remember that there is always something to be learnt in every experience, even the 'bad ones' like rejection. See rejection as an opportunity to grow."
Dancer and teacher Alex Little, as quoted in an article in danceinforma.com

successful. Recall the audition that won you a part, the choreographer who praised your dancing, the role you performed with panache: Learn from these accomplishments.

- Be happy with and take pride in the roles you do have. Still in the corps de ballet? Remember you're an important part of the choreographer's vision and the audience's expectations: What would *La Sylphide* be without the sylphs?

- Delve deeper into the parts you have. Work at refining a difficult combination, improving your acting, and enjoying rehearsals to take your mind off disappointments.
- Ask to be an understudy. Time spent watching another dancer introduces new skills and challenges you'll need to conquer to earn featured roles.
- Believe in yourself. Be ready next time to "prove them wrong."
- Pay attention and take note. What about the other dancers' technique, energy, or acting worked in their favor?
- Support the other dancers. Congratulate them on new parts.

An integral part of the dancer's life is learning to cope with disappointment. Stand up, get back into class, and keep working on your technique and routines.

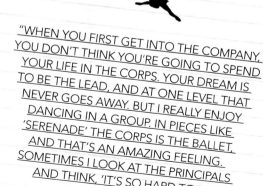

"WHEN YOU FIRST GET INTO THE COMPANY, YOU DON'T THINK YOU'RE GOING TO SPEND YOUR LIFE IN THE CORPS. YOUR DREAM IS TO BE THE LEAD, AND AT ONE LEVEL THAT NEVER GOES AWAY. BUT I REALLY ENJOY DANCING IN A GROUP. IN PIECES LIKE 'SERENADE' THE CORPS IS THE BALLET, AND THAT'S AN AMAZING FEELING. SOMETIMES I LOOK AT THE PRINCIPALS AND THINK, 'IT'S SO HARD TO BE OUT THERE ALONE.'"

Dena Abergel, dancer with New York City Ballet, as quoted in an article in the *New York Times*

DANCING IN PLACE

After a while, many dancers reach a point at which they feel bored, stuck, or uninspired. Perhaps they're dancing the same role every night while on tour and sense their performance is getting stale. Or despite their best efforts to seek promotion, they've stuck in the corps de ballet for many years. Their mind begins to wander in class, or the momentum they enjoyed while quickly progressing from one part to the next has stalled.

A dancer may also feel as though they're dancing in place because an injury is prohibiting their progress, the troupe is working with choreographers whose aesthetic and work processes don't match their own, or the company is cutting back on opportunities due to limited resources. Almost every dancer gets stuck at some point in their career, whether because of internal or external circumstances.

Keeping the dance life—and one's dancing— fresh and invigorating can be difficult, despite the constant push to improve technically, perform with greater artistry, and land bigger, juicier roles. When dancers hit the wall in their career, which is different from burnout (see pages 228–229), the time for renewal, change, and re-evaluation may be near.

Overcoming boredom

- Be creative. Experiment to go beyond or add expressiveness to the usual moves.
- Break out of routine. Add a new acting or technique class to your schedule.
- Improvise to new music. Rehearse choreography with other dancers to pick up new ideas.
- Keep an open mind. Visit another dance studio, watch another company's rehearsal, attend professional dance performances in styles different from your own to inspire creativity.

"I WOULD THINK, 'I'M NOT TALL ENOUGH, I NEED TO GET MY LEG HIGHER.' I WASN'T LOOKING AT MY DEVELOPMENT AS AN ARTIST. I HAD THIS FIRE INSIDE; I WANTED TO BE THE STAR. I FELT STUCK WITH MY PARTS; IT BECAME A JOB AND I WAS JUST PUNCHING IN.... FEELING STUCK WAS ABOUT NOT BEING PRESENT. IT WAS MY BLIND FOCUS ON THE FUTURE."

Abdul Latif, dancer with Donald Byrd/The Group, The Lion King, Hairspray, and JM/TW

If you reach a plateau in your dancing, be creative. Watch another company rehearse, study a new style of dance, or imagine a new challenge for yourself.

- Get out of your comfort zone. Take a workshop or master class that's above your skill level, or in a different style of dance.
- Change cross training. Try a new style of yoga, another somatic practice; swim at the weekend instead of running.

Getting unstuck from the corps, or how to get out in front

1. Remain passionate, not passive, about your love of dance and your dance career.
2. Meet with the artistic director, choreographer, or producer. Talk to them about your goals. Ask them what, in their opinion, is holding you back. Ask them what you need to do, learn, or accomplish to advance in the company.
3. Set new goals for learning and/or improvement.

4. Find a teacher or coach who will give you private lessons so you can reach those goals.
5. Seek out guest artist gigs (an agent can help, see pages 202–203) in which you're a soloist or featured dancer.
6. Consider auditioning for another company if you continue to be passed over.

Keeping performances fresh

- During class and rehearsals, keep working on technique, tricky steps, and difficult partnering; you may surprise yourself in performance.
- Connect more deeply with your part or character, to bring more nuance to the role.
- Make your movement more integral or organic, to ground its expressiveness.
- Stay authentic. If you're not true to your dancing, the audience will know.
- Eliminate another layer of self-protection while on stage; open yourself up more to audiences.

HAVING A FAMILY

Since dance became a discipline and performing art, women have been largely discouraged from becoming pregnant—particularly in ballet. The celebrated Italian/Swedish ballerina Marie Taglioni, for example, explained her absence from the stage in 1835 (because of pregnancy) as a knee injury.

Dance remains a difficult profession to combine with having a family. Not only is a female dancer's performing life short, so too is her period of fertility. While both male and female dancers can be conflicted about whether, or when, to combine a performing career with parenthood, for a woman dancer the decision to become pregnant, and carry and bear a child, can have a significant impact on the trajectory of her professional career.

Dance is an art form of the body. Dancers maintain their bodies for optimal physical performance and as a means of artistic expression. A woman dancer's body, however, undergoes a significant transformation during pregnancy, and those changes can linger.

In addition, pregnancy necessitates that a dancer maintain healthful eating habits. The dancer's responsibility for her body intensifies during pregnancy, as she balances the expectations of her profession with the requirements of her developing fetus.

Changes during pregnancy

- Decreases in muscle strength and stamina
- Weight gain
- Ligaments loosen in the pelvis, hips widen
- Loss of core strength
- Loss of balance
- Blood flow increases, heart works harder
- Emotions heighten because of hormones
- Feet flatten
- Breasts and ankles swell
- More arch develops in lower lumbar

"THE KEY IS TO LISTEN TO YOUR BODY. IF YOU ARE PLANNING TO HAVE A CHILD, IT IS VERY IMPORTANT THAT YOU YOURSELF ARE HEALTHY AND FIT. DANCING IS DEFINITELY ONE OF THE BEST WAYS TO STAY FIT. IT IS BETTER THAN A MECHANICAL WORKOUT IN A GYM, AS IT ALLOWS CREATIVE EXPRESSION AND EMOTIONAL BALANCE AS WELL. AN EXPERIENCED DOCTOR WHO UNDERSTANDS A DANCER'S BODY IS DIFFERENT MUST BE CHOSEN CAREFULLY."

Veena Basavarajaiah, a Bangalore-based solo dancer and choreographer, as quoted in an interview in narthaki.com

Many dancers continue to perform well into their pregnancies.

Returning to dance
- Maintain good nutrition and hydration
- Ease back into exercise: walking, swimming, easy stretching, gentle yoga, Pilates
- Reduce calorie intake only after finishing breastfeeding
- Return to dance: normal delivery, three to four weeks
- Return to dance: cesarean section, at least six weeks

Balancing dance and family
Any working mother or father knows what a challenge such a balance is, but parents in the arts—particularly dancers—face unique obstacles. Dancers invest years, often from a young age, in learning, practicing, and preparing for a career on stage, in which their every move is watched and critiqued. They've dedicated their lives to dance, to the exclusion of almost everything else.

Now more than ever, women are adept at having it all. And dancers—whether male or female—are no longer expected to choose between family and career. Still, for dancers, taking time off to deliver a baby and recover, or enjoy parental leave with a newborn is just the first adjustment of many.

Although some companies happily accommodate dancers with children, others do not. For freelance dancers, who already juggle disparate jobs and dance gigs, adding children to the mix means coordinating an already overcommitted schedule. Touring can be especially challenging, with family and friends providing much-needed child care for dancing parents.

Despite the inevitable guilt while at the studio or on the road, many dancers end up embracing their new role as parents. Such life experiences as pregnancy, partnership, and family deepen one's emotional attachments, which can enhance a dancer's art.

LEAPING INTO CHOREOGRAPHY

Many dancers get the urge to start creating their own choreography while a member of a company. Or they may be inspired to make their own dances, and begin to choreograph (sometimes for the companies in which they dance) as a way of exploring their creative potential.

For those who can't seem to progress in a studio or company, but have a vision for dance and the ability to craft movement into kinetic art, choreography may be a more fruitful nonperformance option. And for older dancers ready to exit a performing career, choreography can be a smooth transition to a different role in the dance profession.

Choreographers typically work on a freelance basis, unless they're also the artistic director of their own company. They choreograph for theater companies, music-theater productions, festivals, dance

Funding for emerging choreographers
- Princess Grace Awards (USA)
- Marion North Mentoring Awards, Bonnie Bird Choreography Fund (UK)
- Jerome Foundation (USA)
- Frederic and Robin Seegal Fund for Emerging Choreographers (International)
- Emerging Choreographers Initiative, Australian Arts Council
- Prix Jardin d'Europe Emerging Works Summit, 4Culture (Romania, Europe)
- Mariam McGlone Emerging Choreographer Award (International)
- Emerging Choreographer Fund, Asia Dance Magazine (Malaysia)

studios, fashion shows, music videos, films, live-music concerts, and international events like the Olympics—in addition to dance companies.

Choreographers generally specialize in one dance style, such as ballet (classical, neoclassical, and/or contemporary); modern; jazz, tap, and/or musical theater; hip-hop; ballroom; African; or if from

Choreographer Jamal Sims has worked on films, including *Footloose* and *Step Up 3D*.

India, a single style such as Odissi, Bharatanatyam, or Kathak. Many dance instructors are choreographers as well, as they create and teach choreography in classes, for competitions, and for recitals.

How to begin choreographing

- Study how choreographers generate, teach, and organize their material.
- Watch how choreographers dictate to or collaborate with dancers.
- Analyze how choreographers create combinations, sequence combinations into sections, and edit their own work.
- Start improvising with a favorite piece of music or inspirational image.
- Ask friends or colleagues if you can choreograph on them.
- Seek out opportunities to show your work and choreograph new work.
- Be patient. Like learning to dance, learning to choreograph takes time, work, and dedication

Many dancers get the urge to choreograph and start by making work for themselves.

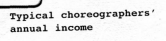

Typical choreographers' annual income

USA	$25,000–$55,000
Australia	
(part-time)	$17,100
(full-time)	$24,500
UK	£450 a week

"MOST CHOREOGRAPHERS START AS DANCERS, AND MY ADVICE WOULD BE TO PERFORM AS MUCH AS YOU CAN. THAT'S THE HEART OF IT—IF YOU CAN PUT YOURSELF IN THE MOMENT AND LEARN TO INTERPRET OTHER PEOPLE'S IDEAS THROUGH DANCE, YOU'LL BE A BETTER CHOREOGRAPHER. BUILD YOUR SKILLS AS A COMMUNICATOR BY KEEPING UP A REGULAR, OPEN DIALOGUE WITH OTHER ARTISTS IN OTHER DISCIPLINES, LIKE PAINTERS AND WRITERS, SO YOU DON'T GET HOT-HOUSED. TRUST YOUR CREATIVE PROCESS, AND BE OPEN TO MAJOR TRENDS. WE ARE CONTEMPORARY ARTISTS, SO WE SHOULD BE AWARE OF WHERE WE ARE IN A COMPLEX WORLD."

Choreographer Ben Wright, as quoted in an article in *The Independent*

11

REALITY CHECK

"Dance has never been a particularly easy life, and everybody knows that," choreographer Twyla Tharp once said. Ask any dancer: Beneath the seemingly effortless movements, the spangled or flowing costumes, the smiles and vitality are years of hard work, discipline, disappointment, injury, and pain, along with long hours and low pay. In some cases, eating disorders, drug abuse, and sexual harassment enter the mix, as well. This chapter delves into the dark side of the dance profession, the realities that dancers generally don't care to discuss for fear of appearing weak, of lacking commitment, or of appearing unsuited to the rigors of dance.

DANCE: A SHORT, DIFFICULT, UNDERVALUED CAREER

In her blog *What a Body Knows*, published in psychologytoday.com/blog, Dr. Kimerer L. LaMothe, a dancer, writes, "To dance is a radical act. To think about dance, to study dance, or to practice dance in this twenty-first century is a radical act. Why? Because if dancing matters—if dancing makes a difference to how we humans think and feel and act—then dancing challenges the values that fund modern western cultures."

For one thing, explains Dr. LaMothe, dancing defies the Western privileging of mind over body. "To dance is a radical act because dancing reminds us that the bodily movements we make, make us who we are." Western culture also prioritizes the individual over the collective, she continues, whereas dance is about relationships.

Cultures of the West also favor the written word and speech as modes of discourse, rather than physical expression. Work that entails sitting, and thus privileges the intellect, is more valued than work that uses the body.

Dance: the underfunded art

A lack of funding affects dancers all over the world. In the United States, researchers have found that dance is in fact the most underfunded of all the performing arts. When a country's national economy goes into recession, arts programmers are less likely to feature newer artists and companies, and focus instead more on well-known artists. At the same time, however, organizations in countries throughout the world continue to develop new programs. Canada has a program that encourages creativity-based partnerships between presenters and artists, and France has provided funding for young choreographers to establish companies in regional centers.

Why do people do it?

With all these difficulties, why do people dance? Dr. Kim Vincs, director of the Deakin Motion.Lab, has investigated the "factors that influence how and why people become—and stay—dance artists." She found that dance artists in Australia earned an average of $27,000 per year, of which only $16,700 was dance-related, meaning that, for most dancers, the career choice is driven by more than just economic reasons. She suggests that "things to do with the value, satisfaction and quality of life dance artists get from what they do—might be as significant, if not more significant, drivers of sustainability than pure economics."

DOWNSIDES TO A DANCE CAREER

- A dancer's career is intense and short. Most dancers need to retire from dancing on stage by age forty, as the physical tolls of continued overexertion, repeated injury, and normal aging cause loss of technique, speed, and flexibility.
- At the age when a dancer's performing career ends, his or her nondance friends are entering their peak earning years as they progress in their professions.
- Financial insecurity is endemic to careers in dance.
- Students graduating from a college, university, or conservatory dance program enter the job market with substantial debt.
- Competition is fierce. The number of applicants exceeds the number of openings. Only the highly talented are likely to secure stable employment.

- Dancers have one of the highest rates of nonfatal on-the-job injuries of any profession.
- Dance requires long hours. Freelance dancers often work other jobs during the day, and take class, rehearse, and perform at night. Company dancers take class and rehearse all day, and perform at night.
- Dancers can spend much of the year on the road, whether as company members, dancers in a touring production, or hired for a cruise ship or theme park.
- Studios and performance venues can be cold and drafty, non-air-conditioned, and have unsuitable flooring.
- Many dancers, especially freelance, do not receive health insurance.

For many dancers, the considerable downsides to a dance career are outweighed by the thrill of performing onstage in front of an audience.

FINANCIAL REALITIES: DANCER PAY

Around the world, a professional dancer's average annual pay varies widely, depending on a number of factors: type of dance; dancer experience; union or nonunion position; number of days, weeks, or shows; payment per week, show, tour, or year; benefits (health insurance, workers' compensation).

Unions

At many large dance companies, and within commercial ventures, union contracts often stipulate dancer salaries and benefits. Union representatives and dance directors and producers negotiate contracts that specify salary, work hours, benefits, overtime, touring, and other conditions. Some producers and venues require union membership —for example, only members of the Actors' Equity Association can access many Broadway auditions.

Benefits of union membership include
- help with negotiating contracts;
- incorporating provisions for sick and family leave;
- ensuring safe working conditions;
- providing health insurance; and
- communicating between employers, dancers, and union.

Downsides to union membership include
- initial joining fee;
- annual fees; and
- restrictions on working on nonunion productions.

SOME DANCE-RELATED UNIONS

- Equity (UK): dancers in musical theater, clubs, opera, dance companies, other commercial theater
- Canadian Actors' Equity Association: dancers in commercial ventures and nonprofit companies
- American Guild of Musical Artists, AFL-CIO (US): professional ballet, opera, modern dancers who work with a company
- American Federation of Television and Radio: dancers on televised performances or perform professionally on television
- Screen Actors Guild: dancers in film
- Actors' Equity Association, AFL-CIO: dancers in musical theater
- American Guild of Variety Artists: dancers in circuses, Las Vegas showrooms and cabarets, dance revues, theme parks, and arena and auditorium performances
- EuroFIA Dance Passport: gives members of International Federation of Actors (FIA) union, guild and associations of professional performers employment assistance
- UNI MEI: dancers in media, entertainment and arts in 100 union and guilds in over seventy countries

> **It can be frustrating. You see all your friends with real jobs and they make decent money, enough to say, 'I'm going to go buy a new couch today.' And I'm like, 'Well I'm going to go buy myself a cheeseburger today.'**
>
> Dancer Linnea Schlegel, quoted in an article in *Daily Finance*

Contracts

In addition to name and contact information, agreed-upon payment, and length of employment, a dancer contract may also include additional responsibilities like participating in lecture demonstrations, residencies, or press interviews. Free days during tours are specified, along with parameters for travel from the hotel. Health insurance and liabilities may be covered, as well as salary gradations.

Such details as ongoing practice and training, types of rehearsals and required attendance, and rest time during intermissions are included. A code of conduct is often integral to a contract. Before Britney Spears' "Femme Fatale" tour, the backup dancers signed contracts banning them from consuming alcohol and drugs anywhere near the star, and subjecting them to random drug testing.

Because most dancers can't live on their income as a company member, they take on extra jobs and must manage their budget and schedules well.

MOONLIGHTING: MAKING ENDS MEET

Working full-time with a professional dance company often involves touring, teaching, and residencies, as well as daily technique class, learning new choreography, maintaining repertory, and performing. Because of the company's workload and expectations, dancers' salaries often cover living expenses.

But freelance dancers, those who can't find full-time work, dancers who can find gigs only sporadically throughout the year, or dancers just starting out often supplement their income with other jobs. The primary criterion for supplemental work is flexibility, allowing performers to keep dance at the forefront of their lives.

Dance-related jobs

- Teaching in a school, studio, college, or university dance program, community education, or neighborhood program
- Teaching yoga, Pilates, or a somatic practice at a school or studio
- Teaching on the dance convention circuit
- Dancing as a guest with other companies
- Working at a dance school or studio, or in a dance program, in a nondance capacity (as a receptionist, tour coordinator, administrator, or administrative assistant)
- Creating and performing in a Fringe Festival show
- Costume designer and/or sewer
- Lighting designer or technical supervisor for a theater or dance company
- Writing about dance for local print or online publications

GRANTS

Philanthropic organizations around the globe offer financial support to individual dancers (as well as choreographers and dance companies) for the research and development of new work. Emerging and professional dancers can advance their careers by applying for grants from nonprofit organizations. Competition for funding is fierce. Submission guidelines vary and must be followed to the letter. Applications (much like audition applications) are often accompanied by cover letter, CV, references, and demo reel. Listed below are some organizations that provide funding to individual dancers:

- Arts Council of England
- Arts Council of Wales
- Arts Decree/Arts Flemish Parliament Act
- Creative Capital
- Guggenheim Memorial Foundation
- Herb Alpert Foundation
- Ireland Arts Council/An Chomhairle Ealaion
- Jacob's Pillow Award
- McKnight Fellowship for Dancers
- Mid-Atlantic Arts Foundation
- New England Foundation for the Arts
- PEW Charitable Trusts
- Princess Grace Awards
- USA Fellows

Nondance-related jobs

In addition to part-time office positions and waitressing, dancers can be extremely creative in coming up with jobs that pay the bills:

- DJ-ing at clubs and special events
- Commercial salmon fisherman
- Bank teller
- Model
- Receptionist
- Accountant
- Massage therapist
- Marketing/communications

Additional costs for freelance dancers

- Costumes, accessories, hair, makeup, shoes
- Classes (to refine technique, learn new choreography, advance skills and artistry)
- Rehearsal space
- Music CDs

Working as a server is probably the most common way dancers supplement their incomes.

Being a professional mambo dancer may fulfill many dreams, but making a living is not necessarily one of them.

Manny Siverio in *salsanewyork.com*

SUBSTANCE ABUSE

In 1986, ballerina Gelsey Kirkland parted the curtains on substance abuse in the ballet world with her cocaine-infused, tell-all memoir, *Dancing on My Grave*. A dancer with New York City Ballet and American Ballet Theater during the 1970s, Kirkland revealed—in addition to the eating disorders, disregard for health, and extreme physical demands dancers submitted to—drug use and addiction in the dance world.

New York City Ballet founder George Balanchine gave Kirkland amphetamine-laced "vitamins" during a tour in the Soviet Union, to boost her stamina. Fellow Ballet Theater dancer Patrick Bissell introduced her to cocaine, which became the basis of their relationship. In addition to abusing alcohol and marijuana, she wrote, "I was a speed freak, a Valium addict, a coke casualty, and a total wreck. Even my teeth were falling out."

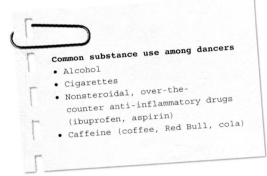

Common substance use among dancers
- Alcohol
- Cigarettes
- Nonsteroidal, over-the-counter anti-inflammatory drugs (ibuprofen, aspirin)
- Caffeine (coffee, Red Bull, cola)

Drugs may seem like an immediate solution to many of the pressures dancers experience, but substance abuse can lead to serious problems, including addiction and injury.

Nevertheless, she wrote, "Cocaine still seemed to be a godsend. The social setting of the dance world had insulated me, and I had isolated myself. I mistakenly identified my artistic ideals as the cause of all my maladies. The drug allowed me to adjust, to adapt to anything and anyone… Cocaine enabled me to avoid misery, the agony that existed in a theater that rejected perfection in favor of expediency and box-office receipts."

The jury is still out about whether Kirkland's autobiography testified to one dancer's addiction and downfall, an era of

Cigarettes and alcohol are among the substances most abused by dancers.

excess, or a systemic problem in the dance world—or perhaps all three. In 2011, an internal report on cocaine use at the Royal Danish Ballet was leaked to the *Copenhagen Post*. The dancers' drug use was tied to artistic director Nikolaj Hübbe's alleged cocaine abuse.

One paragraph, in translation, noted "escalating drug abuse problems among dancers over the past two years, among these escalating problems with cocaine abuse. It is important to emphasize here that people not employed by the ballet, but with various connections to the ballet, have also reported rising concerns about the escalating drug abuse problems."

Still, because of books like Kirkland's, dancers now better understand the side effects and health risks of drugs and alcohol, and substance abuse in many dance companies is minimal. "I wish I had racier stories for you," Linnette Roe, a former dancer with the Pacific Northwest Ballet, told the *New York Times*. "But the No. 1 performance-enhancing drug today is coffee."

Why do dancers use drugs?
- Pressure to stay thin (appetite suppressants, including cocaine, cigarettes, diet pills)
- Stimulate energy and stamina (amphetamines, cocaine)
- Pain (painkillers such as Vicodin, Percocet, and OxyContin, muscle relaxants)
- Performance anxiety, increase confidence (cocaine)
- To relax from stimulants (alcohol, marijuana, Valium, sleeping pills, barbituates)
- Peer pressure among dancers
- To hide an injury, which can lead to more serious injuries

Consequences of long-term drug use
- Malnutrition
- Bone loss
- Injury
- Loss of energy, stamina, motor function
- Lack of rest, sleep
- Heart problems
- Addiction
- Arrest
- Depression
- Psychosis
- Loss of income

OVERCOMING BURNOUT

According to Drs. Robert S. Weinberg and Daniel Gould, researchers in sport sciences and exercise psychology, burnout is "an exhaustive psychophysiological response exhibited as a result of frequent, sometimes extreme, and generally ineffective efforts to meet excessive training and competitive demands."

In other words, burnout is a stage beyond fatigue (see pages 106–107), when dancers' mental and physical demands exceed their emotional, psychological, and physical capacity to keep up. Although dancers' minds and bodies are trained to work beyond capacity, to adapt to an extreme and then push on, this process can overload a dancer and result in burnout. Burnout can be debilitating.

Experiencing burnout can also be accompanied by feelings of helplessness and despair. Dancers diagnosed with burnout must reduce their workload and increase rest and recovery for three to four months, or risk relapsing.

Factors contributing to burnout

- Added dance commitments in class, rehearsals, performances
- Lack of recovery time (i.e., rest) from dance commitments
- Dance culture's emphasis on ignoring fatigue, overexertion, pain
- Need to overachieve, surpass the quality of the last performance
- Stress caused by finances, personal life, family relationships
- Frequent injuries or chronic injury

Symptoms of burnout

- Feeling as if dancing has plateaued
- Dreading performing
- Passion for dance is gone
- Loss of technique

Burnout is a stage beyond fatigue and debilitating if not addressed.

- Lack of motivation, energy, excitement
- Insomnia, restless sleep, nightmares

Negativity
- Lack of appetite
- Irritability, dramatic mood swings
- High blood pressure and/or heart rate
- Excessive sweating
- Increased susceptibility to infections, viruses
- Malfunctioning metabolism

Two types of burnout

Acute: short-term burnout, often less than a month; can occur during summer intensives, workshops, at the start of a season, after a series of performances.

Chronic: long-term burnout, as a result of cumulative imbalances in workload and demands versus rest and recovery time.

Take the symptoms of burnout seriously and make changes in your lifestyle, commitments and schedule if necessary.

STRATEGIES FOR OVERCOMING BURNOUT

- Reduced commitments/workload
- Rest, relaxation, recovery
- Good nutrition
- Dance and nondance support systems
- Short-term break
- Change in schedule
- Counseling
- Temporarily assume a nondance role in the company
- Consulting with a dance coach on goals

"I'VE BEEN TEACHING/SHARING DANCE WITH KIDS IN SCHOOLS THIS WEEK, ESPECIALLY UNDERPRIVILEGED KIDS, WHICH COMPLETELY HEALS THE BURNOUT. IT OFFERS BALANCE AND PERSPECTIVE FOR ME, AND CONNECTS ME WITH MY HEART AND THE LOVE OF DANCE BEYOND THE PERFORMANCE/ BUSINESS/COMPETITION/SELF-FOCUS. AMAZING. IT'S A BEAUTIFUL THING."

Dancer and choreographer Tamara Ober, member of Zenon Dance Company

DANCERS BEHAVING BADLY: RIVALRIES

Naima Akef, an Egyptian belly dancer in the mid-twentieth century, became a star at Badeia Masabny's famous nightclub—until the other dancers, jealous of her success, attempted to beat her up and Akef was fired. In the South Korean film *Wishing Stair*, a friendship turns lethal when two girls compete for a single spot in a Russian ballet school. In American ballet films from *The Turning Point* to the Australian television teen drama *Dance Academy* and the Hollywood *Bring It On* cheerleading movies, to competitive dance reality shows broadcast from India to Poland, the fierce rivalries among dancers are legendary, whether fictive or real.

In dance competitions, academies, departments, studios, and companies around the world, rivalries abound. Healthy competition is an integral part of becoming a dancer, and can spur dancers to continually improve and realize their career objectives. Jealousy, however, is a complicated and destructive emotion. A manifestation of fear, vulnerability, insecurity, and feelings of inadequacy, jealousy can bloom into hatred, bitterness, and depression.

Some dancers, rather than admit they're jealous of another dancer's role, promotion, or performance, will attempt to discredit the other dancer. Be aware that the teachers, choreographers, artistic directors, and producers you're working with have seen it all. They've all experienced healthy competition and vicious jealousy themselves, and their responses will range from disinterest to resolving the rivalry.

Competition, jealousy, and gossip can be rife in a dance company, and damage a performer's self-esteem.

Ways to overcome jealousy

If you are experiencing feelings of jealousy
toward someone you work with, there are
some simple ways to make yourself feel better
about the situation.

1. Be aware: Admit you're jealous.
2. Identify your real feelings: anger, fear,
   humiliation, vulnerability, insecurity.
3. Are you often jealous? Is the envy a new
   feeling or an old one? Did it start with
   competitive parents who asked questions
   like, "Why can't you dance more like her?"
   or "Why didn't you get that part"?
4. Recognize the ways in which you excel in
   dance. Write them down. Affirm them to
   yourself.
5. Consider jealousy a wake-up call to work
   harder on your technique, acting, and roles.
6. Learn to compliment other dancers on their
   promotions and performances.

Signs of jealousy

- Gossip
- Rumors
- Eye rolling and glaring
- Whispering
- Intimidation

> I do not try to dance better
> than anyone else. I only try
> to dance better than myself.
>
> Mikhail Baryshnikov

SEXUAL HARASSMENT

Because dance is an art form of the body; touch is integral to learning, partnering, and performing; and dance is a business in which competition is fierce and power is unevenly distributed, knowing if and when sexual harassment is occurring is critical to a dancer's peace of mind and physical well-being. Although infrequent, cases of sexual harassment in dance schools and companies have been made public through lawsuits.

A lawsuit filed against the North Carolina School of the ARTS alleged a male instructor seduced a student into a sexual relationship. A principal dancer with the Houston Ballet alleged "unwelcome, unsolicited and untoward sexual advances" from the artistic director, that her complaints to the company were ignored, and that she was "subsequently retaliated against and subjected to a hostile work environment."

Many companies, however, generate and implement successful sexual harassment policies. Dance Aotearoa New Zealand is an organization that has created codes of practice for dance teachers, dancers, and choreographers. As part of good professional practice, the organization suggests schools and companies publicly post codes of compliance, which also include New Zealand laws on sexual harassment and abusive behavior.

Sexual harassment includes any type of attention that is sexual and unwanted, from looks to physical touching to verbal abuse.

What is sexual harassment?

Any type of verbal or physical attention that is sexual and unwanted is a form of sexual harassment. Sexual harassment can be inflicted by a teacher on a student, or producer or artistic director on a company member, or between dancers (whether students or professionals). It also crosses gender and sexual orientation lines.

Even if you feel extremely uncomfortable or distressed after experiencing sexual harassment, it's important to report your experience by phone, email, letter, or in person.

How to address sexual harassment

- **Pair up.** Don't be alone with the person; always insist on having someone with you.
- **Vocalize.** In a firm, confident, and clearly audible voice say "No," "Your behavior is inappropriate," or "What you just said/did to me is offensive."
- **Document.** Write down every incident in a notebook, journal, or computer file. Include the date, time, place, what occurred, how you responded, and how the perpetrator responded. Include how you felt.
- **Report.** Talk with the executive director, business manager, or personnel director at the school or company about incidents, and their sexual harassment policy. Ask them to intervene on your behalf.
- **File a complaint.** If the perpetrator continues the harassment after intervention, file a formal complaint with the company or school.
- **Bring a lawsuit.** If the complaint doesn't cause the harasser to stop, consult with legal aid/a lawyer about addressing the situation with a lawsuit.

Sexual harassment isn't as much about sex as it is about power. It's perpetrated as a way of exercising control over another person. Sexual harassment of a minor is illegal and a criminal offense. Here are some examples:

- Teacher, director, or producer to a dancer: sexually explicit comments; sexual proposition; repeated requests for a date; unwanted touching (beyond in-class or rehearsal corrections); verbal abuse of a sexual nature.
- Between dancers/students/ colleagues: repeated requests for a date, despite stated lack of interest; gossip; whispering; rumors of a sexual nature; unwanted sexually explicit comments; unwanted and/or forcible touching.

12
LIFE AFTER DANCING

As the adage goes, life is short. For dancers, the performing life is even shorter. Although some remarkable dancers continue performing into their forties and fifties, most retire from dancing while in their thirties—if not before, because of injury. The continual mental and physical rigor, stress, and strenuousness of a performing career takes its toll on dancers, who may reach their prime just a few years before retirement. Retirement can feel like a devastating loss, and amidst such sadness, dancers wonder, "What do I do next?" Despite the difficulty of transitioning out of performance, most dancers find a fulfilling second career. Many become choreographers, dance writers, or scholars; others become teachers, coaches, or mentors in dance or related areas. Some start their own dance companies, for which they choreograph. Others go farther afield, into professions ranging from therapy and counseling to law to business.

THE TRANSITION

Because of dancers' commitment and dedication to their art, often to the (expected, or even required) exclusion of everything else, they're particularly vulnerable when becoming older, while facing retirement at an age much younger than their nondancing peers. In their single-minded devotion to dance, some dancers forgo college or live on a shoestring without any savings—which makes planning for a second act more difficult. And after living in the limelight, in front of an audience, transitioning to a less-public, less-visible career can be challenging.

Several organizations throughout the world were created specifically to help dancers transition into new careers. Professionals from these organizations urge dancers to begin planning for retirement, or even to start working at a second career, while still performing. If permanently sidelined by injury, this strategy can help ease the trauma of losing one's identity as a dancer early on, and provide some financial stability and breathing room as one embarks on the next stage of professional life.

Research findings

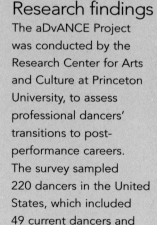

The aDvANCE Project was conducted by the Research Center for Arts and Culture at Princeton University, to assess professional dancers' transitions to post-performance careers. The survey sampled 220 dancers in the United States, which included 49 current dancers and 171 former dancers.

Career-transition challenges faced by respondents:

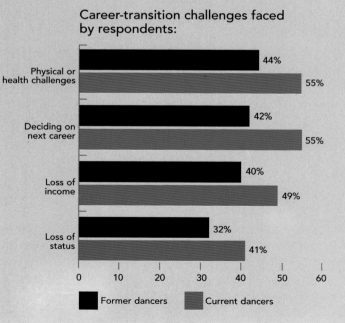

Physical or health challenges — 44% (Former dancers), 55% (Current dancers)

Deciding on next career — 42% (Former dancers), 55% (Current dancers)

Loss of income — 40% (Former dancers), 49% (Current dancers)

Loss of status — 32% (Former dancers), 41% (Current dancers)

Former dancers   Current dancers

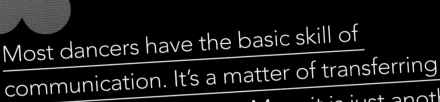

Most dancers have the basic skill of communication. It's a matter of transferring it into a different career. My suit is just another costume and [my job] is another role I'm playing.

Geon van der Wyst, former principal dancer with the National Ballet of Canada who transitioned into selling real estate, as quoted in thestar.com

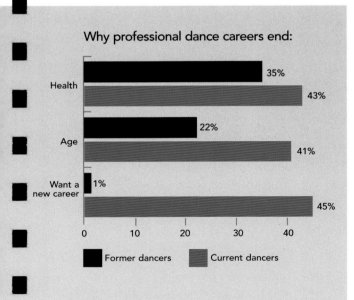

Why professional dance careers end:

	Former dancers	Current dancers
Health	35%	43%
Age	22%	41%
Want a new career	1%	45%

Dancer qualities applicable to a new career

- Self-discipline
- Motivation
- Dedication, commitment
- Reliability, responsibility
- Focus, concentration
- Attention to detail
- Collaboration, teamwork

ACTING AND CHARACTER ROLES

Some dancers transition from virtuosic movement-intensive parts on stage to character roles, or into acting. Neither option is as physically rigorous or as taxing to the aging body as pure dance, although both continue to use the body as a form of physical expression. Instead, character roles and acting place a greater emphasis on the face, gesture, mime, and other ways of embodying the personality and motivations of a character, rather than communicating more abstractly through dance.

Character dance

Character roles help drive and enhance the narratives of ballets or other dances. The characters may be comic or tragic, central to the story or a diversion. These roles might be demure, such as the partygoers and parents in *The Nutcracker*, or quite outré as the Queen of Hearts in the Royal Winnipeg Ballet's extravaganza *Wonderland*.

The costumes are usually extravagant and colorful. Rather than wearing pointe shoes or ballet slippers, dancers performing character roles may wear shoes that fit their characters' work or personality: from boots to glittery platform shoes to modest character shoes with heels.

Older members of a company usually play character roles. The San Francisco Ballet has a special title for these esteemed professionals: principal character dancer. George Balanchine even performed character roles: the mysterious Drosselmeyer in

The Nutcracker, and Don Quixote in the ballet of the same name.

At the Royal Danish Ballet, dancers may transition into character roles when they turn forty. These roles are critical to the RDB, particularly in the ballets created by Danish choreographer August Bournonville. By retaining long-time dancers to perform character roles, RDB also preserves its institutional memory, keeps on dancers with the experience to mentor younger dancers, and can turn to these professionals for help in teaching and staging repertory works with younger dancers.

Tips for transitioning into acting
- Develop and hone acting skills learned in dance through theater or film acting classes
- Discuss the transition with your agent
- Audition and promote yourself as a performer (not just a dancer or actor)
- Go after roles close to your former profession (e.g., dancer, dance teacher, yoga instructor)

> Young boys and girls are lucky today! There are a bevy of dance reality shows on television nowadays. If you observe, most of the participants end up foraying into television. The reverse is also true, that most actors we see on TV are winners of dance reality shows. And why not?
>
> Actress Resshmi Ghosh, as quoted in *The Times of India*

Penélope Cruz is one film star who began her performing career studying dance.

FILM STARS WHO TRANSITIONED FROM DANCING TO ACTING

Summer Glau (Ballet San Antonio)
Lyndsy Fonesca (IMTA's runner-up for "Young Miss Dancer of the Year")
Zhang Ziyi (trained at Beijing Dance Academy)
Lea Thompson (dancer with American Ballet Theatre)
Penélope Cruz (studied at Spain's National Conservatory)
Alexander Godunov (principal with Bolshoi Ballet)
Jeremy Sheffield (The Royal Ballet)
Gregory Hines (Broadway jazz tap dancer)

ESTABLISHING A DANCE COMPANY

A dancer does not create a dance company, team, or crew to make money or become famous. Much like being a professional dancer, starting a group of one's own requires tireless dedication, creativity, and the resilience to overcome disappointment and adversity—but also a clear vision, and an array of management and business skills.

Dancers start companies to expand their commitment to dance into another realm, to realize their talents in choreography, and/or to advance their creativity through the direction of a dance company. Only the singularly talented and wildly ambitious, however, acquire fame or financial stability through their companies. Instead, the rewards of running a dance company lie in the collaboration and creativity it brings to those involved.

Creating your own dance company can be an artistic, financial, and business challenge—but tremendously satisfying.

Essential skills

- Passion and desire (to start a company and keep it running)
- Vision and philosophy (to differentiate your company from others)
- Choreographic ability (to make dances for the company, or hire and assist choreographers working with the company)
- Management skills (to oversee and direct staff and dancers)
- Business acumen (to manage finances)
- Leadership (as the founder, figurehead, and director of the company)
- Communication skills (so staff and dancers know what you want and why)

- Networking ability (to find and engage dancers, members for the board of directors, donors/funders, staff, audiences)

Budget basics

- Earned income: revenues from ticket sales, advertisements placed in show programs, classes and workshops offered
- Contributed income: foundation and government grants, donations
- Expenses: salaries for staff and dancers; rental fees for office space and performance venues; fees paid to graphic

NONPROFIT STATUS

The economic realities of founding and managing a concert dance company are as daunting as those of living a dancer's life: Generally, one has more expenses than income. For this reason, most artistic directors in the United States run their dance companies as nonprofit organizations, which means the company structure meets the requirements of Section 501(c)(3) of the Internal Revenue Code. A nonprofit dance group

- is exempt from taxes;
- is eligible for reduced postal rates;
- can apply for grants from government agencies and foundations;
- can solicit money from donors;
- can protect company members and directors from personal liability;
- must form a board of directors that, in effect, governs the organization;
- puts all employees on the payroll (which means paying for unemployment and disability and workers' compensation insurance, and withholding federal, state, and local taxes and Social Security); and
- must submit documentation and undergo auditing to ensure compliance.

Instead of becoming a 501(c)(3), some small dance companies align with a service organization as a fiscal agent. For a fee or percentage of income, the service organization provides selected nonprofit benefits.

and website designers, lighting designers, videographers, photographers, lawyers, accountants, IT and publicists; marketing and advertising costs; costs for costumes, sets, music, office supplies

Considerations

- What is driving your desire to start a company, team, or crew?
- What is your mission? What do you hope to achieve?
- What kind of company is it? How is the company different from others?
- What is the brand?
- Who is the audience?
- How will the company fit into/ benefit the dance ecosystem in the community?
- Are you the choreographer? If so, what is your style and purpose?
- Are you commissioning choreographers? Who? Where will you find them? How will their work build the repertory?
- What will the repertory reflect?
- What is the troupe's name? What does the name tell people? (Again, the brand.)
- What kind of performers are you looking for? How will you find them?
- Where will funding come from?
- In what venues will the company perform?
- Who can help you realize your vision?

Dancers start companies to expand their commitment to dance into another realm, to realize their talents in choreography, and/or to advance their creativity.

TEACHING DANCE

Dance-teacher training actually begins the day aspiring dancers take their first class. The moment they begin paying close attention to their teacher, watching his or her movements, practicing those motions with their own bodies, and taking in and making corrections, young dancers are in fact learning how (or how not) to teach. Which is why the transition into dance teaching is so natural and easy for retired performers: The dancer has already spent years observing, absorbing, and critiquing others' training methods.

Sharing one's dance experience through teaching is not only altruistic, but a way to expand one's skill set, earn income, and stay in the studio. In order to teach, dancers must have choreography skills, know how to format classes to advance students' learning, and in some cases have acquired additional education, training, or accreditation.

Although some retired performers find stable employment with one institution or organization, most teach on a freelance basis for a number of different schools and studios. Teaching is also a good second-income stream for dancers while they're still performing, and can ease the transition into teaching full-time as a post-performance career.

Where to teach
- Private dance schools
- Dance company schools
- Dance studios
- Colleges, universities, conservatories
- High schools, schools for the arts
- Education or community centers
- During workshops, summer intensives

Teacher training
Depending on the studio, school, college or university, conservatory, workshop, or summer intensive you're applying to, different teaching credentials may be required. In addition to professional dance experience, these may include the following:
- Bachelor's degree in education or Bachelor of Fine Arts in dance
- State teacher certification
- Master's degree in dance education, choreography

"I LOVE HAVING FUN AND PASSING ON MY PASSION OF DANCE. I LOVE WATCHING THE STUDENTS WHEN THEY HAVE THE 'AHA' MOMENT AND GET WHAT I AM TEACHING BOTH PHYSICALLY AND MENTALLY."
Tony Czar, choreographer for Britney Spears and Jason Derulo, who teaches in Australia, Poland, Taiwan, Russia, Japan, Korea, and Guam

Many dancers teach, while performing and in retirement from the stage, to share their knowledge.

- Knowledge of specific dance techniques or styles
- Certification in teaching a specific style, technique, or approach to dance
- Qualifications from a dance-teacher training program
- Accreditation from a dance-teacher training organization
- Teaching internship or ITT (initial teaching training) certification

Financial realities

Many dance teachers are self-employed, running their own business or working freelance for several different schools. Income varies depending on the amount of work.

US: $9.68–$35.52 per hour; median annual income $37,570

UK: £21,500 to £36,000 (full-time in state schools)

Dance-teacher skill set
- Dance background and experience
- Teaching experience, certification, educational degree
- Understanding of educational frameworks, progressive learning
- Knowledge and application of anatomy, alignment in teaching
- Knowledge of various teaching styles, approaches
- Develops own distinctive approach to teaching (methodology)
- Teaching methods are safe; knows first aid
- Applies multiple learning strategies for different students
- Creativity in explanations using metaphor, other descriptions
- Teaches beginning to advanced levels
- Creates curricula and lesson plans
- Choreographs in-class combinations and sequences; choreographs dance works for recitals, programs, competitions, concerts
- Manages confidential and injury information
- Provides constructive feedback
- Good interpersonal skills, patient, manages and diffuses conflict
- Operates according to school, studio, or country's ethic codes for teaching
- Promotes/markets self and classes

TEACHING MIND–BODY PRACTICES

Throughout a performing career, many dancers seek to improve their alignment, mind–body awareness, technique, and understanding of anatomy by incorporating the study of an additional mind–body practice into their schedule. They may study yoga or Pilates (see pages 76–77). Or they may begin investigating Laban Movement Analysis (see pages 98–101) or Bartenieff Fundamentals^{SM} (see page 100). Others learn one of the imaging or somatic practices described in Chapter 6, such as the Alexander Technique, Skinner Releasing Technique, Ideokinesis, or Body-Mind Centering.

When it's time to find a new career, these ex-performers often transition into teaching a body practice other than dance. The one they choose is usually the practice in which they've invested the most time, found the greatest meaning, or that enlightened their integrative understanding of movement and image, body and mind.

Transitioning from student to teacher

While a student, one's attention is on the teacher's direction and instruction, and incorporating those lessons. The focus is on the self and self-improvement. The student is concerned with learning and cultivating a deeper understanding of the practice, in order to improve his or her performance.

Teachers undergo training, during which they transform such lessons into their own instructional methodology. They're responsible for clearly explaining and describing the practice to their own students, and ensuring students learn and progress without injury. They manage various proficiencies and individualities within groups of students while keeping the entire group on the same progressive track. And they create engaging classes

Skill set
- Knowledge of anatomy and alignment
- Safe teaching practices, first aid
- Confidence
- Creativity
- Ability to give constructive feedback
- Teaching experience
- Enthusiasm for the practice
- Breathing and meditation techniques
- Openly communicates
- Ability to adapt approach to students with less strength and flexibility, students with injuries
- Create curricula that advances student learning and ability
- Develop a specialized approach and niche
- Promotion and marketing (for yourself as a teacher and for your classes)

that maintain students' enthusiasm and interest.

Education

To teach such practices usually requires certification, which varies widely in price, length of training, and quality of instruction. The various yoga styles may require 200 hours of teacher certification through a qualified studio or school. Pilates teacher training through qualified centers is often divided into mat certification and comprehensive certification (the latter of which includes all of the Pilates equipment), both of which require practice teaching.

Teaching a mind-body practice related to dance is a good way of earning extra income or transitioning into a career off the stage.

Some colleges and universities offer two-year certificates in somatic studies. The somatic practices also have their own studios and schools throughout the world. Would-be teachers undergo extensive training in order to meet specific criteria, learn training methods, and acquire practice-teaching experience.

After graduating with a certificate, teachers are often required to participate in continuing education. The Feldenkrais Method, for example, requires at least 100 hours of professional practice in the method and 20 hours of documented continuing education each year.

Where to teach
- Dance studios, schools
- Colleges, universities, conservatories
- Centers where the practice is taught
- Health centers and wellness institutes
- Community centers
- Theaters and acting studios

Dancers who have cross trained in Pilates, yoga, or somatic practices will often acquire accreditation in order to teach those practices to others.

BECOMING A BODYWORKER

After years of undergoing bodywork to improve alignment, decrease pain, ease movement, and recover from injury, some former dancers may find their calling is to become a bodywork practitioner themselves. Whether the goal is to work with the general population or with dancers and other performers, the ex-dancer brings a range of experience and knowledge about the body to a practice before undergoing training. Many bodyworkers who practice a specific modality or technique may teach it as well.

Bodywork refers to treatment approaches that emphasize manipulation and realignment of the musculoskeletal structure in order to improve function. Such therapies can also be preventive, in that they adjust the body before injuries (such as those caused by repetitive stress or overuse) can occur.

Dancers who sought out bodywork therapies to improve motion, enhance technique, and heal injuries during their performance careers can provide invaluable insights to those they treat. More people are turning to holistic treatment therapies as noninvasive, integrative, and mind–body alternatives to conventional medicine. Bodywork practitioners who distinguish themselves as former dancers with specific insights can do well in this post-performance career.

EXAMPLES OF BODYWORK THERAPIES

- massage
- acupressure, acupuncture, shiatsu
- Rolfing or structural integration (deep manipulation of soft tissue to realign and balance the body's myofascial structure)
- craniosacral (gentle manipulation of the skull and spine)
- Trager (release of tension patterns in the body followed by dance-like exercises called Mentastics)
- Klein and Klein/Mahler (developed by dancers, for dancers, to learn optimal and balanced integration of experience and intellect in use of the body)
- MELT Method® (Myofascial Energetic Length Technique, uses foam rollers and balls to lengthen connective tissue and balance the nervous system)
- Alexander Technique
- Feldenkrais
- Rosen Method (nonmanipulative touch and words to encourage physical and emotional awareness, tension release, and healing)

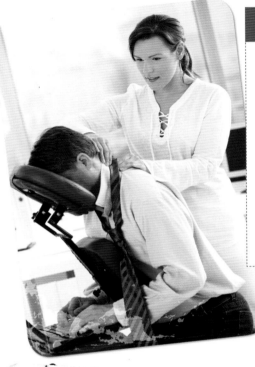

EDUCATION

Training as a bodywork therapist often involves education, certification, and licensing, as well as continuing education. Massage therapy schools and colleges throughout the world offer distinctive training in specific modalities. Specialized techniques such as Alexander, Feldenkrais, and Rosen operate their own training institutes, but students can also study with licensed practitioners who hold educational workshops and classes. Schools of holistic medicine offer certificates in massage, acupuncture/ acupressure, and other bodywork modalities.

By training in various styles of massage, a former dancer can establish a practice that caters specifically to dancers and other performers.

"IN 1971, WHEN I WAS NINETEEN YEARS OLD, I BECAME A PROFESSIONAL DANCER, BUT I SOON LOST MY LOVE OF DANCE AS A PERFORMANCE. INSTEAD I BECAME INTERESTED IN HOW PHYSICAL MOVEMENT RELATED TO MY PERSONAL SENSE OF SELF-EXPRESSION AND HOW TO USE IT FOR MEDITATION. SOON AFTERWARDS, I BEGAN TO STUDY STRUCTURAL INTEGRATION (ROLFING), A STYLE OF BODYWORK THAT FOCUSES ON BRINGING THE BODY INTO ALIGNMENT AND BALANCE THROUGH DEEP MASSAGE."

Satyarthi Peloquin, creator of the body therapy
Holistic Pain Healing

Where to practice bodywork
- Your own business or office
- Health and wellness center
- Spa, health club, gym
- Massage or bodywork center
- On staff with a dance company
- As a traveling specialist who visits homes, schools, offices

WRITING, CRITICISM, SCHOLARSHIP

Some dancers turn to writing after retiring from the stage. The most prominent genre of writing is the memoir, most famously (and often notoriously) by former prima ballerinas, iconic choreographers, and Broadway sensations. Although these autobiographies may at times be gossipy tell-alls, they also impart lessons learned, wisdom accumulated, and insights into dance training and the profession.

Former dancers have also written nondance books: cookbooks (Heather Watts and Jock Soto, Jigyasa Giri), instructional books on creativity and collaboration (Twyla Tharp), books on the dancer's body and nutrition (Allegra Kent), and books for young dancers (Suki Schorer, Lise Friedman). In addition, dancers who retire from the stage have moved into careers as editors of dance publications, and as dance critics/writers and scholars.

Dance criticism and writing

Former dancers bring unique insights to the practice of dance criticism, which is the process by which a writer watches, considers, and critiques a dance performance. The written critiques or reviews are published in magazines, newspapers, or online, but dance critics may articulate their reviews on radio or television. Most dance critics are journalists; many early dance critics, starting in the late 1800s, were music or theater critics who took on dance out of interest, or need (most likely, a publication asked them to review a prominent ballet company).

The profession of dance criticism gained recognition, in addition to full-time salaried positions in print media, in the mid-twentieth century with the rise of modern and postmodern dance. Beginning in the late twentieth century, however, with the advent of the Internet, which changed the business of print media, most print publications eliminated the

"I HAVE ALWAYS BELIEVED THAT A PERSON SHOULD KNOW EITHER EVERYTHING OR NOTHING. EVERYTHING ALLOWS YOU TO PLACE YOUR OPINIONS IN CONTEXT AND LINK THE DANCE EXPERIENCE TO WIDER ISSUES. NOTHING ALLOWS YOU TO SEE MOVEMENT FRESHLY AND PENETRATE EMPTY DANCE RHETORIC. BUT THE TERM 'A DANCE BACKGROUND' IS ESSENTIALLY MEANINGLESS. WHAT GIVES YOU 'A DANCE BACKGROUND'? RUSSIAN CLASSICAL BALLET? BUTOH? FLAMENCO? GRAHAM-MODERN? KATHAK? KHON? KABUKI? HULA?"

Dance critic Lewis Segal

In an age when anyone with a computer and Internet access, or a smart phone and a signal, can voice their thoughts and opinions—whether via a blog post, status update, or Twitter—dancers (whether retired or not) are finding ways of expressing themselves in cyberspace. While none of these ventures comes with a paycheck, they can act as a gateway to finding paying work as a dance critic or writer by serving as a platform for articulating and honing one's thoughts in writing.

position of dance critic. Today, most dance critics and writers work on a freelance basis and are paid per piece.

Dance writers are those who, rather than doing criticism, write previews of upcoming performances or feature stories on a dancer, choreographer, or new work. Dance critics and writers almost always have a dance background; either they studied dance before becoming journalists/critics, or they are former professional dancers. In some cases, dance writers still occasionally perform or choreograph.

Dance scholarship

Some dancers pursue academic scholarship after retiring from performance (or while they're still performing). Dance scholars may be affiliated with a university or college, or work independently. They spend considerable time, energy, and resources investigating a dance topic of significant interest to them, whether a person or

Former dancers bring unique insights to the practice of dance writing, criticism, and scholarship.

performance, dance style or tradition. Their investigations may involve library research, travel to other cities or countries to observe and/or research dance, interviewing people with insights into their research topic, and locating photos and illustrations that support their findings or evidence.

Once they have assembled the results of their research, scholars craft the information into an article, paper, or book-length text, with ample documentation (footnotes, endnotes, bibliography) that credentials their work. Dance scholars also present their research to peers at academic conferences, and/or publish their work in academic journals or books.

DANCERS AS ENTREPRENEURS

It's clear: The world loves dance. Whether the fascination is with ballerinas or b-boys, Kabuki or Kathak, competitive ballroom or battling dance crews, the world's fascination with dance is displayed in theaters, classrooms, studios, blogs, and advertisements, and on stages and screens around the globe.

Some former dancers capitalize on the dance boom by exploring entrepreneurial opportunities within the dance industry. Others use their considerable skill sets and acumen as former performers, especially if they worked as freelancers, to create their own businesses far afield from the dance profession.

Although dancers possess the discipline and dedication to innovate an entrepreneurial career, those who choreographed also have the ability to envision, create, manage, and promote large-scale productions. Setting up one's own shop or business as a bodyworker or teacher of somatic practices is also an entrepreneurial venture.

Whether a former dancer decides on a bricks-and-mortar setting or does business online in cyberspace, the entrepreneurial route can be a lucrative and satisfying second career.

Grants and scholarships

Many of the organizations around the world for transitioning dancers provide financial assistance for those seeking retraining in a new

career area, or for starting a new business. Career Transition For Dancers has awarded more than $4 million in educational scholarships that help pay for tuition, books, and related expenses. The organization has also awarded more than $400,000 to entrepreneurial dancers.

Entrepreneurial dancers have established mail-order costume and dance-shoe companies, and developed energy bars for performers.

Crossover skill set

The characteristics and skills essential to a career as a performing artist are the same as those required to become an entrepreneur:

- Creativity
- The ability to be improvisational, flexible, adaptive
- Motivation
- Commitment
- Resourcefulness
- The ability to be collaborative, yet self-directed
- Risk taker
- Self-promotion and audition techniques
- Market research

Additional skills needed by entrepreneurs

- Business acumen
- Strategic planning
- Negotiation
- Verbal and written communication
- Multitasking
- Management

DANCERS AS ENTREPRENEURS

- Chan Hon Goh, dancer with the National Ballet of Canada, with her husband, Chun Che (a Toronto ballet teacher), developed a line of pointe and slipper shoes for women and men called Principal Shoes.
- Julia Erickson, principal dancer, Pittsburgh Ballet Theatre, developed Barre energy bars, including Pirouette, Pirouette Crunch, and Black Swan.
- Sae La Chin, dancer with the Metropolitan Opera Ballet and the Rockettes, created SayBayBee, a baby planning business that also features pre- and postnatal dance fitness workouts.
- Christopher Coffee, former dancer with Oregon Ballet Theatre, started Gotham Lasik with ophthalmologist Brian Bonanni, and later Gotham Skincare, a medical spa.
- Cindy Pasky, a former ballet student, started Strategic Staffing Solutions or S3, a staffing information technology company, with branches in the United States and Europe

Jock Soto, former principal dancer with NYCB, is one of the beneficiaries. After retiring from the stage, he received a grant to attend culinary school. He has since written a cookbook with his former dance partner, Heather Watts. And while Soto teaches at the School of American Ballet, he also manages a catering events company.

Andrey Kasatsky, former dancer with Moscow Classical Ballet, studied digital effects and 3D animation, and now teaches at The DAVE School of computer animation.

INDEX

Figures in italics indicate images.

CREDITS

All other images are the copyright of Quintet Publishing Ltd. Unless otherwise noted, all illustrations are by Claire Scully and Dawn Painter at The Quiet Revolution. While every effort has been made to credit contributors, Quintet Publishing would like to apologize should there have been any omissions or errors—and would be pleased to make the appropriate correction for future editions of the book.

6, 7 © Stephanie Colgan, courtesy of Zenon Dance Company; 8 © Ed Bock, courtesy of Ramgamala Dance; 9 © Steve Niedorf, courtesy of Zenon Dance Company; 36, 37 © William Cameron, courtesy of Zenon Dance Company; 40 © Dan Rosenfeld, courtesy of Collage Dance Theatre; 41 © Ahmad Masri courtesy of Mary Lee Hardenbergh; 47 © Danny Buraczeski; 48 © V. Paul Virtucio, courtesy of Ananya Dance Theatre; 49 © Ed Bock, courtesy of Ragamala Dance; 50 Photo courtesy of the Walker Art Cente; 52 © Jeff Austin, courtesy Zorongo Flamenco Dance Theatre; 53 © Perry Hanson, courtesy Ethnic Dance Theatre; 100, 101 © Laban/Bartenieff Institute of Movement Studies, LIMS®; 141 © Saliq Savage; 143 © Hugo Lortacher; 145 © Naomi Sher; 150 © Tim Summers / The Heidi Duckler Dance Theater; 151 © Jeff Kurt Peterson, courtesy of Collage Dance Theatre; 171 © Stefan Iwaskewycz, courtesy Ethnic Dance Theatre; 177 by Jane Laurie; 199 © Elena Murchikova / The Ballet Bag.

Shutterstock: 12 © Hector Conesa / Shutterstock.com; 15 © Doug James / Shutterstock.com; 19 © Gianluca Curti / Shutterstock.com; 21(t) © ChipPix; 21(b) © Bishwambers' / Shutterstock.com; 23 © AISPIX by Image Source; 26 © Val Thoermer / Shutterstock.com; 27 © Igor Bulgarin / Shutterstock.com; 28 © ostill; 32 © Sean Nel; 33 © Bocman1973 / Shutterstock.com; 35 © criben / Shutterstock.com; 39 © lev radin / Shutterstock.com; 42 © Mark Hayes; 43 © Viciousgambler; 44 © Andrey Bayda / Shutterstock.com; 45 © Jack.Q / Shutterstock.com; 56 © Kaziyeva-Dem'yanenko Svitlana; 57 © Igor Bulgarin / Shutterstock.com; 59 © runzelkorn; 60 © olly; 61 © margo_black; 62 © 6348103963; 65 © manzrussali / Shutterstock.com; 68 © Felix Mizioznikov; 69 © Felix Mizioznikov; 71 © Jon Kroninger; 72 © Kaziyeva-Dem'yanenko Svitlana; 75 © Albina Tiplyashina; 76 © Ozger Aybike Sarikaya; 77 © Serg Zastavkin; 81 © Linda Bucklin; 83 © Randall Reed; 84 © AYakovlev; 85 © AYakovlev; 87 © Sehenswerk; 89. © Chad Zuber; 90 © Elena Schweitzer; 91 © Yuri Arcurs; 92 © Kletr; 95 © Featureflash / Shutterstock.com; 97 © Cleo; 104 © Ariwasabi; 107 © Sean Nel; 109 © Yuri Arcurs; 111 © Yuri Arcurs; 112 © wavebreakmedia ltd; 115 © Juriah Mosin; 116 © Orrza; 119 © hxdbzxy / Shutterstock.com; 122 © ArTono; 124 © Arvind Balaraman / Shutterstock.com; 126 © Nejron Photo; 127 © Mayer Vadim; 128 © Matthew Strauss; 129 © lev radin / Shutterstock.com; 132 © paul prescott / Shutterstock.com; 134 © Lauren Jade Goudie; 135 © trekandshoot / Shutterstock.com; 149 © Sean Nel; 152 © 6348103963; 155 © Entertainment Press / Shutterstock.com; 161 © criben / Shutterstock.com; 162 © Morgan Lane Photography; 163 © Tracy Whiteside; 167 © .shock; 172 © Jack.Q / Shutterstock.com; 175 © AlexAnnaButs; 190 © vhpfoto; 200 © Rido; 201 © stocknadia; 203 © wavebreakmedia ltd; 207 © kojoku / Shutterstock.com; 211 © Luna Vandoorne; 213 © bezikus; 216 © Joe Seer / Shutterstock.com; 217 © Sean Nel; 221 © Jack.Q / Shutterstock.com; 223 © JanVlcek; 227 © Kravtsov Sergey; 228 © auremar; 230 © konstantynov; 231 © Luba V Nel; 232 © Edw; 239 © cinemafestival / Shutterstock.com; 240 © Piotr Marcinski; 241 © Jack.Q / Shutterstock.com; 243 © Kaziyeva-Dem'yanenko Svitlana; 245(t) © AISPIX by Image Source; 245(b) © Franck Boston; 247 © StockLite; 249 © BestPhotoStudio.